LIFE AMONG THE CHINESE:

WITH

CHARACTERISTIC SKETCHES AND INCIDENTS

OF

MISSIONARY OPERATIONS AND PROSPECTS IN CHINA.

BY REV. R. S. MACLAY, M.A.,

THIRTEEN YEARS MISSIONARY TO CHINA FROM THE METHODIST EPISCOPAL CHURCH.

New York:

PUBLISHED BY CARLTON & PORTER,

200 MULBERRY-STREET.

1861.

PREFACE.

THE important events which have transpired in China during the past few years have awakened, both in Europe and the United States, an unprecedented interest with reference to that ancient and remarkable empire.

In the spring of 1858 the government of China formed treaties of amity and commerce with the respective governments of England, France, Russia, and the United States. The provisions of these treaties are of the most liberal character, and initiate a new and most auspicious era in foreign intercourse with China. In 1859 the treacherous attack of the Chinese on the English fleet at the mouth of the Peiho seemed to jeopardize these cheering prospects; but in 1860 the brilliant successes of the allies in the north of China, commencing with the destruction of the Taku forts, and terminating with the burning of the imperial summer palace near Pekin, dissipated all anxiety on this subject, and, by procuring additional privileges and guarantees from the Chinese government, placed foreign relations with China on a basis which is likely to prove permanent and satisfactory to all parties.

Coincident with the dawning of this new era in Chinese politics, we notice that the wonderful triumphs of steam navigation and telegraphic communication are bringing into close proximity the most widely separated portions of the human family. There is now direct and continuous steam transit from New York to Jeddo. Calcutta, by telegraph, is only six days from London; and, by the proposed Pacific railroad through the United States, with its supplementary line of steamers across the Pacific, the traveler will be able to pass in twenty-two days from New York to China.

The volume herewith offered to the reader contains the results of observations and researches during a residence of about twelve years in China. Familiar intercourse with the people, the ability to converse freely with them in their own dialect, and personal visits to nearly all the cities open to foreign trade, gave the author ample opportunities for forming reliable opinions on the subjects he has discussed, and he ventures to hope that the information communicated may prove acceptable to all classes of readers.

The author begs to express his indebtedness, in the preparation of this volume, to the writings of Sir John Davis, Rev. Dr. Medhurst, Dr. S. W. Williams, Rev. M. S. Culbertson, Rev. J. Edkins, W. C. Milne, Esq., and others who have preceded him in this department of literary effort, and to their entertaining works he would refer the reader for fuller information concerning some of the topics discussed in the following pages.

To those whose earnest and oft-repeated suggestions induced the author to prepare this volume for publication, to those who are interested in the evangelization of the Chinese, and to all who desire information concerning the oldest nation in the world and one of the grandest empires on which the sun has ever shone, the following pages are now presented, in the earnest hope and with the fervent prayer that they may contribute somewhat toward the ushering in of that glorious period when China, clothed and in her right mind, shall be found sitting at the feet of Jesus.

R. S. Maclay.

New York, *April* 26, 1861.

CONTENTS.

CHAPTER V.

LAWS OF CHINA.

CHAPTER VI.

RELIGIONS: CONFUCIANISM.

CHAPTER VII.

RELIGIONS: RATIONALISM AND BUDHISM.

CHAPTER VIII.

CHARACTER OF THE CHINESE.

CHAPTER IX.

CITY OF FUHCHAU.

CHAPTER X.

BUILDINGS, LAND-TENURE, ETC.

CHAPTER XI.

TRIP INTO THE COUNTRY.

CHAPTER XII.

PREACHING AND CHURCHES.

CHAPTER XIII.

SCHOOLS.

CHAPTER XIV.

JOURNAL, TRANSLATIONS, ETC.

CHAPTER XV.

THE PEACH FARM.

CHAPTER XVI.

INCIDENTS.

CHAPTER XVII.

INCIDENTS.

CHAPTER XVIII.

CHINA AS A MISSION FIELD.

CHAPTER XIX.

APPEAL TO THE CHURCH.

ADDENDUM.

Illustrations.

LIFE AMONG THE CHINESE.

CHAPTER I.

GENERAL VIEW OF CHINA.

A GLANCE at a map of the world will show the interesting geographical position of the Chinese Empire. It occupies the southeastern portion of the continent of Asia, comprising an extent of territory greater than that of all modern Europe, or about one tenth of the surface of the habitable globe. It stretches through some thirty-five degrees of latitude and about seventy degrees of longitude, from the Beloor Mountains on the west, to the sea of Jeddo on the east; and from the great Altay Mountains on the north to the Gulf of Tonquin and the Himalaya Mountains on the south. The superficial area comprised within these limits is *five millions of square miles*, of which about one fifth lies within the tropics, and all the rest within the north temperate zone. It possesses about two thousand miles of seacoast, affording some of the finest harbors in the world. Nearly one half of its southern frontier touches on the great empire of British India; its northern and western boundaries are formed almost entirely by the Asiatic possessions of Russia; a few days' sail to the southward lies the vast continent of Australia; while eastward, across the Pacific, and within some ten days of its coast by steam navigation, it faces the western coast of the United States of America.

The internal resources of China are almost boundless; the treasures of the mineral, animal, cereal, and vegetable kingdoms have been lavished upon her with profuse liberality. Gold, silver, copper, tin, lead, iron, coal, gypsum, limestone, the ruby, diamond, amethyst, garnet, opal, agate, and other stones, abound. Most of the animals, birds, and fishes found in the temperate zones, and many of those peculiar to the tropics, exist in China. Lions, tigers, leopards, etc., are now rarely met with; but the domestic animals, as the horse, cow, goat, sheep, pig, dog, cat, etc., abound. They have also the camel, wolf, fox, wild-cat, hare, rabbit, martin, ermine, silver-fox, ratel, wolverine, sea and land otter, squirrel, porcupine, hedgehog, marmot, weasel, rat, mouse, etc. Less is known of the *birds* of China than of its mammiferæ. We may mention, however, the eagle, hawk, crow, magpie, pheasant, owl, butcher-bird, grackle, thrush, goat-sucker, swallow, sparrow, robin, cuckoo, jay, kingfisher, parrot, peacock, dove, goose, duck, chicken, pigeon, snipe, plover, rice-bird, (a species of ortolan,) heron, egret, stork, curlew, cormorant, grebe, pelican, etc. The *ichthyology* of China is, perhaps, one of the richest in the world, comprising shark, ray, sturgeon, porpoise, torpedo, a kind of cod, salmon or bynni-carp, pomfret, sole, mackerel, shad, carp, eel, goldfish, sun-fish, yellow-fish, pipe-fish, pike, mullet, file-fish, anchovy, oyster, clam, prawn, shrimp, crab, craw-fish, cuttle-fish, etc. Among the *gramineous* plants cultivated in China we enumerate rice, wheat, barley, oats, millet, buckwheat, Indian-corn, sugar-cane, a coarse grass used for weaving floor-matting, and another kind used for fuel, hemp, tobacco, bamboo, and palm. "The bamboo is cultivated about villages for its pleasant shade and beauty, and a grove furnishes from year to year culms of all sizes for the various uses to which it is applied. No plant imparts so oriental and rural an aspect to a garden or village as the clumps of this graceful and stately grass; the stalks shoot up their wavy plumes to the height of fifty feet and upward, and swaying themselves to every breeze, form an object of great elegance, well befitting so useful a plant.

"This plant may well be called useful, for it is applied by the Chinese to such a vast variety of purposes (some of them indeed better accomplished elsewhere by different materials) that it may justly be called their national plant. It is reared from shoots and suckers, but after it has once rooted is not much attended to. The common yellow species extends over all the southern and eastern provinces, but the varieties mentioned by Chinese writers amount to sixty, of which the black skinned sort, used in making furniture, and the low, fine-branched one, affording the slender twigs employed in the manufacture of writing pencils, are the best known. The tender shoots are cultivated for food, and are, when four or five inches high, boiled, pickled, and comfited; but not the 'tender buds and flowers, cut like asparagus,' as represented by Murray. The roots are carved into fantastic images of men, birds, monkeys, or monstrous perversions of animated nature, cut into lantern-handles and canes, or turned into oval sticks for worshipers, to divine whether the gods will hear or refuse their petitions. The tapering culms are used for all purposes that poles can be applied to in carrying, supporting, propelling, and measuring, by the porter, the carpenter, and the boatman; for the joists of houses and the ribs of sails, the shafts of spears and the wattles of hurdles, the tubes of aqueducts, and the handles and ribs of umbrellas and fans.

"The leaves are sewed upon cords to make rain cloaks, swept into heaps to form manure, and matted into thatches to cover houses. Cut into splints and slivers of various sizes, the wood is worked into baskets and trays of every form and fancy, twisted into cables, plaited into awnings, and woven mats for scenery of the theater, the roofs of boats, and the casing of goods. The shavings, even, are picked into oakum, and mixed with those of rattan, to be stuffed into mattresses. The bamboo furnishes the bed for sleeping, and the couch for reclining; the chopsticks for eating, the pipe for smoking, and the flute for entertaining; a curtain to hang before the door, and a broom to sweep around it; together with screens, stools, stands, and sofas for various uses of convenience and luxury in the house. The mattress to lie upon, the chair to sit upon, the table to dine from, food to eat, and fuel to cook it with, are alike derived from it: the ferule to govern the scholar, and the book he studies, both originate here. The tapering barrels of the *sâng*, or organ, and the dreaded instrument of the lictor, one to make harmony, and the other to strike dread; the skewer to pin the hair, and the hat to screen the head; the paper to write on, the pencil handle to write with, and the cup to hold the pencils; the rule to measure lengths, the cup to guage quantities, and the bucket to draw water; the bellows to blow the fire, and the bottle to retain the match; the bird-cage and crab-net, the fish pole and sumpitan, the water wheel and eave-duct, wheelbarrow and hand-cart, etc., are one and all furnished or completed by this magnificent grass, whose graceful beauty when growing is comparable to its varied usefulness when cut down."*

The *trees* of China embrace the pine, yew, cypress, willow, oak, chestnut, walnut, hazlenut, banian, camphor, olive, juniper, thuja, and some others. The *vegetables* comprise a large variety, though the quality is inferior to that of the same kinds in the United States. Those most generally cultivated are peas, beans, tomatoes, cabbage, radish, cucumbers, onions, celery, carrot, water-caltrops, spinach, cockscomb, green basil, rhubarb, sweet potato, yam, etc. The *fruits* are abundant, but in most instances deficient in flavor. Orange, pumalo, pomegranate, pear, peach, plum, apple, (very inferior,) plantain, pineapple, mango, custard-apple, lichi, lungan, and other kinds abound.

The *population* of China, according to the latest and most reliable information on this subject,

* Middle Kingdom, vol ii, p. 216.

amounts to *four hundred millions.* It is difficult to form an adequate conception of such a mass of human beings. Comparing it with the populations of other portions of the earth's surface, we find that it exceeds the combined populations of Europe, Africa, and the entire continent of America. It constitutes, in fact, more than one third of the human race. This estimate is derived from the official papers of the Chinese government. In China the people furnish the data for the census returns of the government; and as the government avails itself of these statistics of population in levying conscriptions for military service, and in demanding subsidies to replenish its exhausted exchequer, there is everything to induce the Chinese to *understate* rather than *overstate* the amount of their population. We accept, then, as correct and reliable, the statement that there exist to-day within the Chinese empire at least one third of the human race. Says the Rev. M. S. Culbertson, while writing on this topic: "The mind cannot grasp the real import of so vast a number. *Four hundred millions!* What does it mean? Count it. Night and day, without rest, or food, or sleep, you continue the weary work; yet eleven days have passed before you have counted the first million, and more than as many years before the end of the tedious task can be reached." He also supposes this mighty multitude to take up its line of march in a grand procession, placed in single file at six feet apart, and marching at the rate of thirty miles a day, except on the Sabbath, which is given to rest. "Day after day the moving column advances, the head pushing on far toward the rising sun; now bridge the Pacific, now bridge the Atlantic. And now the Pacific is crossed, but still the long procession marches on, stretching across high mountains, and sunny plains, and broad rivers, through China and India, and the European kingdoms, and on again over the stormy bosom of the Atlantic. But the circuit of the world itself affords not standing room. The endless column will double upon itself, and double again and again, and shall girdle the earth eighteen times before the great reservoir which furnishes these numberless multitudes is exhausted. Weeks and months and years roll away, and still they come, men, women, and children. Since the march began the little child has become a man, and yet on they come, in unfailing numbers. Not till the end of forty-one years will the last of the long procession have passed."

Four hundred millions! Who are they? Our brethren; bone of our bone, flesh of our flesh. *What are they?* Heathen, athwart whose gloomy night of error no ray of light ever shines; *idolaters*, bowing down to senseless images, the workmanship of their own hands. *What are they?* Men, created by God; fallen, ruined, helpless; victims, morally, of a foul and relentless malady; sinking into guilt and woe unutterable, inconceivable; *immortals*, objects of the divine compassion, subjects of Christ's mediation, into the mysteries of whose redemption angels desire to look, and for whose eternal salvation all heavenly intelligences are moved with a profound and ceaseless solicitude.

How are we to classify the Chinese? What character and position shall we assign them among the nations of the earth? They are not savages; they are not barbarians. Viewed from a heathen standpoint, we must call them a civilized people; viewed from a Christian standpoint, they are at least semi-civilized. They are a fixed, stationary people, not migratory or nomadic. They dwell in hamlets, towns, and immense cities, successive generations following each other on the old manor or homestead. They possess social order, an educational system, and political government. They practice most of the industrial arts, and produce nearly all the necessaries, together with many of the luxuries of life. Their writers on political economy distribute society into *five* classes: farmer, artisan, scholar, merchant, and soldier.

The *farmer* is, theoretically, the first or most honorable class in Chinese society. At a very early period of their history the Chinese turned their attention to agriculture; and in subsequent ages they apotheosized those ancient monarchs who first taught their subjects the rudiments of the art. Each successive dynasty seeks to stimulate the agricultural spirit and enterprise of the people, and to this day every emperor is required annually to perform the ceremony of "holding the plow" in a small plat of ground near Pekin, the capital of the empire. But, notwithstanding these advantages, Chinese agriculture, even in our day, is still in a primitive state, and, as a class, the farmers are not distinguished for enterprise or influence. As generally characteristic of the members of this class, we may say they are ignorant, superstitious, industrious, frugal, deferential to superiors, and furnish the nearest approximation to honesty that we meet with in Chinese society.

"Notwithstanding the encouragement given to tillage, vast tracts of land still lie waste, some of it the most fertile in the country; partly because the people have not the skill and capital to drain and render it productive, and partly because they have not sufficient security or prospect of remuneration to encourage them to make the necessary outlay.

"Landed property is held in clans or families as much as possible, but it is not entailed, nor are overgrown estates frequent. The land is held as a freehold so long as the sovereign receives his rent, which is estimated at about one tenth of the produce, and the proprietors record their names in the district magistrate's office as responsible for the tax, feeling themselves secure in the possession while that is paid. The paternal estate and the houses upon it descend to the eldest son, but his brothers can remain upon it with their families, and devise their portion in perpetuo to their children, or an amicable composition can be made. Daughters never inherit, nor can an adopted son of another clan succeed. A mortgagee must actually enter into possession of the property, and make himself personally responsible for the payment of the taxes before his mortgage is valid. Unless explicitly stated, the land can be redeemed any time within thirty years on payment of the original sum. Sections XC to C of the Code contain the laws relating to this subject, some of which bear a resemblance to those established among the Hebrews, and intended to secure a similar object of retaining the land in the same clan or tribe.

"The Chinese are rather gardeners than farmers, not only in the small size of their grounds, but in their ignorance of those operations whereby soils naturally unfruitful are made fertile, those which produce few kinds of plants made to bring forth a greater variety, and their natural fertility sustained at the cheapest rate by a proper manuring and rotation of crops. They make up for the disadvantages of poor implements by hard work, repeatedly turning over the soil, and sustaining its productiveness by constant manuring. Their agricultural utensils are few and simple, and are probably now made similar to those used centuries ago. The broad hoe, a less efficient tool than our spade, is used more than any other; the edge of the large wooden blade is guarded with iron, and the weight adds impetus to the blow. Spades, shovels, and mattocks are employed in kitchen gardening, and the plow and harrow in rice cultivation. The plow is made of wood, except the iron-edged share, which lies so flat that it cannot penetrate the soil more than five inches. The whole implement is so simple and rude that one would think the inventor of it was a laborer who, tired of the toil of spading, called the ox to his aid, and tied his shovel to a rail; fastening the animal at one end, and guiding the other, he was so pleased with the relief that he never thought of improving it much further than to sharpen the spade to a coulter, and bend the rail to a beam and handle. The harrow is a heavy stick, armed with a single row of stout wooden teeth, and furnished with a frame-work to guide it, or a triangular machine, with rows of teeth, on which the driver rides.

"The buffalo is most used in rice cultivation, and the ox and ass in dry plowing; horses, mules, cows, and goats likewise render service to the farmer in various ways, and are often yoked in most ludicrous combinations. But the team which Nieuhoff describes, of a man driving his wife and his ass yoked to the same plow is too bad for China often to present, though it has been so frequently quoted that one almost expects on landing to see half the women in the harness."*

In the *Fuh-kien* province, and perhaps elsewhere in China, the farmer raises three crops of grain from the same soil within twelve months. It is done in this way: about the middle of April the first crop of rice is set out in the fields, after the manner of transplanting cabbages, beets, etc., in the United States. This crop grows till about the middle of June, when the second crop is set out in the same fields, the rows coming between those of the first crop. The two crops then grow together till about the middle of July, when the first crop is harvested. After the removal of the first crop, the second comes forward rapidly, and about the middle of September it is gathered. The ground is now plowed, and prepared for the winter crop of wheat, which is sowed about the first of October, and is reaped about the first of the following April, thus

* Middle Kingdom, vol. ii, page 102.

leaving the soil to be prepared for the summer rice crops.

Artisans constitute a most numerous class, and their efforts are directed to almost every conceivable branch of human industry and enterprise. Their skill in many departments of handicraft is universally recognized, and some of their fabrics and wares command the admiration of the world. It is worthy of remark that what are considered by Europeans as the three great discoveries or inventions of modern times, the art of printing, the manufacture of gunpowder, and the mariner's compass, had their origin in China. Printing was practiced in China during the tenth century of the Christian era. The Chinese name for gunpowder is fire-medicine, or fire-drug; and though it is probable they received from western nations the knowledge of applying it to firearms, it is nevertheless certain that its composition was known to the Chinese in very ancient times. There is reliable evidence that as early as the third or fourth century of the Christian era the Chinese were acquainted with the properties and use of the mariner's compass; and even the variation of the needle had not escaped their observation.

The use of inflammable gas for artistic and other purposes is with us a very recent measure; and as we look at our dwellings and cities thus lighted, we take to ourselves great credit for ingenuity and enterprise. But here, also, it appears the Chinese have anticipated us, though they have failed to apply it on as grand a scale as their western brethren.

Fire Wells.

"In the province of Sze-chueu, one of the western provinces, there are very deep wells, the water of which is like brine, from flowing through beds of rock salt. This brine is boiled down in great pans. In some parts of the province there are hot salt water wells, and what are called fire-wells. The mouths of these wells are closed, and a bamboo pipe is passed into the well. Through this a large quantity of gas passes, and if a light be applied it takes fire and burns constantly, just like the gas-pipes in our towns. Now the Chinese are very clever, and therefore they make use of this natural gas manufactory for lighting the villages near it, conveying it to them in hollow bamboos instead of iron pipes.

"The chief use, however, which they make of the gas is to lead it, by the pipes, under the salt-pans; but to keep the pipe from burning they fix an earthenware nozzle in the end of the bamboo pipes, and thus the water is evaporated or boiled away. In this manner salt is produced very cheaply, because there is no expense for fuel, and in this district the quantity of gas is so great that as many salt-pans can be worked as the people choose to make. The gas is something like our coal gas. It is produced by some volcanic action under ground, and probably comes from some burning layers of coal, which throw off gas in greater or smaller quantities. Perhaps there is no other instance where so much gas flows continually from the ground as in this."

Even "table-turning and spiritual manifestations are not unknown in China. In this, as in many other things, they are in advance of the practitioners among ourselves. The mode of carrying on this operation is somewhat different from that in vogue in the United States. The table is turned upside down upon a pair of chopsticks laid at right angles over the mouth of a mortar or bowl filled with water. Four persons lay one hand upon each leg of the table, while the other clasps the free hand of one of the four, and thus the circle is completed. An incantation is now chanted by the 'medium,' and soon the table begins to move. The 'circle' move with it, and in a minute it is whirling violently upon its axis, until it is thrown violently off its balance, and falls upon the floor. The motion of the table is universally attributed to supernatural agency, but it seems not to have been used as a means of communication with the spiritual world.

"There is no necessity for resorting to so clumsy a method of communication with the dead. The spirits have been induced to write their communications. A table is sprinkled with some kind of powder, or flour, or bran, or dust. Then a small basket, without a handle, is armed with a pencil or chopstick, which is tied to its edge, or thrust through its interstices. The basket is then turned upside down, its edges resting upon the tips of one or two fingers of two persons standing on opposite sides of the table, and in such a manner that the pencil touches the powdered surface. In a short time the pencil moves, leading after it the basket and the fingers on which it rests, and tracing upon the dusty table lines and figures in which a good linguist easily recognizes the characters of the Chinese language. In this way information is communicated on subjects of which the operators have no knowledge. Sometimes, indeed, a ghost thus invoked may be unable to write Chinese, or may be unwilling to exercise its powers, and then nothing can be discovered but unmeaning lines and angles. But in general the composition is good and the information valuable." *

The *scholar* has always been held in very high estimation by the Chinese. It is interesting to notice at what an early period they directed their attention to letters. Before Cesar led his conquering legions into Britain, or Cecrops introduced the first colonies into Greece, the Chinese had their schools of learning, whose halls were crowded with ingenuous youth. Their written works on natural history, mathematics, agriculture, silk-weaving, tea-culture, and kindred subjects, contain in a crude state a considerable amount of curious and useful information. Their national history is voluminous, minutely elaborated and generally trustworthy. Their poetry furnishes some fanciful conceptions and neat similes, though in dreary settings of vapid commonplace and attenuated sentimentalism. Their metaphysical writings afford some specimens of searching criticism, subtle analysis, correct generalization, and the occasional enunciation of sound principles in morals and politics, interwoven, however, in all these departments, with much that is empirical, vitiating, and false. Their genial atmosphere and brilliant sky early invited their attention to the motions of the heavenly bodies; and we find their oldest historic records associated with notices of eclipses and other celestial phenomena.

* China: Its Religions and Superstitions. Pp. 186, 187.

The Chinese, however, have never made much progress in scientific investigations, and in view of the advanced position of modern Christian nations in these departments, an acquaintance with the higher sciences can scarcely be predicated of them. They are eminently a practical people, and have made quite creditable progress in most of the useful and many of the fine arts.

The *merchants* of China comprise a large and highly respected class of society. They are characterized by tact and shrewdness in business transactions, fertility of resources and expedients, and by patient energy and perseverance in overcoming difficulties. The great varieties of their climate, soil, and productions, soon excited the spirit of trade among the Chinese, while their admirable facilities for internal navigation furnished every encouragement to the development of commercial enterprise. While Jehoshaphat was building his ships for the gold trade with Ophir, the counterparts of those specimens of naval architecture were sailing on the rivers and estuaries, or along the coast of China. The maritime position of the empire, and the value of its productions, early attracted the attention of other nations; and even during the first centuries of the Christian era we find evidences of its commercial intercourse with foreign countries. In subsequent ages the Chinese fostered this trade with other nations, and it was not till the accession of the present dynasty, A.D. 1644, that the government of China introduced its exclusive policy on this subject. Notwithstanding this governmental opposition, and the embarrassing difficulties it originated, foreign trade was never wholly extinguished; and to-day merchants of all lands resort to China, and the ships of every civilized nation enter her ports. So important, indeed, are the productions of China in the world's commerce, that recently the four great representative nations of Christendom combined their flags and their diplomacy in a grand effort to open up the empire to foreign intercourse. The scene enacted in the *Peiho* during the spring of 1858 is probably unparalleled in the history of nations. There, side by side, lay the splendid frigates of England, France, Russia, and the United States, their national ensigns floating out in the breeze of that northern gulf. The smoke had scarcely rolled away from the battlements of Sebastopol, the graves were still fresh that had closed over the victims of the ensanguined battle-fields in the Crimea, the divergent and frequently conflicting home policies of their governments were still active and unharmonized; and yet there in the extreme east, the high embassadors of those lately contending nations now meet in friendly council, and combine their prestige and power to draw within the circle of Christian nations the oldest and mightiest heathen nation in the world.

The *soldier* occupies the lowest position in the Chinese classification of society, and this arrangement, we think, is in accordance with the true sentiment of the nation on this point. The Chinese do not regard it as at all derogatory to their character to be told that they are deficient in the elements of warlike strength. "We are not a military people," say they, "we are a literary nation. With us reason, and not force, defines rights and privileges; argument, and not the sword, decides controversies." It is not strange then that in China the military art is lightly esteemed, and that their soldiers are indifferently trained, poorly paid, ludicrously inefficient, and frequently disgustingly vicious.

During the summer of 1854 the western portions of the Fuh-kien province were greatly disturbed by local banditti, who, taking advantage of the great insurgent movement, and sometimes following in its wake, proceeded to pillage the people and devastate the country. To put down these disturbances the governor sent out occasional detachments of troops, who invariably returned after a brief campaign, reporting the troubles all settled. In one of the detachments thus sent out were a goodly number of persons who lived near one of our chapels. It was quite interesting to see them robe themselves in military costume, and bidding adieu to their families and neighbors, start for the scene of danger. About two months after their departure, as I was closing the services in the chapel, it was announced that the soldiers were returning, and everybody rushed to the street to see them. As the beggarly looking squad came straggling along I noticed that all my neighbors were home again, and to all appearances unharmed. "What!" said I, with some surprise, "are you all back again?" "Yes," they replied, "all save two or three who died of dysentery from eating too much fruit." "And what of the campaign?" I continued. "Ah, we had a dangerous time of it."

"What!" said I, "did you succeed in finding the enemy?" "Finding them," they replied with some earnestness," why we fought some fifty pitched battles!" "Fifty battles," I exclaimed, "and nobody hurt." "Hurt!" they indignantly rejoined, "why just look here!" and they held up their tattered garments and scratched skins with an expression of countenance at once doleful and ludicrous. The appeal was irresistible, and I dropped the subject.

CHAPTER II.

ANCIENT RELIGIOUS FAITH OF THE CHINESE.

Any one who carefully analyzes the character of the Chinese must notice its unique and, in some respects, apparently anomalous traits. This character is manifestly the product of forces, some of which at least are now extinct, the result of influences, some of which are now inoperative. Confucianism, Rationalism, or Buddhism, acting either singly or conjointly, could never produce such a character. Rationalism and Buddhism are palpably incompetent to perform such a work; and with regard to Confucianism, its influence in this direction is due quite as much to those ancient principles which underlie and antedate it as to the ethical and political maxims which Confucius has deduced from them. Conceding to the three religious systems of China all the influence in the formation of the national character which can fairly be claimed for them, there still remain mental and moral traits for which these systems indicate no adequate cause, furnish no satisfactory explanation. It is, we think, to what might be called the ancient religious faith of the Chinese that we must look for the true type of their character. Much has been written with reference to ancient

Chinese civilization; and modern infidelity, with its accustomed avidity and recklessness, seized upon it as an argument against the Bible. "The Bible," said they, "is not essential to human progress; man can civilize himself. There is in man an innate power by virtue of which he rises from barbarism to refinement;" and to substantiate the truth of these propositions they referred to China. "There," said they, "is a vast people who have grown up from barbarism to civilization without any contact with or influence from the teachings of the Bible." Within the past few years Europeans and Americans have enjoyed unprecedented facilities for studying Chinese character and history; and, as one gratifying result, we are now able to explode errors and enunciate correct views on subjects formerly distorted by exuberant fancy or polished malice. Without wishing to deny or undervalue the just claims of ancient Chinese civilization, we do deny most unequivocally the statement that it has been obtained independent of "any contact with or influence from the teachings of the Bible." We assert that all the elements of progress and conservatism which have given to Chinese civilization its high character and position have been drawn directly or indirectly from the primitive teachings of the Bible. In support of this assertion we present the following facts and considerations.

In view of the ascertained and reliable facts of early Chinese history, it is, we think, entirely *probable* that the founders of the Chinese empire possessed a traditional knowledge of some of the ancient doctrines and facts of the Bible. We shall hereafter see that the early authentic records of the Chinese carry us back to a period just sufficiently remote from the deluge and the dispersion to account for the eastward migration, through central Asia, of this ancient colony, and its permanent political organization in the great plain of China. It is not improbable that some of the founders of this great empire were the immediate children of those who started from western Asia on the great eastward migration. Coming thus directly from the primeval seat of the race, these colonies must have taken with them some knowledge of the early teachings of the Bible, and some recollection of the more prominent events of sacred history. This view is corroborated by the references to these topics which we find in the mythological history of the Chinese. Their account of the creation of the heavens and the earth by Pwanku is only a reflection of the Mosaic narrative of that stupendous creative act by the Almighty; and with reference to the subsequent events of sacred history, says Dr. Medhurst, "the coincidence of ten generations having passed away, the institution of marriage, the invention of music, the rebellion of a portion of the race, and the confused mixture of the divine and human families closed by the occurrence of the flood in the time of Yau, might lead us to conclude that, in their allusions to this period, the Chinese are merely giving their version of the events that occurred from Adam to Noah." "The mention made in their early history of the draining of the land as one of the first acts of the primitive rulers of China, and the allusion to the discovery of wine about the same period, show that their first kings must have synchronized with the immediate descendants of Noah; and the recorded fact that a seven years' famine took place in China nearly coeval with that of Egypt, proves that their chronicles are entitled to some degree of credit."

But we have still stronger evidence on this subject. Some of the oldest and most reliable books of the Chinese furnish conclusive evidence that in ancient times they possessed some correct knowledge of the true God. This Being is designated *Shangti*, (Upper Ruler,) and to him are ascribed many of the attributes which we predicate of the true God. We admit that subsequent Chinese philosophers have sought to explain away all these allusions to the Upper Ruler, and that in our day this ancient knowledge has utterly faded from the national consciousness of the Chinese; but there stands the record on the subject, embalmed in their sacred writings, as a sure witness against them; "because that, when they knew God they glorified him not as God, neither were thankful; but became vain in their imaginations, and their foolish heart was darkened. Professing themselves to be wise they became fools, and changed the glory of the incorruptible God into an image made like to corruptible man, and to birds, and fourfooted beasts, and creeping things." Sir John Davis, referring to this subject, says: "Notwithstanding the general aspect of materialism that pertains to the Chinese philosophy, it is difficult to peruse their sentiments regarding *tien* (heaven) without the persuasion that they ascribe to it most of the attributes of a supreme governing intelligence." In the ritual for public worship in what has been termed the state religion of China, there are certain prayers, used by the emperor, which afford light on this subject. The following is a translation of the ancient form of prayer with which the emperor, at the round altar, in the southern suburbs of Pekin, the capital of China, greeted the approach of the spirit of Shangti to the sacrifices offered at the winter solstice. The translation is by the Rev. Dr. Legge, of the London Mission at Hong-kong, China.

"To thee, O mysteriously working Maker, I look up in thought. How imperial is the expansive arch (where thou dwellest.) Now is the time when the masculine energies of nature begin to be displayed, and with the great ceremonies I reverently honor thee. Thy servant, I am but a reed or willow; my heart is but as that of an ant; yet have I received thy favoring decree appointing me to the government of the empire. I deeply cherish a sense of my ignorance and blindness, and am afraid lest I prove unworthy of thy great favors. Therefore will I observe all the rules and statutes, striving, insignificant as I am, to discharge my loyal duty. Far distant here, I look up to thy heavenly palace. Come in thy precious chariot to the altar. Thy servant, I bow my head to the earth, reverently expecting thine abundant grace. All my officers are here arranged along with me, joyfully worshiping before thee. All the spirits accompany thee as guards (filling the air) from east to west. Thy servant, I prostrate myself to meet thee, and reverently look up for thy coming, O Te!

O that thou would vouchsafe to accept our offerings, and regard us while we worship thee whose goodness is inexhaustible!"

In A. D. 1832 China was visited with a long and severe drought, and the emperor, Tau-Kwang, thus prays for relief: "I, the minister of heaven, am placed over mankind, and am made responsible for keeping the world in order and tranquilizing the people. Unable as I am to sleep or eat with composure, scorched with grief and trembling with anxiety, still no genial and copious showers have as yet descended. . . . I ask myself whether, in sacrificial services, I have been remiss; whether pride and prodigality have had a place in my heart, springing up there unobserved; whether from length of time I have become careless in the affairs of government; whether I have uttered irreverent words, and deserved reprehension; whether perfect equity has been attained in conferring rewards and inflicting punishments; whether, in raising mausoleums and laying out gardens, I have wasted property and distressed the people; whether in the appointment of officers I have failed to obtain fit persons, and thereby have rendered the government vexatious to the people; whether the oppressed have found no means of appeal; whether the largesses conferred on the afflicted southern provinces were properly applied, or the people left to die in the ditches. . . . Prostrate, I beg imperial Heaven to pardon my ignorance and dullness, and to grant me self-renovation; for millions of innocent people are involved by me, a single man. My sins are so numerous that it is hopeless to escape their consequences. . . . Prostrate, I implore imperial Heaven to grant a gracious deliverance!"

While the ancient writings of the Chinese show conclusively that they possessed, originally, some correct knowledge of the nature and attributes of God, it is interesting to find that in the consciousness of the Chinese, even in our own day, there lingers a tradition or impression of the divine law. In preaching to the Chinese the missionary frequently refers to the decalogue, and presents its requirements and enactments as the *divine* law. Speaking one day on this topic in the chapel of our mission, in the city of Fuh Chau, a Chinese gentleman present interrupted me with the remark, "We also have a heavenly law." The expression "heavenly law" (tien tëû) was new to me at the time, and I eagerly inquired about it. "We all know," continued the speaker, "about the heavenly law," and the entire congregation corroborated the correctness of the statement.

"Where is this statute or law?" I inquired.

They replied: "We cannot tell where it is."

"Is it not found," I proceeded, "in some of your books?"

"No," they answered; "our books give us no information on the subject."

"Cannot some of your scholars or learned men explain the matter?"

"They know nothing more on the subject than we do."

"How then," I asked with some earnestness, "do you know there is such a law as that to which you refer? You have never seen it, have never read it, are ignorant of its precise import; how do you know there is such a law?"

"Why," said they, "every one says there is a heavenly law, and we never heard of one who had any doubt on the subject."

Pursuing these inquiries, I ascertained that all with whom I conversed were informed on the subject. This statute is a kind of unwritten higher law to them; they accept it as the standard of morals, the authoritative rule of faith. They consider it a sufficient condemnation of any man or enterprise to say, "Ah, he or it violates the heavenly law!" When urged to give the import of this law, their reply is, "We know it enjoins the performance of virtuous actions, and forbids vicious conduct;" and those who have some knowledge of Christian doctrines say that it must be similar to the precepts of the decalogue.

Whence did the Chinese obtain this profound impression of a heavenly law? and how happens it that the abrasion of successive centuries has failed to obliterate it from their minds? From the Bible standpoint alone can satisfactory answers be given to these inquiries. The sublime scenes enacted on Sinai rise before us as we dwell on this subject, where, we are told, "all the people saw the thunderings, and the lightnings, and the noise of the trumpet, and the mountain smoking: and when the people saw it, they removed and stood afar off. And they said unto Moses, Speak thou with us, and we will hear, but let not God speak with us, lest we die. . . . And the people stood afar off; and Moses drew near unto the thick darkness where God was." We can conceive somewhat of the impressions this terrific scene would produce on the minds of all present on that occasion; and when we add the influences of those stupendous miracles by which, subsequently, the law was magnified, and of those terrible judgments by which all violations of its statutes were punished, it is not strange there even now exists among the Chinese a recollection of the "heavenly law."

I was preaching one day to a Chinese congregation on the fourth commandment, and while endeavoring to explain and enforce the claims of the Sabbath, a Chinese gentleman present in the congregation startled me by saying:

"May I inquire whether your Sabbath is the same as our 'heavenly day?'"

"Heavenly day!" said I in reply; "what do you know about a heavenly day?"

"Why," responded the speaker, "we have always heard of a heavenly day, but we cannot say much on the subject."

Following up this interesting topic, I ascertained that there is in general use among the Chinese of Fuh Chau a proverb which runs thus: "Ah, you are ignorant of the heavenly day!" This proverb is employed by old men when reproving the youth of the land. No one seemed to have any clear idea of the proverb's precise meaning.

"What is this heavenly day?" I inquired.

The uniform answer was: "We cannot tell what it is."

"When does it occur? Does it come once a year, once a month, or how often?"

The same answer still met me: "We cannot tell you anything about it."

"Do your books say nothing on the subject?"

"Nothing, so far as we know."

"And why," I proceeded, "in the absence of all direct evidence on the subject, do you believe there is a heavenly day?"

My effort to develop any latent skepticism was utterly futile. "Every one believes it," said they, "and it must be true."

We should not be authorized, perhaps, to infer from this proverb that the Chinese once had some acquaintance with the fourth commandment; and yet the fact is interesting and suggestive. Pertinent to this subject, let us now notice a few other illustrative and corroborative circumstances.

In the ancient history of China we are told that when a certain king ascended the throne he instructed the different portions of his subjects, "On the *seventh* day come and pay your obeisance." Chinese physicians, in their diagnosis of diseases, lay it down as an axiom that every case of sickness assumes a new phase on every *seventh* day. Again, when a Chinese dies, his friends, if able to do so, will employ priests to celebrate mass for the repose of the departed spirit on the *seventh* day after the death of the party, and this mass is performed on successive *seventh* days for *seven* times. This use of the number *seven* by the Chinese is the more remarkable because in China everything goes by decades or decimals. Their dozen is ten; their sets of plates, cups, saucers, etc., comprise ten pieces or pairs; in fact, you constantly hear of tens. But in the instances to which I have referred we find the number *seven* introduced. Now, connecting this singular fact with their proverb about the heavenly day, are we not authorized to infer that, in some former period of their history, the Chinese were acquainted with the divine command, "Remember the Sabbath-day," etc.?

The *filial piety* of the Chinese has an important bearing on this view of the subject. The doctrine of filial piety, that is, respect of children for their parents, is one of the most important and prominent features of Chinese civilization. It is scarcely necessary to remind the reader that the Chinese have pressed their theories on this subject to an unjustifiable extreme; that their filial piety is rank idolatry; and that, in genuine regard and love for their parents, the theory and practice of the Chinese are utterly divergent and hopelessly conflicting. Notwithstanding these sad drawbacks, however, it is still true that the position of the Chinese on this interesting question is far in advance of that of any other heathen nation in the world. The doctrine underlies and supports their entire social and political systems, and it has developed that form of idolatry to which, of all others, the Chinese are most firmly and sincerely attached. We may say, indeed, that the Chinese are the only heathen people who have given to this doctrine an important place in their civilization and government. While other heathen nations entirely ignore this subject, or openly sanction practices utterly opposed to its beneficent teachings, the Chinese have accepted it as a primary truth, and have invested it with all ethical and political honors. In this regard their civilization is unique among all the heathen nations of the world. What has given to the Chinese this distinguishing characteristic? There can be, we conceive, only one answer to this question: It has sprung from their early connection with the old Bible records, and particularly with the fifth command of the decalogue.

The *marriage institution*, as recognized in the laws of China, contributes evidence on this subject. The intelligent reader is prepared for the statement that in this respect, also, the Chinese stand entirely above all other heathen nations; but it is probable even he will be surprised to observe how nearly the Chinese view of this subject harmonizes with the one contained in the Pentateuch. A Chinese husband can have at one time only one legal wife. At her death, the bereaved husband may make a second marriage. This wife is taken with established ceremonies, and she is the recognized head of the domestic household. Concubinage is allowed, and freely practiced in China; but the concubine cannot take from the wife her authority or position in the family. His marriage is one of the most important events in the life of a Chinese. Its preliminaries are arranged with anxious solicitude, and with profound deference to all the influences, terrestrial and celestial, which are supposed to affect so important an enterprise. The nuptials are celebrated with all the display which the resources of the parties can command, and the ceremony is invested with judicial sanctions, social festivities, and ancestral honors. It is certainly as remarkable as singular to find such sentiments on this subject prevailing so extensively among a heathen people, and the bearing of this fact on the question before us is sufficiently evident to the reader. We might refer to other sources of testimony on this point. The industrial and fine arts, agriculture, commerce, architecture, literature, jurisprudence, political economy, proverbs, social system, and the manners and customs of the Chinese, all furnish evidence, palpable, cumulative, and convincing, that the original Chinese came from the old homestead of the human race, in Western Asia, and were acquainted with the doctrines and facts of the early Bible records. It does not fall within the plan of this work to present this evidence in detail. We simply indicate the sources from which additional testimony on this subject may be drawn, and now pass to notice another remarkable feature of Chinese civilization.

It is a noteworthy fact, that of all those ancient empires founded immediately subsequent to the deluge China alone remains. The Assyrians, Egyptians, and, in later times, the Grecians, have severally attained to a comparatively high degree of intelligence and refinement; but their star soon culminated and sank into utter darkness. China, however, has never been wrecked, her civilization has never retrograded; paradoxical though it seems, her star has remained in its zenith for at least three thousand years. Through all this long lapse of centuries the Chinese have kept up, fairly and steadily, to their original civilization; and to-day they present all the essential elements of those social, literary, and political traits which characterized them in those early epochs when the Assyrians built their magnificent cities, the Egyptians developed their subtle theory of the metempsychosis, or the Greeks were thundering at the gates of Troy. It must certainly be interesting to inquire how such a result has been reached, and to ascertain, if we can, at least some of the causes which have contributed to it. In solving this interesting problem we observe that the civilization of the Chinese is distinguished from all other heathen civilizations by the fact that its primitive elements were derived from the Bible, and that the necessary tendency of these elements is to conserve and perpetuate the system. A prominent characteristic of Chinese civilization is the total absence of those revolting and cruel rites which form the leading traits of other heathen systems of civilization. As illustrative of this remark, we may refer to the deification of vice and the offering of human victims in sacrifices, practices which, though characteristic of nearly every other heathen nation, constitute no feature of Chinese civilization. The connection between these abominations and the destruction of the nations guilty of them, is shown in Leviticus xviii, 24, 25: "Defile not ye yourselves in any of these things: for in all these the nations are defiled which I cast out before you; and the land is defiled: therefore I do visit the iniquity thereof upon it, and the land itself vomiteth out her inhabitants." As a further contribution to the solution of this question we refer to the length of days promised by the Almighty to those who observe the command: "Honor thy father and thy mother." No heathen nation has ever approximated the Chinese in their respect for parents; and notwithstanding the wide divergence of the Chinese, both in theory and practice, from the true import of the fifth commandment, we conceive it is neither fanciful nor farfetched to suppose that even their imperfect observance of it has had much to do with the permanence of their institutions and the perpetuity of their national existence. Finally, on this topic, we observe that God may have preserved the Chinese nation in its integrity for the elucidation of some great principle, or the fulfillment of some prophecy connected with the progress and triumph of his Son's kingdom in the world. There are intimations that in the latter days the Church, in her graces, accomplishments, and triumphs, will be surpassingly beautiful and glorious. "Therefore thy gates shall be open continually; they shall not be shut day nor night; that men may bring unto thee the forces of the Gentiles, and that their kings may be brought. For the nation and kingdom that will not serve thee shall perish; yea, those nations shall be utterly wasted." "Behold, these shall come from far: and lo, these from the north and from the west; and these from the land of Sinim." (China?) "Who hath heard such a thing? who hath seen such things? shall the earth be made to bring forth in one day? or shall a nation be born at once?" For the accomplishment of these and similar prophecies no nation has ever furnished such grand and essential elements as the Chinese, and in no age of the world have the signs of ultimate and immediate success been so grand and auspicious as at the present hour.

CHAPTER III.

HISTORY OF CHINA.

THE history of China has proved to many writers a fruitful source of perplexity and misconception. While some have decried it as altogether unworthy of credence or study, others have lavished upon it the highest encomiums. It has had, indeed, the somewhat singular fortune of being alternately unduly extolled or indiscriminately disparaged. Disgusted with its harsh and unintelligible nomenclature, and with the *outré* garb in which its scenes and heroes appear before us, the man of refined taste has usually dismissed the subject from his thoughts; while the skeptic, eager for plausible arguments in support of his views, has seized with avidity on its high-sounding claims to antiquity as a triumphant refutation of the claims of the Bible. Some of our readers can doubtless remember the confident utterances of the infidel oracles in France and Germany on this subject not many years ago: "The Bible chronology unreliable;" "the Bible history contradicted by the authentic records of ancient nations;" "the Bible proved to be false!" These and kindred statements supplied at once the text and key-note for innumerable philippics against the Christian religion. "The

Mosaic record," said these writers, "is utterly at fault, for the ancient records of China assure us that the ancestors of that people were laying the foundations of the Chinese empire at the time when, according to the Mosaic narrative, the Almighty was creating the heavens and the earth; and that the Chinese husbandman was tilling his farm at the time Adam is represented as cultivating Eden." The issue was thus fairly presented, and, admitting the premises assumed, the conclusion is inevitable. If the ancient annals of China are authentic, the Mosaic record is invalidated. The only question is, "Are the ancient records of China authentic?" This question has now been thoroughly investigated, and a unanimous verdict has been given by both Chinese and foreigners, missionaries and diplomatists. The substance of this verdict is that all the historic records of China anterior to *Fuhhi*, supposed to be B. C. 2852, are utterly fabulous; that from *Fuhhi* to the commencement of the *Chau* dynasty, about B. C. 1100, they are extremely vague and uncertain, and that it is not till you come to the times of the Chau dynasty, about B. C. 1100, that they become entirely reliable.

Sir John Davis, referring to this subject, says: "The period of authentic history may be considered as dating from the race of Chau, in whose times Confucius himself lived; for although it might be going too far to condemn all that precedes that period as absolutely fabulous, it is still so mixed up with fable as hardly to deserve the name of history." Says the late Rev. Dr. Medhurst: "It has been generally supposed that the Chinese maintain an antiquity of myriads of years, and that their historical records, stretching far back into the vista of more than a thousand ages, are at such variance with the comparatively recent account of Moses as to oblige us either to question the one or the other. The fact is, however, that the Chinese, like most other heathen nations, have a mythological as well as a chronological period; the one considered by themselves as fabulous, and the other as authentic; the one connected with the history of their gods, and the other with that of their men. In the former they speak of their celestial emperor, who reigned forty-five thousand years; their terrestrial emperor, who reigned eighteen thousand years, followed by their human emperor, who reigned as long; without condescending to enlighten us as to the names, characters, events, or circumstances of these wonderful individuals, or their still more extraordinary reigns; nay, without so much as telling us whether their dominions were established in heaven or on earth, or whether they referred exclusively to China, or included other nations. In short, the vague account they furnish us of these fancied emperors shows that they were merely the figment of the imagination, introduced to supply a deficiency and to amuse the credulous. Indeed, so little credit is attached to this fabulous period by the Chinese themselves, that one of their most respectable historians, *Chu-Fu-Tsz*, does not venture to allude to it, but, passing by these extravagant assumptions, commences his relation at a much later period, when events and circumstances of a connected character stamp the records of the age with greater marks of credibility." Another Chinese historian waxes indignant over these absurd claims to antiquity, and declares they "are contrary to all sense and reason."

The entire period from Fuhhi, supposed to be B. C. 2852, to the beginning of the Chau dynasty, B. C. 1100, is so full of the marvelous, its notices are so vague, its dates so arbitrary, and the general character of the period so fanciful and obscure, that it is impossible to receive its records as reliable history. We are not authorized, perhaps, to reject this period of Chinese history as fabulous, and yet we are utterly unable, from its dim historic lights, to ascertain with certainty the chronological position and order of its events; and we can only hope that future researches and discoveries in the lands of the East may multiply the lights of these shadowy centuries, and guide the honest inquirer to truthful and reliable conclusions on this interesting subject.

Such, then, is the verdict which stern historic truth has given with reference to the vaunted antiquity of the Chinese empire. The ante-mosaic pretensions of Chinese records vanish into thin air, while all the facts of their reliable history are in beautiful and perfect harmony with the teachings of divine revelation.

It does not come within the plan of this work to give a detailed account of the history of China, and for full information on this subject we would refer the reader to the excellent works of Sir John Davis, Dr. S. Wells Williams, and others. It is sufficient for our present purpose to state that according to the Chinese records, commencing with Yu the Great, about B. C. 2205, there have existed twenty-six dynasties, covering an entire period of about four thousand years to the present time. The earliest records of China point to the province of HONAN as the original seat of its founders, and a glance at the physical geography of the country suggests the route over central Asia, through the mountain passes on the northwest of China, and down the waters of the Yellow River, along which they passed in reaching that position. From this point the Chinese gradually extended to the northward and southward over the area of their present empire. At times, as we pursue their history, they present the appearance of a consolidated government under a central and authoritative head; and then, again, they appear split up into petty and frequently contending states or kingdoms, of which at one time the number was one hundred and twenty-five. It is a noteworthy circumstance, that at the time our Lord and Saviour, Jesus Christ, was born into the world, China was under the sway of an emperor whose name was Peace. In A.D. 585, the territory north and south of the YANG-TSZ River, the Mississippi of China, was united in one empire. *Taitsung*, one of the most celebrated emperors of China, reigned at this period, and "during his reign the limits of the empire were extended over all the Turkish tribes lying west of Kan-suh, and south of the Tien-shan, as far as the Caspian Sea, which were placed under four satrapies or residences. West of these many smaller tribes submitted and rendered a partial obedience to the emperor, who arranged them into sixteen governments under the management of a governor-general placed over their own chieftains. His frontiers reached from the borders of Persia, the Caspian Sea, and the Altai of the Kirghis steppe, along those mountains to the north side of Cobi, eastward to the inner Hingan. Sogdiana and part of Khorassan, and the regions around Hindu-kush, also obeyed him. The rulers of Nipal and Bahar in India sent their salutations by their embassadors; and the Greek emperor, Theodosius, sent an envoy to Si-ngan in A. D. 643, carrying presents of rubies and emeralds, as did also the Persians. The Nestorian missionaries also presented themselves at court. Taitsung received them with respect, and heard them rehearse the leading tenets of their doctrines; he ordered a temple to be erected at his capital, and had some of their sacred books translated for his examination, though there is no evidence now remaining that any portion of the Bible was done into Chinese at this time."

The empire has been twice overrun and subjugated by the northern hordes, who for centuries have hovered along its northern frontiers. In A. D. 1280 the Mongolians, under Kublai-Khan, obtained the ascendancy, and for ninety years governed the empire. Marco Polo visited China during the reign of Kublai, and on his return to Europe gave a glowing description of the splendid magnificence of that eastern monarch's court. Possibly this description had something to do with Coleridge's poem, which, he says, was composed while he slept:

"In Xana-du did Kublai-Khan
A stately pleasure dome decree,
Where Alph, the sacred river, ran
Through caverns measureless to man
Down to a sunless sea."

In A. D. 1644 the Manchu Tartars, from Manchuria, obtained the throne and founded the dynasty which governs the empire to this day.

The Chinese have not grown up in complete independence of the other nations of the earth. There is sufficient evidence that some of the ancients were not ignorant of the existence of such a nation. Arrian speaks of the *Sinæ* or *Thinæ*, in the remotest parts of Asia, who exported the raw and manufactured silks which were brought westward by way of Bactria or Bokhara. It is recorded in the Chinese annals, that in A. D. 94 an envoy was sent by the then reigning emperor of China to seek intercourse with western nations. Marcus Antoninus, A. D. 161, made an unsuccessful attempt to send, by sea, an embassy to the eastern country which produced the splendid silk fabrics so much admired and coveted by the luxurious Latins. Nestorianism was introduced into China, about A. D. 635, by some bishops of that faith who had been driven eastward by persecutions in the Roman provinces. Two Arabian travelers visited China in A. D. 850 and 877, and published their itineraries, which Renaudot has translated, giving an account of the extensive commerce then carried on between Arabia and China. In A. D. 1246 Pope Innocent IV. dispatched, by the overland route through Russia, Giovanni Carpini, a monk, to the court of China to labor for the conversion of the emperor to the Roman Catholic faith. Carpini, it is said, was astonished at the immense treasures everywhere displayed, and having been courteously treated, was sent back by the emperor with a friendly letter to the pope. He was pleased rather than scandalized by the near resemblance of the rites of the Chinese Budhists to the forms of Roman Catholic worship, inferring from thence that they either already were, or very soon would be, Christians. Matthew and Nicholas Polo, two noble Venetians, visited China, were kindly received by the emperor, and on their departure for Europe were invited to return to China. They did return in 1274, carrying with them letters from Pope Gregory X., and accompanied by young Marco Polo, son to one of them. Young Marco became a favorite with the emperor, lived at his court for seventeen years, obtained liberty with some difficulty to return to Europe, and on his appearance in Venice gave an account of the vastness, resources, and splendor of the Chinese empire, which at the time was received with utter incredulity, but is now regarded as trustworthy.

"Abundant evidence," writes Sir John Davis, "is afforded by Chinese records that a much more liberal as well as enterprising disposition existed in respect to foreign intercourse than prevails at present. It was only on the conquest of the empire by the Manchu Tartars, 1644, that the European trade was limited to Canton; and the jealous and watchful Tartar dominion established by this handful of barbarians has unquestionably occasioned many additional obstacles to an increased commerce with the rest of the world. We have already noticed the Chinese junks which were seen by the Arabian traveler, Ibn Batuta, as far west as the coast of Malabar, about the end of the thirteenth century. Even before the seventh century it appears, from native records, that missions were sent from China to the surrounding nations, with a view to inviting mutual intercourse. The benefits of industry and trade have always been extolled by the people of that country; the contempt, therefore, with which the present Tartar government affects to treat the European commerce must be referred entirely to the fears which it entertains regarding the influence of increased knowledge on the stability of its dominion."

The Portuguese led the van of modern European nations in opening up trade with China. They appeared at Canton soon after their discovery (A. D. 1516) of the passage to the far east by way of the Cape of Good Hope; and their government sent, in 1520, the first embassy to the Court of China ever dispatched by sea from a European court. It was most unfortunate that the character and performances of nearly all these early adventurers were not calculated to give the Chinese a very exalted conception of foreigners. Thirsting for wealth, and often reckless as to the means of acquiring it, they usually scrupled not to resort to any practices, legal or illegal, that promised to fill their coffers. Eager to monopolize the tempting harvest before them, they were extremely jealous of all competition, and by the hostile attitude which they assumed toward the efforts of other European nations who sought to establish commercial relations with the Chinese, they taught them to fear and discountenance all intercourse with foreigners. It is truly wonderful to observe with what stern impartiality evenhanded justice commends the poisoned chalice to the lips of those who have mixed its contents. The Portuguese, through the entire period of their intercourse with the Chinese, have reaped the bitter fruit of the narrow and unjust policy toward foreigners with which they so unwisely contributed to indoctrinate the rulers of China; and at this day their position and influence in China are but little in advance of what they were centuries ago, while other nations, who sought to initiate a more magnanimous and truthful policy, have risen steadily in importance and influence, and to-day their counsels are almost omnipotent in the imperial cabinet.

The Dutch, in 1624, established themselves on the west coast of Formosa, a large island on the coast of China, but were finally driven from thence by the Chinese, and in 1662 they returned to Java. At the present day they have an extensive and lucrative trade with China. The Russians, as early as 1693, sent overland an important embassy to China; in 1719 another was sent by Peter the Great; in 1727 Catharine I. dispatched an embassador extraordinary to China, who concluded a treaty with that nation, and to the present time they have always wielded a powerful influence in China.

The English early directed their attention to China. Unsuccessful attempts to open a trade with the Chinese were made in 1637 and in 1664; but in 1670, just eight years after the Dutch had been driven from that island, they succeeded in establishing trade with the Chinese on the island of Formosa.

In 1685 they opened trade at Amoy and Canton, two important cities on the seaboard of China. Since that time England has always occupied a prominent position in the foreign commerce and diplomacy of China, and, in the main, her policy toward that government has been magnanimous, honorable, and just. It is chiefly due to her influence and efforts that the Chinese government is laying aside its exclusive policy, that China is rapidly coming to take her position in the circle of Christian nations, and that now the empire is thrown open to foreign commerce and Christianity.

The trade between the United States and China commenced in 1784, and has continued to expand quietly and rapidly to the present time. The practical energy and peaceable proclivities of the American character, complementing in the Chinese mind the more stately and powerful resources and characteristics of the English, have doubtless contributed much toward giving the Chinese an adequate and worthy conception of foreigners.

CHAPTER IV.

GOVERNMENT OF CHINA.

"EXTREMES MEET," says the old proverb, and every department of knowledge and experience corroborates the truthfulness of the sentiment. We doubt, however, whether any one ever fancied that a comparison between the respective governments of China and the United States of America would furnish a striking illustration of this popular adage. And yet, incredible as the statement may seem, we are prepared to show that, in form at least, an analogy exists between the most recent system of representative government and the oldest political despotism in the world. The existence of a central government as the supreme authority in the empire, the division of Chinese territory into provinces or states, counties, townships, and wards; the presence of regularly organized provincial or state governments, their independence as between themselves, and their subordination to the central government; the brief tenures of office prescribed for state officers, and the regulations controlling rotation in office; the existence of municipal organizations among the people, and the large amount of freedom and authority they exercise in the management of local matters; all these features of the Chinese government, and others to which we might refer, find, partially at least, their correspondences in the government of the United States of America. The *contrasts*, however, between these two governments are obvious and radical. The government of China is thoroughly despotic. The emperor is the sole and supreme head of the Chinese constitution and government. He is regarded as the vicegerent of Heaven, chosen by divine authority to govern all the world, and is called "The August Lofty One," "Celestial Ruler," "Sacred Sovereign," "Son of Heaven," "Sire of Ten Thousand Years," etc. Theoretically he is supreme in everything, possessing without limit or control the highest legislative and executive powers; practically, however, there are limits to this apparently irresponsible authority. Although the emperor is the fountain of all power, rank, honor, and privilege to all within his dominions; although he is the recognized head of religion, the only one qualified to adore Heaven, the source of law, and the dispenser of mercy; still the people regard him as bound to rule according to the published laws of the land, and his power is yet further circumscribed by public opinion, the want of an efficient standing army, poverty, and the venality of his own official agents.

There is in the Chinese government nothing fully analogous to a congress, parliament, or tiers état; still necessity compels the emperor to consult and advise with some of his officers. There are two imperial councils, which may be regarded as the organs of communication between the imperial head and the body politic; namely, the Cabinet or Privy Council, and the General or Public Council. Subordinate to these two councils are the administrative parts of the supreme government, consisting of the six boards, the Colonial Office, Censorate, Courts of Representation and Appeal, and the Imperial College.

The *Cabinet* or Privy Council is composed of six chancellors, under whom are six grades of officers, amounting in all to upward of two hundred persons, more than half of whom are Manchus. The imperial statutes state that the duties of this cabinet are, "to deliberate on the government of the empire, proclaim abroad the imperial pleasure, regulate the canons of state, together with the whole administration of the great balance of power, thus aiding the emperor in directing the affairs of the nation."

The *General Council* is of more recent organization, and is probably the most influential body in the Chinese government. It is composed of princes of the blood, the chancellors of the cabinet, the presidents and vice-presidents of the six boards, and the chief officers of all the other courts in the capital, selected at the emperor's pleasure. The number of members in this General Council probably varies according to his majesty's pleasure; but as no list of them is given in the Red Book, it is impossible to tell the proportion of Chinese and Manchu officers constituting this mainspring of the Chinese government.

Under the foregoing two councils at Pekin, the national capital, are the six boards, departments of long standing in the government, having originated during the ancient dynasties of the empire.

1. *The Board of Civil Office* "has the government and direction of all the officers in the civil service of the empire, and thereby assists the emperor to rule the people." It further takes charge of "whatever appertains to the plans of selecting rank and gradation, to the rules of determining degradation and promotion, to the ordinances of granting investitures and rewards, and the laws for fixing schedules and furloughs that the civil service may be supplied."

2. *The Board of Revenue* "directs the territorial government of the empire, and keeps the lists of population, in order to aid the emperor in nourishing the people, controls whatever appertains to the regulations for levying and collecting duties and taxes, to the plans for distributing salaries and allowances, to the rates for receipts and disbursements at the granaries and treasuries, and to the rights for transporting by land and water, that sufficient supplies may be provided for the country."

3. *The Board of Rites* "examines and directs concerning the performance of the five kinds of ritual observances, and makes proclamation thereof to the whole empire, thus aiding the emperor in guiding all the people. Whatever appertains to the ordinances for regulating precedence and literary distinctions, to the canons for maintaining religious honor and fidelity, to the orders respecting intercourse and tribute, and to the forms of giving banquets and granting bounties, are reported to this board in order to promote national education." The five rites referred to are the propitious, the felicitous, the infelicitous, the military, and the hospitable rites.

4. *The Board of War* "has the government and direction of all the officers within and without the provinces employed in the military service of the nation, for the purpose of aiding the emperor in protecting all the people. Whatever appertains to the ordinances for taking away, giving, and resuming office or inheriting rank, to the plans of the post-office department, to the rules of military examination and discipline, and to the rates and enrollments of actual service, are reported to this board in order to regulate the hinge of state."

5. *The Board of Punishments* "has the government and direction of punishments throughout the empire for the purpose of aiding the sovereign in correcting the people. Whatever appertains to measures for applying the laws with leniency or severity, to the task of hearing evidence and giving decisions, to the rights of granting pardons, reprieves, or otherwise, and to the rates of fines and interest, are all reported to this board, to aid in giving dignity to national manners."

6. *The Board of Works* "has the government and direction of the public works throughout the empire, together with the current expenses of the same, for the purpose of aiding the emperor to keep the people in a state of repose. Whatever appertains to plans for buildings of wood or earth, to the forms of useful instruments, to the laws for stopping up or opening channels, and to the ordinances for constructing the mausolea and temples, are reported to this board, in order to perfect the national works."

The Colonial Office, or court for the government of foreigners, "has the government of the external foreigners, orders their emoluments and honors, appoints their visits to court, and regulates their punishments, in order to display the majesty and goodness of the state." This office has the superintendence of all the tribes in Mongolia, Cobdo, Ili, and Koko-nor. These tribes are called external foreigners, to distinguish them from the tributary tribes in Sz Chuen and Formosa, who are called internal foreigners.

The Censorate, or "all-examining court," has "the care of manners and customs, the investigation of all public offices within and without the capital, the discrimination between the good and bad performance of their business, and between the depravity and uprightness of the officers employed in them; taking the lead of other censors, and uttering each his sentiments and reproofs, in order to cause officers to be diligent in attention to their daily duties, and to render the government of the empire stable."

The Court of Representation is composed of six officers, whose duty it is to receive memorials from the provincial authorities, and appeals from their judgment by the people, and present them to the cabinet. This court is also the channel through which the people can appeal directly to the emperor, and it is not a rare occurrence for even women and girls to travel from remote places in the empire to present their petitions for redress before the throne.

The Court of Appeals has the duty of adjusting all the criminal courts in the empire, and somewhat resembles a supreme court in the government.

The Imperial College is intrusted with the duty of drawing up governmental documents, histories, and other works; its chief officers take the lead of the various classes, and excite their exertions to advance in learning, in order to prepare them for employments, and fit them for attending upon the sovereign."

The *provincial* or *state* governments of China have been constructed with considerable ingenuity, and have proved to be remarkably stable and efficient. The territory of China proper is divided into *eighteen* provinces or states, and each province is subdivided into what may be termed *counties*, *townships*, and *wards* or *tithings*. The high civil authorities in each *province* comprise the viceroy or governor-general, lieutenant-governor, treasurer, judge, literary chancellor, and commissioners of rice and salt. In each province there are also what are termed intendants of circuits, who act as deputies for the viceroys and lieutenant-governors. The *county* authorities are the prefects, and in some cases the superintendents of customs. At the head of each *township* is the district magistrate, and at the head of each *ward* is the constable or centurion. The military officiary in each province is thoroughly organized, and has charge of both the land and sea forces. The highest military officer in the province is the Tartar-general, who resides in the provincial capital, takes rank with the viceroy, but whose jurisdiction is usually limited to the city where he resides. Inferior in rank, but superior in power to the Tartar-general, is the major-general, who, in conjunction with the viceroy and lieutenant-governor, directs the movements of the forces. Under this major-general are various grades of officers, corresponding in the main to the organization of armies in Europe or the United States.

The *nobility* of China comprise the members of the imperial house and clan, of which there are twelve orders, the five ancient orders of nobility designated duke, count, viscount, baron, and baronet, and, finally, some other orders which, in consequence of rarity or peculiar privileges, are deemed even more honorable than the preceding, and correspond in some degree to the orders of garter, thistle, bath, etc., in Europe. The nobility of China, as a body, is destitute of power, land, wealth, office, or influence. The members of the imperial house and clan comprise two branches: the lineal descendants of the first emperor of the reigning dynasty, and the lineal descendants of his uncles and brothers. The management of the clan of imperial relatives appertains solely to the emperor, and he has constituted what may be called the clansmen's court, whose duty it is to direct whatever pertains to the imperial kindred.

The civil officers in the Chinese government are chosen by the emperor from the literary class of society, and in nearly every instance from those who have obtained the three literary degrees corresponding to our bachelor of arts, master of arts, and doctor of laws. The highest civil officers of the government are generally selected from those who have received the *fourth*, or highest literary degree known in China. It is not surprising, then, that the great majority of Chinese officials are men of good natural abilities, thoroughly trained in their schools, and intimately acquainted with both the theory and practice of their own government. Literary attainments are considered absolutely essential to official position and preferment; they constitute, in fact, the only aristocracy that exists among the Chinese. The literary class in China is first in social position, civic honors, and political influence; it is a power behind the throne greater than the throne itself. The state papers of China, written by her officers and covering every department of legislation, will compare favorably, in many respects, with the diplomatic productions of any government in Christendom. Some of the most accomplished statesmen of Great Britain and the United States have been sent as ministers to the Court of China, and they have invariably returned from their Eastern mission with a cordial respect for the business talent, logical acumen, and general intellectual ability of their Chinese diplomatic confreres.

The foregoing sketch of the government of China would be incomplete without a brief reference to some of the practical anomalies with reference to this subject which exist among the Chinese. The government of China is intensely despotic, and yet, coincident with this unmitigated despotism, there exists among the Chinese a strong democratic element, which finds expression and scope for action in their municipal regulations. Every ward in China has its elders, its public hall, where the people meet for the transaction of business, and its placards or public manifestoes, in which the popular sentiments are boldly expressed; and both unpopular officers and offensive acts of government are sometimes criticised and denounced with irresistible logic and overwhelming ridicule. These elders are chosen by the people, either by seniority or by the sentiment of the ward, and their authority is potent and generally ultimate in adjudicating the cases brought before them. In all important festivals and processions, whether civic or religious, these elders, in appropriate costume, march at the head of the people and act as their representatives. The government regards them as the patriarchs of the people, and holds them responsible for the acts of the ward in which they reside. If a riot or serious casualty occurs in any ward where the enforcement of the laws is difficult, the government will require the elders to arrest and hand over the guilty parties for punishment; and in case of failure to comply with these demands, it will proceed to arrest and confine the elders until the guilty or suspected parties are delivered up to the proper authorities. Public meetings may be convened in the ward at any time, and notice is usually given by sounding a gong through the streets, or by written placards posted in public places. At these meetings all the people may be present and participate in the proceedings. Tea, tobacco, wine, and sometimes a substantial feast, form the accompaniment to these gatherings of the people. The presence of the literary class in these meetings gives additional dignity and authority to their proceedings; but it is a rare thing for a literary gentleman to take part in any meeting where either the acts or officers of the government are to be criticised and opposed. During the earlier years of our missionary operations in Fuhchau we had most convincing evidence of the existence and influence of these ward meetings. Instigated and controlled by a few crafty and interested parties in the ward where we lived, the people assumed an attitude of decided hostility toward us and our operations. Meetings innumerable were held by them to discuss the subject and arrange their plans; interminable remonstrances against us were sent up to the government authorities, and formidable committees were appointed to take charge of the matter. The result was that for about two years we were utterly unable to do anything in the way of obtaining residences for additional families of missionaries, or even native houses for chapels and school-rooms in that part of the city.

In the spring of 1858 there was a popular insurrection in Fuhchau, illustrative of the reserved sovereignty claimed and exercised by the Chinese. The government officials in that city had obtained large sums of money from the people for the purpose of protecting the place against the insurgents, who were approaching from the westward; but instead of using the money for the object designated, it was ascertained that the greater part of it was embezzled by the officers. At this juncture the imperial commissioner, on his way from Pekin to Canton, arrived at Fuhchau. On the morning of his intended departure from the city, the authorities were desirous of displaying the troops provided for the defense of the city; but, as the force in actual service would furnish a most startling contrast to the official reports on the subject forwarded to the emperor, they resorted to the following device to meet the emergency. A large quantity of military caps and coats were purchased or hired for the occasion, and then the occupants of every shop in the entire line of streets along which the commissioner would pass were ordered to furnish a man to wear the uniform, and stand in front of the shop while the procession was defiling through the street. The plan was ingenious, and thoroughly Chinese; but unexpected difficulties were encountered in endeavoring to enforce it. The people cried out against such barefaced imposition, and one man persistently refused to comply with the requisition. The police arrested him and proceeded summarily to punish him. This was too much even for the Chinese, and all the people promptly united to resist the execution of the odious order. This precipitated a collision with the government, and the excitement instantly spread throughout the whole city. Business was suspended, all the shops were closed, the streets were filled with the excited populace; the government offices were surrounded by vociferating crowds, unpopular officers were attacked in the street, their sedans were broken and their sedan-bearers were beaten. The imperial commissioner was unable to leave the city, the people declaring they would capture him if he made the attempt; the people forced their way into the viceroy's palace, defacing the furniture and rudely jostling his excellency; and thus, for about two days, the people defied the government, and the city was entirely in their power. During all this time the great mass of the people were quiet and orderly, and even those who were active in the insurrection demeaned themselves with studied propriety, stated calmly and carefully the circumstances necessitating their present proceedings, and, availing themselves of this favorable opportunity, presented a list of their grievances for the consideration of the government. The issue of the movement was that the government authorities promised free and full pardon to all who were engaged in these violent proceedings, and also agreed to redress promptly all the grievances of which the people complained.

We have seen that the Chinese believe their emperor to be the vicegerent of Heaven, and that he rules the empire by divine right. In case of a local disturbance, where the conflict lies between the people and the local authorities, the friends of the movement will seek to justify it by charging the authorities with defrauding and oppressing the people against the instructions of the emperor, and without his knowledge, and that hence this popular outbreak is only an appeal to the emperor against the treachery of his agents. But any direct and avowed infringement of the imperial prerogative, any organized resistance of the imperial mandates, they characterize as both treason and sacrilege. All who participate in such movements are called thieves, and their leaders head-thieves or robbers. When the rumors of the great rebellion first reached Fuhchau in 1852, the people spoke of the movement with evident disapprobation; but when it began to assume gigantic proportions, when half the empire had succumbed to its prowess, I observed that the people gradually changed their nomenclature and began to use respectful language in speaking of it. Conversing one day with an intelligent Chinese on the subject, I inquired:

"How does it happen that the insurgent chief makes such rapid progress, if the emperor holds his authority and position by divine right?"

After thinking a few moments he gravely replied:

"The emperor *claims* to be the vicegerent of Heaven, ruling the empire by divine right, and he *proves* it by keeping possession of the empire against all enemies; but if the insurgent chief can defeat the imperial armies and seize upon the throne, that disproves the emperor's claim, and shows that with the insurgent chief now rests the divine right to govern the empire."

CHAPTER V.

LAWS OF CHINA.

"THE *laws* of China," says Dr. Williams, "form an edifice, the foundations of which were laid by *Li Kwei* twenty centuries ago. Successive dynasties have been building thereon, adding, altering, pulling down, and building up, as circumstances seemed to require. A history of the changes and additions they have undergone, if there were materials for such an account, would contribute much to show the progress of the Chinese in civilization and good government." The Chinese entertain a profound respect for the laws contained in their national code. Sir George Staunton remarks that "all the Chinese seem to desire is the just and impartial execution of these laws, independent of caprice and uninfluenced by corruption. That the laws of China, on the contrary, are very frequently violated by those who are their administrators and constitutional guardians, there can be, unfortunately, no question; but to what extent, comparatively with the execution of laws in other countries, must at present be very much a matter of conjecture. At the same time it may be observed, as something in favor of the Chinese system, that there are substantial grounds for believing that neither flagrant nor repeated acts of injustice do, in point of fact, often, in any rank or station, ultimately escape with impunity."

This code of laws is called by the Chinese *Ta Tsing Liuh Li*, that is, Statutes and Rescripts of the Great Pure Dynasty, and contains all the published laws of the empire. The laws are classified under seven leading heads, namely, General, Civil, Fiscal, Ritual, Military, Criminal, and those relating to public works; and are subdivided into four hundred and thirty-six sections, called *liuh*, to which are appended the *li*, or modern clauses, which limit, explain, or alter them. These *li*, or modern clauses, are now much more numerous and voluminous than the original statutes. The clauses are attached to each statute, and have the same force; but there are no authorized reports of cases and decisions, either of the provincial or supreme courts, published for general use, though a record of them is kept in the court where such decisions are made, and in some instances these adjudged cases have been published as a guide to officers. A new edition of this code is published by imperial authority once in five years, and to the edition published in 1799 an extensive collection of notes, comments, and cases illustrating the practice and theory of the laws was appended. A very brief sketch of this body of laws is all we can here present to the reader.

The *General Laws*, in forty-seven sections, contain the principles and definitions which guide the administrator in the construction and application of the entire code.

The *Civil Laws*, in twenty-eight sections, are divided into two books, one of which refers to the system of government, the other to the conduct of magistrates, etc.

The *Fiscal Laws*, in eighty-two sections, contain rules for enrolling the people, for succession and inheritance, for regulating marriages between different classes of society, for guarding granaries and treasuries, for preventing and punishing smuggling, for restraining usury, and for overseeing shops.

The *Ritual Laws*, in twenty-six sections, contain the regulations for state sacrifices and ceremonies, for the worship of ancestors, and for whatever pertains to heterodox and magical sects or teachers.

The *Military Laws*, in seventy-one sections, provide for the protection of the imperial palace, for the government of the army, the guarding of frontier passes, the management of the imperial cattle, and the forwarding of dispatches by the couriers.

The *Criminal Laws* are arranged in eleven books, containing in all one hundred and seventy sections, and constitute the most important division in the whole code. These laws relate to robbery, high treason and renunciation of allegiance, to homicide and murder, quarreling and fighting, abusive language, indictments, disobedience to parents, and false accusations, bribery and corruption, forging and frauds, incest and adultery, arrests and escapes of criminals, their imprisonment and execution, and lastly, miscellaneous offenses.

The laws referring to public works and ways, in thirteen sections, contain regulations concerning the weaving of interdicted patterns, the repairing of dikes, and the construction and preservation of government edifices, canals, forts, walls, mausolea, granaries, manufactories, etc.

A writer in the Edinburg Review has pronounced the following encomium on this code: "When we turn from the ravings of the Zendavesta or the Puranas, to the tone of sense and business in this Chinese collection, it is like passing from darkness to light; from the drivelings of dotage to the exercise of an improved understanding; and redundant and minute as these laws are in many particulars, we scarcely know a European code that is at once so copious and so consistent, or is nearly so freed from intricacy, bigotry, and fiction." Dr. Williams, referring to the same subject, says: "A broad survey of Chinese legislation, judged of by its results and the general appearance of society, gives an impression of an administration far superior to that of any other Asiatic country. The defects in this remarkable body of laws arise from several sources. The degree of liberty that can safely be awarded to the subject is not defined in it, and his rights are unknown in law. The government is despotic, but having no efficient military power in its hands, it resorts to a minuteness of legislation upon the practice of social and relative virtues and duties which interferes with their observance; though it must be remembered that there is no pulpit or Sabbath-school in China to expound and enforce them from a higher code, and the laws must be the chief guide in most cases. The code also exhibits a minute attention to trifles, and an effort to legislate for every possible contingency, which must perplex the judge when dealing with the infinite shades of difference occurring in human actions. There are now many vague and obsolete statutes, ready to serve as a handle to prosecute offenders for the gratification of private pique; and although usage and precedent both combine to prove their disuse, yet malice and bribery can easily effect their reviviscence and application to the case.

"Sheer cruelty, except in cases of treason against the emperor, cannot be charged against this code as a whole, though many of the laws seem designed to operate chiefly *in terrorem*, and the penalty is placed higher than the punishment really intended to be inflicted, that the emperor may have scope for mercy, or, as he says, for leniency beyond the limits of the law." The principle on which this is done is evident, and the commonness of the practice proves that such an exercise of mercy has its effect. The laws of China are not altogether unmeaning words, though the degree of efficiency in their execution is subject to endless variations. Some officers are lenient, others severe; the people in some provinces are industrious and peaceable, in others turbulent and averse to quiet occupations, so that one is likely to form a juster idea of their administration by looking at the results as seen in the general aspect of society, and judging of the tree by its fruits, than by drawing inferences applicable to the whole machine of state from particular instances of oppression and insubordination, as is so frequently the case with travelers and writers."

The Chinese government has evidently sought to obtain and perpetuate a just and equitable administration of its laws. To effect this, it selects its civil officers only from the literary class of society; it distributes the civil officers of the empire equally between the Manchus and Chinese, who are required to inform on each other; it forbids any man to hold office in his native province; it requires constant rotation in office, no officer being allowed to remain more than three or four years in one office; it prohibits its officers from marrying in the jurisdictions under their control, from owning land there, and from employing son, brother, or near relative as an officer under them. Censors are appointed by the emperor, whose duty it is to point out all errors of administration; members of the imperial clan attend the meetings of the boards at Pekin, to observe and report whatever they may deem amiss, or of interest, to the emperor and his council; and in all the upper departments of the general and provincial governments a system of espionage is strictly enforced. In addition to this, there is made out, triennially, by the board of civil office, a catalogue of the merits and demerits of all the officers in the empire, for the imperial inspection. The imperial code ordains "that if any officer of government, whose situation gives him power and control over the people, not only does not conciliate them by proper indulgence, but exercises his authority in a manner so inconsistent with the established laws and approved usages of the empire that, the sentiments of the once loyal subjects being changed by his oppressive conduct, they assemble tumultuously and openly rebel, and drive him at length from the capital city and seat of his government, such officer shall suffer death." It would seem as though these provisions were amply sufficient to secure the desired end, and yet, notwithstanding all such safeguards and penalties, the administration of the laws in China must be characterized as, in the main, venal, tricky, extortionate, and cruel. Magaillans, who, after residing nearly forty years in China, ought to be good authority on such questions, has left on record his opinion touching this point. "It seems," says he, "as if the legislators had omitted nothing, and that they had foreseen all inconveniences that were to be feared; so that I am persuaded no kingdom in the world could be better governed and more happy, if the conduct and probity of the officers were but answerable to the institution of the government. But in regard that they have no knowledge of the true God, nor of the eternal rewards and punishments of the other world, they are subject to no remorses of conscience, they place all their happiness in pleasure, in dignity, and riches; and therefore, to obtain these fading advantages, they violate all the laws of God and man, trampling under foot religion, reason, justice, honesty, and all the rights of consanguinity and friendship. The inferior officers mind nothing but how to defraud their superiors, their superiors how to defraud the supreme tribunals, and all together plot how to cheat the king, which they know how to do with so much cunning and address, making use in their memorials of words and expressions so soft, so honest, so respectful, so humble, and full of adulation, and of reasons so plausible that the deluded prince frequently takes the greatest falsehoods for solemn truths. So that the people, finding themselves continually oppressed and overwhelmed without any reason, murmur, and raise seditions and revolts, which have caused so much ruin and so many changes in the empire. Nevertheless, there is no reason that the excellency and perfection of the laws of China should suffer for the depravity and wickedness of the magistrates."

The Chinese themselves speak out boldly on this subject. One of the imperial censors says: "Among the magistrates are many who, without fear or shame, connive at robbery and deceit. Formerly horse-stealers were wont to conceal themselves in some secret place, but now they openly bring their plunder to market for sale. When they perceive a person to be weak, they are in the habit of stealing his property and then returning it to him for money, while the officers, on hearing it, treat is as a trivial matter, and blame the sufferer for not being more cautious. Thieves are apprehended with warrants in their possession, showing that when they were sent out to arrest thieves, they took advantage of the opportunity to steal for themselves. At a village near the imperial residence there are very many plunderers concealed, who go out by night in companies of twenty or thirty persons, carrying weapons with them; they frequently call up the inhabitants, break open the doors, and having satisfied themselves with what food and wine they can obtain, they threaten and extort money, which if they cannot procure they seize the clothes, ornaments, or cattle of the people and then depart. They also frequently go to shops, and having broken open the shutters, impudently demand money, and, failing to get it, they set fire to the shop with the torches they carry in their hands. If the master of the house apprehends a few of them and sends them to the magistrate, he merely imprisons and beats them, and before half a month allows them to run away." Another censor, in speaking of the police, says: "They no sooner get a warrant to bring up witnesses than they assail both plaintiff and defendant for money to pay their expenses, from the amount of ten taels (ounces) of silver to several scores of taels. Then the clerks must have double what the runners get; and if their demands are not met they contrive every species of annoyance. Then, again, if there are people of property in the neighborhood, they will not fail to implicate them. They plot also with pettifogging lawyers to get up accusations against people, and threaten and frighten them out of their money."

The effect of all this upon the minds of the people may be readily imagined. With such flagrant perversions of justice before their eyes, the people have become afraid of all contact with the officers of government. Their great study is to keep out of the clutches of the law, and they will submit to almost anything rather than fall into the hands of those myrmidons who surround the government offices. The government of China, in fact, is an unmixed despotism. Resting on the patriarchal theory, and constructed with all the functions of a refined and ubiquitous tyranny, it has grown up into a vast and powerful system of government, the necessary effect of which is to destroy all confidence, and infuse universal suspicion among the people.

The following incident, which came under the personal observation of the writer, is pertinent to this aspect of the subject:

In the *Fing-hua* prefecture of the Fuh-kien province, some fifty miles southward from Fuhchau, there are two factions, known as the black flag and white flag parties, between whom a bitter feud has existed for many years. The frequent collisions between these hostile factions keep the prefecture in a state of perpetual excitement and alarm, and, as a natural consequence, business is frequently suspended, the harvests become uncertain, and at times it is unsafe for travelers to enter the territory. The government has frequently sought to adjust the difficulty, but with only indifferent success; indeed, it has often occurred that the approach of government troops produces a temporary combination of the rival factions, with a view to a joint onslaught on the common foe. During 1850–3 these factions seemed to be constantly at war with each other. Everything was thrown into confusion, and the government's local authorities were utterly unable to restrain the people or enforce the laws. At this point the lieutenant-governor of the province collected an army, proceeded to the disturbed prefecture, and after a campaign of perhaps four months, returned in triumph to Fuhchau, proclaiming the entire pacification of the belligerent factions. The rejoicings consequent on this gratifying consummation had scarcely ceased, when it was reported and extensively credited that the recent adjustment of difficulties had been effected by the most disreputable means; that, in short, the contending factions had bribed the governor to withdraw his troops, and forward to the emperor a glowing but utterly mendacious report of the victories won by the imperial troops, and the complete settlement of the whole affair. A literary gentleman in possession of all the facts in the case, memorialized the emperor on the subject. The memorial reached the emperor, and a commissioner was immediately dispatched to Fuhchau to investigate the matter. On arriving at Fuhchau, the commissioner was waited on by the lieutenant-governor, who soon arranged the preliminaries of the investigation entirely to his own satisfaction. The lieutenant-governor then sent for the author of the memorial, and partly by threats, but chiefly by bribes, induced him to write out a voluntary confession of his guilt, stating that the charges against the governor contained in his memorial to the emperor were utterly false, that the governor is in all respects a most upright and virtuous officer, that he can offer no justification for the malicious slanders contained in his memorial, and that he now begs the emperor to inflict upon him the severest punishment. Strange to say, this "voluntary confession" was duly embodied in the commissioner's official report of the case to the emperor, and in a short time an imperial rescript was received at Fuhchau, exonerating the governor from the charges preferred against him, and sentencing the author of the memorial to immediate banishment beyond the northern frontiers.

Another characteristic incident on this subject may close this chapter. When Europeans and Americans first went to live at Fuhchau, under the provisions of the treaties formed by their respective governments with the emperor of China, some of the people of the city, influenced by the bad precedent established at Canton, announced that foreigners could not be allowed to reside within the city wall. The English consul, however, failing to obtain a suitable residence in the suburbs, and having found an eligible and picturesque situation within the city wall on a hill called *Ushih-shan*, (black stone hill,) proceeded at once to occupy it. This gave great offense to the literary gentry of Fuhchau, and they ceased not to send up to the emperor the most urgent and elaborately written remonstrances against this invasion of their intra-mural city precincts by the ruthless foreigner. They stated that the residence of foreigners on the hill within the city wall was exerting a most deleterious influence on the trade and health of the city, and that it was every way exceedingly offensive to the people. Yielding at length to these persistent appeals, the emperor dispatched a commission to Fuhchau, to examine and report upon the subject. When the members of the commission reached Fuhchau, they found that the English Consul was really living on the *Ushih-shan*, that the hill was indeed within the city wall, and that the literary gentry of the city were anxious for his removal. But they soon ascertained it was useless to attempt driving him away. The case was an embarrassing one, but Chinese ingenuity was equal to the emergency. The history of Fuhchau states that in ancient times the *Ushih-shan*, which is now *within* the city wall, was then *outside* the city limits. Availing themselves of this important historic fact, the commissioners in preparing their report for the emperor, gravely stated that, on investigating the subject, they found that the allegations of the memorialists were in the main correct; that the English consul did certainly live on a hill called *Ushih-shan*, and that there is a hill by that name within the city wall. "But," continued the commissioners, "we find there are *two* hills in Fuhchau called *Ushih-shan*, one being *within*, the other *outside* the city wall, and it is on the *Ushih-shan outside* the wall that the English consul is living.

CHAPTER VI.

RELIGIONS: CONFUCIANISM.

THE religious notions and practices of the Chinese have been divided into three systems: Confucianism, Tauism or Rationalism, and Budhism; and the classification is convenient, and sufficiently correct for all practical purposes. This arrangement is in accordance with Chinese ideas on this subject. If you were to ask a Chinese how many systems of religious belief and practice there are in his country he will invariably answer *three*, and will name them in the order just given. And yet if the reader infers from this that there are three distinct classes in Chinese society, distinguished by these religious characteristics, the inference would be incorrect. It is utterly impossible to distribute Chinese society according to this arrangement. All that can be stated with strict propriety on this point is, that in Chinese society there is a class in whose minds the Confucian element predominates; another class in whom Rationalism is the leading characteristic; and a third class with whom the Budhistic element is in the ascendency. At the same time it is true that the so-called Confucian will resort to the teachings and practices of both the Rationalists and Budhists whenever such a step will subserve his own interests; that the Rationalist will avail himself of all the helps which Confucianism and Budhism proffer; and that the Budhist will supplement the teachings of the great sage by the axioms of Confucius and Lau-tsz. We thus reach the seemingly paradoxical conclusion that in the same Chinese mind there co-exist three distinct systems of religious faith. A brief examination of the subject will aid us in appreciating and explaining this mental phenomenon.

Confucianism confines itself to the enunciation and application of the principles of morals and political economy; it aims at teaching a man to govern himself, the child to obey its parents, the citizen to respect and conform to the laws of society, and the subject to revere and implicitly follow the commands of his ruler. All these principles and duties it seeks to substantiate and enforce by constant appeals to what might be called the *moral* sense; and hence it assumes the form and character of a system of moral philosophy underlying and vitalizing their social system and the entire scheme of political economy on which rests the stupendous fabric of their general government. Its sole tendency is to qualify man for society and government; but adduces no divine authority for its teachings, fails to communicate anything with regard to man's origin, nature, responsibilities to a higher power, or future destiny, and is utterly silent touching those questions which in all ages press upon the human mind and indicate the universal and imperative wants of the race. *Rationalism* is an intensified form of human *selfishness.* It practically deifies man, and to him subordinates heaven, earth, and hell. Man is enthroned; all recognized influences, celestial and terrestrial, are held to subserve his purposes, and are valuable and worthy of respect only as they contribute to this end. Resting on an original basis of superb transcendentalism, the system degenerated rapidly and utterly into utilitarianism, epicureanism, and materialism. With it the *quid utile* is omnipotent; *cui bono* is the universal text of excellence. Nothing is good that does not now contribute to man's personal profit; nothing worthy of attention that does not directly aid man in attaining the object of his present desires. Confucianism, it would seem, fails by attempting too much, Rationalism by attempting too little. The former is an effort to erect, on an insufficient basis of merely human authority and motives, the stupendous structures of social order and political government; the latter, starting with magnificent assumptions, suddenly descends to alchymy, jugglery, and buffoonery; the former is a grand effort of mortals to reach the gods, the latter an insane attempt to precipitate both gods and men into utter chaos and ruin. *Budhism* differs from both the preceding systems. It contemns matter, revels in the ideal, and professes to supply aliment for man's spiritual wants. Its doctrine of metempsychosis or transmigration of souls, associated with its belief in a state of future rewards and punishments, furnished a basis for powerful appeals to the popular conscience. Budh, its great object of worship, is invested with a character incomprehensibly sublime; its idols are massive and splendid, and its ritual of worship gorgeous and imposing. The system is admirably adapted to arrest the attention, delight the imagination, and kindle the enthusiasm of its devotees. It opens before the mind a boundless field for metaphysical speculation, and thus addresses a faculty of the human mind unnoticed by the other systems to which we have referred. From this rapid sketch we observe how these three systems complement each other, and hence can readily understand how they co-exist in the same mind, being in fact mutually supporting, instead of mutually destructive. We shall now give a more extended notice of these forms of heathenism which exist in China.

Confucianism, as we have already intimated, is a system of philosophy in the departments of morals and politics, rather than a system of religious faith and practice. It has, however, some characteristics which justify its appearance in this classification as one of the religions of China. The system was founded by Confucius, who, in connection with his immediate disciples, edited or composed the writings which contain its doctrines. Confucius (as his name has been Latinized by the Jesuits) was born about B. C. 550, in the kingdom of Lu, now comprised within the Shantung province, in the northeastern part of the Chinese empire. He was the son of a statesman, was the chief minister of his native kingdom, and spent the larger portion of his life in official employment. He was a reformer, seeking to correct the vices of society and of the government, and proved his sincerity by resigning his official positions when he found his counsels unavailing. He was remarkable for his simplicity, modesty, and uprightness; and his reformatory efforts were so successful that he gathered three thousand disciples, of whom seventy-two distinguished themselves by their devotion to their master and their observance of his precepts. He died in the seventy-third year of his age. Discoursing on the character of Confucius, Dr. Morrison remarks that he "was engaged in politics all his life; and even his ethics dwell chiefly on those social duties which have a political bearing. A family is the prototype of his nation or empire; and he lays at the bottom of his system, not the visionary notions of *independence* and *equality*, but principles of *dependence* and *subordination*, as of children to parents, the younger to the elder, etc. These principles are perpetually inculcated in the Confucian writings, as well as embodied in solemn ceremonies, and in apparently trivial forms of mere etiquette. It is probably this feature of his doctrines that has made him such a favorite with all the governments of China for many centuries past and down to this day. These principles and forms are early instilled into young minds, and form the basis of their moral sentiment. The elucidation and enforcement of these principles and forms are the business of students who aspire to be magistrates or statesmen, and of the wealthy who desire nominal rank in the country; and it is, in all likelihood, owing chiefly to the influence of these principles on the national mind and conscience, that China holds together the largest associated population in the world."

Confucius made very few remarks on religious subjects: he admitted, indeed, that he had no certain knowledge concerning the gods; that they were above and beyond human comprehension; and laid it down as an axiom that we ought to concern ourselves about the duties growing out of the present state of things, concerning which we have certain knowledge, rather than to trouble ourselves about supposed duties growing out of our fancied relations to the future, of which we know nothing. "Not knowing even life," said he, "how can we know death?" He regarded himself as commissioned by Heaven to restore the doctrine and usages of the ancient kings. "If Heaven is resolved that my doctrine shall not fail," said he in a moment of apparent danger, "the men of Kuang can do nothing to me." "There are three things," said he, "to beware of through life. When a man is young let him beware of his appetites; when middle-aged, of his passions; and when old, of covetousness especially." "How can a *mean* man serve his prince?" inquired the sage. "When out of office his sole object is to *attain* it, and when he has attained it his sole object is to *keep* it. In his unprincipled dread of losing his place he will readily go all lengths." In the penal code of China it is provided that "children and near relatives or dependants shall not be punishable for concealing the faults [crimes] of those with whom they dwell." This enactment is manifestly founded on the precept of Confucius: "The father may conceal the faults [crimes] of the son, and the son those of the father; virtue consists in this." On one occasion he replied to a disciple: "He that offends against Heaven has no one to whom he can pray." Another of his aphorisms is: "Life and death are decreed by fate; riches and poverty rest with Heaven."

The influence of these doctrines is almost omnipotent in forming the character of the Chinese. The official and literary classes of China may be regarded as *par excellence* Confucianists; but all classes are powerfully influenced by the teachings of the great sage. In the family, the school, the forum, the courts of justice, and the palace of the mandarin, these doctrines constitute the authoritative standard of propriety, morality, and political economy.

The following graphic account of the ceremonies observed at the annual worship of Confucius is by the Rev. Dr. Wentworth, a member of the Methodist Episcopal Mission at Fuhchau:

"There are sixty-three temples in honor of the great Chinese sage in the Fuh-kien province, and ten in this department, two of which are located within the city of Fuhchau. One of these was burned down eight or nine years ago, and rebuilt by the mandarins on a scale of unusual grandeur and liberality. It is one of the finest buildings in the city, and, according to a tablet near its entrance, cost about fifty thousand dollars. It is constructed similarly to ordinary Chinese buildings, one-storied, in the form of a hollow-square, with a spacious court in the center, apartments on each side, and the main temple at the end, opposite the entrance. This has a fine portico, supported by lofty columns, and the fretted roof within is sustained by columns of solid granite, of enormous size and strength. Here are no idols, but ancestral tablets supply their places in the gilded shrines. In the center is that of Confucius, on the sides are those of twelve of his most celebrated disciples, six on each side, and in the temple apartments, ranging along the outer court, are the shrines and tablets of some seventy followers of lesser fame.

"The worship of the great philosopher is monopolized by the literati; and the mandarins, who are literary graduates of the highest distinction, are the only priests who officiate upon the occasion. The sacrifice takes place twice a year, in the second and eighth months. It is performed before daylight in the morning, and the common people are rigidly excluded. Foreigners having seldom witnessed the ceremony anywhere, and never, we think, in the chief temple of a departmental city, several of us determined to gain access to the rites if possible, though it is very difficult to get into the temple itself during the periods that intervene between the sacrificial days, at which times it is thrown open for a brief space to the gaping public. On the afternoon of September 10, 1858, Rev. M. Fearnley, of the Church of England Mission, Rev. J. Doolittle, of the American Board Mission, and the writer, from the Methodist Episcopal Mission, went to the preparatory *rehearsal* of the rites in an old temple, aside from the actual theater of the contemplated festive display. All the actors were in full dress, and went through their parts under instruction, that there might be no hesitancy or blundering on the following morning.

Mr. Doolittle and myself took beds at Mr. Fearnley's, who lives inside the city wall, and at three o'clock in the morning were roused by our host, and were soon under way, following a man with a lantern along the silent and deserted streets, to the great discomposure of watchmen and dogs, to the scene of action. We were an hour too early; but better that than five minutes too late. Their magnificences, the mandarins, had not yet made their appearance, and we had opportunity to inspect everything unmolested. A burst of music and a shout at length indicated the coming of the magnates. Their first business was to get the 'huang-kiangs,' 'foreign babies,' out of the sacred precincts, and a mandarin of high rank came to request us to go outside, enforcing his errand with the needless plea: 'If you were worshiping in your churches you would not wish us to come in and disturb you.' We replied: 'Certainly not, and we have not come hither to disturb you, but to see the rites, and if we may not remain inside, pray let us stand next one of the great doors on the portico outside, where we may see what is passing on both within and without.' To this he consented, much to the displeasure of the officers' servants, a crowd of whom were driven off the portico without ceremony, though they insisted that they had as good a right there as those 'foreign devils.' They were more anxious to see us than the worship. 'You see them every day in the year,' said the remorseless lictor, under a hat like a sugar-loaf, with a fearful crack of his long whip. The platform was cleared, and the ceremonies began. The darkness was dispelled by rows of gaudy lanterns and a forest of blazing torches. The court was filled with mandarins and their servants. Privileged spectators from the literary class, with their attendants, crowded all the available space below. In front of the great central door of the temple, on the portico, was a band of musicians with flutes and 'soft recorders,' and another of boys fantastically dressed in the regalia of the occasion. Within were musicians chanting vocally, accompanied by the instruments without, the praises of the sage. The loud voice of a crier within the temple, and the loud response of a herald below, indicated that all was ready. Clouds of incense filled the temple, while two or three mandarins, in full official dress and caps, preceded by attendants, ascended the steps and entered the lofty doors on either side, prostrating themselves with the head to the pavement before the shrines successively, and offering the various articles placed in their hands by the attendants for that purpose to Confucius and his favorite followers. This was repeated three times in succession, the officers retiring and re-entering with the same stately ceremony on each occasion. The offerings were animal and vegetable. On a broad table in front of the shrine and altar of Confucius himself, lay shrouded the carcass of a whole ox, denuded of his skin, and on either side of him a pig and a goat. On the altar were vases of flowers and plates of cooked provisions, so that the philosopher might gratify his immediate appetite, as well as lay in a stock for salting down. Before the shrines of the twelve were pigs and goats, but the seventy outsiders were obliged to content themselves with offerings of grain and vegetables alone. We had opportunity before the ceremony to inspect the contents of the urn-like vessels, containing apparently a quart or two each of rice, millet, wheat, and other grains and vegetables; and found our Protestant fondness for the true and the real somewhat shocked by discovering that the mouths of the vessels had been ingeniously pasted over with paper, on which a thin layer of grain had been strewn so as to look like a full vessel. We saw one where a wag or some curious boy had stuck his finger through in experimenting on the depth of the contents. On inquiring after the reason of this rather Romish practice of endeavoring to cheat the denizens of the spirit-world, we were told that the form and the idea were all that were necessary. Perhaps if full vessels were offered in the sixty temples of this province, and as many more in other provinces throughout the empire, the spirit-sage might get more grain than he knew what to do with; but with only a thin layer in each, the aggregate may be no more than he can comfortably dispose of, though one would think, from the herds of oxen offered, that he would have beef to sell. His worshipers, with one eye on this fact and another to a commendable economy, take care to supply kine of such rascally, Pharaoh-like leanness, that his philosophership would feel no compunctions in throwing it to his dogs.

"At one point in the ceremony an official kneeled before the shrine of Confucius at a respectful distance, and in a loud voice chanted a prayer or hymn of praise. The ordinary chants were very sim-

7

ple, consisting of four notes perpetually repeated, thus:

"The last offering was material for clothing; a sort of coarse silk, in large patches, first offered bodily in the temple, and then taken down into the court and burned, that it might become spirit-silk in the other world. The Budhists usually offer ready-made clothing stamped on paper, and burn whole sheets covered with pictures of hats and frocks and pantaloons, with the idea that they become actual hats and coats and pants in the other state, though if the fire does not enlarge the articles, or the souls of the wearers are not shrunk to lilliputian dimensions, the patterns must be rather scanty. The mandarins send Confucius raw material, and thus put him to the expense of making it up; but at the same time give him the advantage of having his garments cut after the newest style, and by fashionable tailors. I saved a piece of the material from the fire to see if it was real silk and not paper, which, after the discovery of one astonishing fraud in their worship, we thought might answer instead of cloth for the 'form and idea.' The same 'form and idea' dictates to Romanists the economy of using, in their churches, *wooden* wax-candles, with a little reservoir of oil at the top sufficient to illuminate daylight during an hour of worship. In this state of being you might as well expect to deceive Satan as a Chinaman; but as soon as he is dead, his relatives send after him the thinnest possible tin and copper-leaf, and even brown paper itself, through fire into the other world, with the apprehension that, if it does not convert into actual silver and gold, the spirits will never know the difference. About the first gray streakings of the dawn of a cloudy morning the ceremonies concluded, the torches were suddenly extinguished, and the officers with their retinues slowly retired."

CHAPTER VII.

RELIGIONS: RATIONALISM AND BUDHISM.

RATIONALISM arose in China simultaneously with Confucianism. *Lau-kiun*, or *Lautsz*, the founder of the system, was born B. C. 604, in the kingdom of *Tsu*, now comprised in the province of *Hupeh*. He has left only one philosophical work, called *Tau-Teh-King*, or Memoir on Reason and Virtue, which embodies his philosophical writings. Some writers have fancied a resemblance and connection between the Rationalists of China, the Zoroastrians of Persia, the Essenes of Judea, the Gnostics of the primitive Church, and the Eremites of the Thebaid. "All material visible forms," says *Lautsz*, "are only emanations from Tau, or Reason; this formed all beings. Before their emanation the universe was only an indistinct, confused mass, a chaos of all the elements in a state of germ or subtle essence." And again: "All the visible parts of the universe, all beings composing it, the heavens and all the stellar systems, all have been formed of the first elementary matter. Before the birth of heaven and earth there existed only an immense silence in illimitable space, an immeasurable void in endless silence. Reason alone circulated in this infinite void and silence." The precepts of

Lautsz are similar in many respects to the teachings of Zeno. They recommend retirement and contemplation as the most effectual means for purifying the spiritual nature of man. The passions must be subjugated, the thoughts disentangled from external objects, that the soul, which they describe as merely a refined form of matter, may be prepared for immortality.

The Rationalists were formerly a numerous and powerful sect, but in modern times they have degenerated into magicians and jugglers, destitute alike of learning and influence. They worship a great variety of idols, among which are found genii, devils, inferior spirits, and deified men. Their highest divinity is *Yuh-Hwang-Shangti*, a corruption of the ancient Shangti of the Chinese classics. The priests of this sect allow the hair to grow on the crown of their heads, and coil it up in a large bow, through which they thrust a large pin. They live in temples, cultivating the grounds attached to them, or wander through the country deriving a precarious livelihood from the sale of charms and medical nostrums. They study astrology, profess to have dealings with spirits, and their books are filled with accounts of their marvelous performances in this department.

Budhism was introduced into China from India about A. D. 66. *Ming-Te*, the eighth emperor of the Han dynasty, influenced by a dream, or by a remarkable sentence in the writings of Confucius, ("The people of the West have a sage,") dispatched an embassy to the West to find the wise man. On reaching India the embassy came in contact with the Budhist priests, and returned with them to China. Budhism, thus introduced to the Chinese by imperial authority, and patronized by successive emperors, spread rapidly among the people, and now the empire is full of Budhist temples, while the land swarms with Budhist priests. Budhism has its trinity. Its disciples say: "Budh is one person, but he has three forms." Its sacred books are chiefly translations into Chinese from the originals in the Pali language, a dialect of the Sanscrit. The *five precepts* or *interdicts* of Budhism are, 1. Do not kill living creatures; 2. Do not steal; 3. Do not marry; 4. Do not speak falsely; 5. Drink no wine. These precepts are addressed to the priests alone. One of the favorite axioms of Budhism is: "All things originated from nothing, and will revert to nothing." Annihilation, to the Budhist, is the summit of bliss; *nirvana*, or nonentity, is his ultimate wish and anticipation. There is a striking similarity between the ceremonies of Budhism and those of the Church of Rome. Among these points of resemblance we may notice the distinguishing dress of the priests, their tonsure, celibacy, professed poverty, and monastic manner of life; the use of the rosary, candles, incense, holy water, bells, images, and relics in their worship; their belief in purgatory, their pretended miracles, prayers in an unknown tongue, with their endless repetitions; the similarity of their altar furniture, and the names of their intercessors, as "Goddess of Mercy," "Queen of Heaven," and "Holy Mother."

The ranks of the Budhist priesthood are recruited in many ways. One class of recruits comprises those who for some reason, as disastrous financial reverses, loss of dear friends, disappointment or remorse, wish to fly from society. By assuming the prescribed vows and costume, all such persons receive a sudden translation to the priestly office. Another class comprises those who in infancy or boyhood were adopted by the priests, and were by them trained up to be their successors in the priesthood. The temples of Budhism are innumerable; they occupy the most picturesque situations, and command views of the most beautiful scenery to be found anywhere in China. There is a celebrated Budhist temple on a mountain about six miles from the city of Fuhchau. It is situated in a most attractive place, and has become a kind of sanatarium for the members of the foreign community at Fuhchau. The following sketch of it may prove interesting to the reader:

At daylight of August 4, 1852, our party, consisting of Rev. Mr. W., of the "Church Mission," Mrs. Maclay, little Ellen, and myself, started for the monastery. One small native boat, with clean white floor, and rowed by a stout Chinaman, while his wife held the rudder with one hand, and with the other wielded an oar, whose movements corresponded to the steady strokes of her husband, was sufficient to accommodate the members of the party. Another boat of the same size received our baggage. The tide is in our favor, and we glide through the span of the great stone bridge, thread our way through the junks, and soon find ourselves below the shipping, quietly passing down the river. In an hour we reach the landing-place, and are surrounded by a crowd of the villagers, some curiously gazing at our person and clothes, others particularly interested in our baggage, while some are earnestly showing us that for carrying our goods up the mountain the very lowest price they can take is a sum which we very well know to be five or six times as much as they expect to receive. My trusty boy will attend to these matters; so we go on. Leaving the boat, we cross some paddy-fields, and soon come to an old temple which stands at the foot of the mountain. It is surrounded by a high wall, and the broad boughs of the banyans almost hide it from view. Several rest-houses here span the road, and there are seats where the weary traveler may refresh himself. A stream of limpid water issues from a stone wall near your seat. Many stone tablets, with long inscriptions, are placed around; but I fear the classic style of the sentences will prevent us from extracting much information from them at present. For the ascent the ladies are indulged with chairs, but the gentlemen must trust to their own muscles and sinews. The road is perhaps ten feet wide, and paved with large flat stones. Where the acclivity is not too abrupt, the road is plain; but there are steep places where steps are necessary. Rising into the clear air, our elevated position affords a fine view of the plain below. It is pleasant to halt at the shaded spots and enjoy the scene. There winds the broad river, on whose placid bosom our boat was moving only a few minutes since. The banks are very low, and the peasant guides his plow close to the water's edge. Branching off from the main channel are small streams, which, after mapping out numerous low islands, return their waters into it at irregular intervals. Canals, too, innumerable, fed by the river, creep through the plain, thus enabling the husbandman to irrigate his fields. Villages, almost hidden by the overhanging foliage of the banyan, are seen in all directions. There are many fruit orchards scattered along the canals, and on the slopes of the hills. Further west we see the hill where some of the missionaries live. On the right of it, and across the plain, lies the great city. Further still to the west the eye looks on successive ranges of dark mountains, whose rugged peaks shoot up far toward the sky. Northward there is the same mountainous prospect; while to the south rise the "Five Tiger Hills," with circling ranges of wild hills beyond, which, as they approach the sea, seem to divide into ten thousand tapering peaks. But we may not now linger; an August sun is sending its first beams athwart our path, and we may not lightly meet its scorching heat.

Three rest-houses, placed at irregular distances along the road, proffer their refreshing shade and seats as we ascend. The trees, mostly pine, throw a pleasant shade over us as we pass on. At the last rest-house an obsequious priest presses upon us most perseveringly a cup of tea and some dried fruits, in return for which he expects an extravagant remuneration. Merchants, officers, etc., from foreign countries, pay a pretty round sum, but from missionaries mine host must content himself with a few tens of cash. Plodding upward on the zigzag road, your high position renders still more distinct the features of the vast plain at your feet. The sun now pours a flood of light on the distant mountains, the broad river, and the city. Boats of various shapes and dimensions are moving on the water. Troops of young villagers are threading the narrow, winding paths of the rice-fields, going to their morning labors. Women, with basket, wood-knife, and rake, are starting for the mountains in search of fuel. The rustic, carrying his plow, and holding in his hand the tether of his faithful buffalo, slowly moves on to his toil. And if my vision is true, I see many a group of merry boys and girls sporting in the shade of the overarching trees that embower the villages.

But the quick pace of the coolies bids us hasten forward. Sure enough, they have reached the summit of the spur behind which the monastery is situated. The road now slightly descends, and sweeps round the southern base of the peak, whose top seems lost in the clouds. After a few minutes of quick walking, we enter a wooded ravine, and are greeted with the sound of falling water. It is a stream which, issuing from the rocks far up the mountain, is conveyed by an artificial channel to the monastery, and then, having supplied the wants of the priests, goes dashing downward to the plains, and discharges its waters into the Min. A little further, and the deep tones of the great bell come floating down the ravine. A low wall, old and covered with vines and bushes, runs along each side of the road. We pass through several gateways, whose columns and architraves present bold inscriptions, full of deep meaning, doubtless; but as the coolies move rapidly, and we pedestrians are pretty thoroughly tired, we shall not stop to read them. As we near the monastery the scenery becomes more beautiful and impressive. The road follows the meanderings of the stream to which we referred a while ago. Hugė camphor-trees, with gnarled trunks and immense boughs, throw a deep shadow over us; the stalwart pines send up their palmlike forms, waving their high tops like the banners of a host; the graceful bamboo, in silvery lines, skirts the course of the mountain stream, or, in thick clumps, clusters and glistens on the slopes of the ravine. Beneath this leafy canopy a luxuriant undergrowth finds a fertile soil and safe protection; while flowers, sweet "wild wood flowers," hang in rich festoons from decaying walls and sheltering boughs, or bud and bloom on the delicate stem that grows at your feet. The high peak towers up just before us, and from the appearance of immense tile roofs, darkened with age and exposure, we infer the immediate proximity of the monastery. A few more steps, and the vast pile of buildings is in full view; the bell sends forth with increased volume its solemn tones, and quickly passing an open space, where the sun pours down in its strength, we enter the first suite of buildings.

The history of this, as of all other places of note in China, is obscured by absurd legends and pompous traditions. According to some accounts, this situation, in the time of the "Three States," (A. D. 190–317) was chosen for the summer palace of the king. The religion of Budh was then highly esteemed, and one of the kings gave this palace to the priests for a monastery. Another statement is, that during the "Sung dynasty," (950–1280,) a literary chancellor erected some buildings on the spot for the use of the Budhists. Still another account refers its origin to the time of the "Three States." On the occasion of his father's death, an officer of high rank selected this situation for the grave, constructed the tomb with his own hands, built for himself a cottage near by, and, giving up his titles and honors, spent his life in watching and weeping over the dust of his beloved parent. The king, hearing of this instance of filial affection, was filled with admiration, and caused large and costly buildings to be erected, the care of which he committed to the Budhists. Others, discarding these accounts, tell of certain miraculous events which drew to this place the attention of the first preachers of Budhism, and entertain themselves with various marvelous incidents which, it is said, have transpired during the history of the institution.

We will now, if you please, look at the temple buildings. And the first thought suggested is, that, however great may be the antiquity claimed for this institution, the present buildings are certainly of quite recent date. In fact, the temple records show that at two distinct times the buildings, in whole or in part, have been destroyed by fire. And though we may discredit these statements, still, the building materials used by the Chinese being of so perishable a nature, we are compelled to attribute to the present compact, sound structures a recent origin.

An area of perhaps an acre is covered by buildings. In the center, and extending from the front to the rear, are three large temples, with open courts, paved with stones, between them. On each side of these principal edifices are the rooms for the priests, apartments for strangers and visitors, smaller temples, the libraries, and other appurtenances. The buildings, we notice, are only one story high; they are in the main well built and of substantial materials. There is, too, a cleanliness about the courts and rooms which reflects favorably on the priests.

A more particular notice of the prominent parts of this collection of buildings will enable us to think of them with greater satisfaction. The main front looks toward the south; and, as we enter the monastery at this point, we may now glance at the first of the three temples already referred to. This structure is about thirty feet deep and one hundred and twenty feet wide. A space in the middle, thirty feet deep by fifty feet wide, is occupied by idols, the rest of the building being otherwise appropriated. There are here six statues of great dimensions. Facing you, on entering, is a figure of Budh in a sitting posture. The pedestal on which it is placed is elevated about five feet from the floor. The statue is made of bricks and cement, with a bronze gilding. On each side of the entrance are placed two images, each being, perhaps, ten feet in height. They stand facing each other, the space between them being the entrance to the temple. These four images represent the ministers of Budh, and are called "Fung," or messenger; "Tieû," or harmony; "Ju," or rain; and "Song," or "propriety" or "fitness." The first grasps a sword in his right hand, the other is raised as in warning, while his black glaring eyes and fierce countenance seem to say, "*Now* or *never!*" He stands upright, and crushes under his feet a black, dwarfish figure, with features horribly distorted, representing an evil spirit. The second, "Tieû," looks down on you with a jocund face, as he twitches the strings of his "guitar" to some fairy strain, which mortals may not hear. Beneath his feet, too, as also of the others, there writhes a black, dwarfish figure. "Ju," the third, stands there with an umbrella half raised, in expectation of a shower. "Song," the last figure, holds in his left hand a struggling serpent, while in his right he holds up a ball, the precious jewel taken from the bowels of the enraged serpent. This figure is to my mind deeply interesting. The Bible tells us of a serpent, of souls lost by the fall, and of One who "bruised the serpent's head." In the figure before me I saw some points of close, striking resemblance to these truths. It is difficult to get the precise idea of this figure, as the priests themselves seem to have confused notions on the subject. They say, however, that this serpent, after living thousands of years, secreted this precious jewel, that man was unable to obtain it, and that this god accomplished the work. Many interesting thoughts are suggested by the analogy between this tradition and the work of Jesus Christ as the Saviour of the world. Whence came the idea embodied in the figure before me? Is it a fragment of those rays which, broken off from the great sun of truth, are ever and anon discovered among the old nations of the East? Budhism being of Indian origin, it is evident that we may trace this tradition to the same country. But whence did India obtain it? The mind of the Christian at once reverts to the "oracles of God." And there is abundant evidence to believe that India owes to the ancient records of the Bible whatever of truth is found in her mythology. "Harcourt," in his "Doctrine of the Deluge," maintains that the "patriarchs were deified in India, beginning with Noah and his sons;" also, that "Noah's grandson, Phut, was Budh, whose name was changed into Fo and Po; hence the river Padus and his Footstep the Sreepad." (Vide "Doctrine of the Deluge," vol. i, Table of Contents.) The Memoirs of Sir Stamford Raffles throw light on this interesting subject; also, Sir William Jones in "The Institutes of Menu."

To return to our story. Immediately in the rear of the image of Budh, and separated from it by a thin partition, is placed another idol, its back being against this partition, and its face looking toward the temples within. This figure holds in its hand a short stick of wood, with which to beat the evil spirits.

Passing through this building you enter a broad stone-paved, open court. As the original site was uneven, the ground has been leveled by forming terraces. In the center is an artificial reservoir for water, spanned by a stone bridge. Along the two sides of the court are covered passages, by which, ascending three short flights of broad stone steps, you go up to the second temple.

This building is about sixty feet deep by one hundred feet wide. It is devoted to the worship of the "Three Precious Budhs." Here the priests assemble, morning and evening, for worship. Against a high gilded screen, near the rear of the building, are placed the three idols. They are seated on gilded pedestals five feet in height. Their size corresponds to those we have already described. Their countenance, however, is very mild, and a kind of diadem is placed on the head of each one. These figures represent the past, present, and future incarnations of Budh. The one in the middle is the *present* incarnation; on its right is the *past;* and on its left is the *coming* or *future* incarnation. In front of the idols is a large altar, with beautiful vases filled with flowers, and censers with incense ever burning. Low stools, with mats, are ranged over the tile floor for the kneeling worshipers. Tassels and long bands of silk are suspended from the roof. On each side are placed nine images, representing the original disciples of Budh. The front of the temple is occupied with large doors, the upper half of which is composed of a kind of tortoise-shell, through which a dull light is admitted.

The third temple is situated on another terrace, about sixty feet behind the second. You ascend to it by two flights of stone steps. The space between the buildings is paved with stone, and there are two artificial ground plats in the center where flowers are cultivated. In this third temple are several images of the "Goddess of Mercy." One, a rather large figure, is placed in the center of the group. On each side is one of smaller size, in a wooden case. The one on the left, made of porcelain, is thought to be very precious, and receives special attention. In times of drought or famine prayers are addressed to it. During times of long drought this image is carried along the public streets of Fuhchau, and worship is paid to it by all, with the expectation of procuring rain. The size of this building corresponds to that of the last one described. Large cases of books stand along the sides. It is only at certain times the priests worship here; as when any one wishes to prefer a petition, or some public emergency arises.

The regular worship is held in the second temple. They meet twice a day for this purpose, at about four in the morning and at the same hour in the afternoon. They repeat prayers, of whose meaning not one in ten of the priests themselves has the slightest conception; sometimes standing, then kneeling, and finally marching, single file, around every row of stools in the temple. Their chanting is accompanied by the jingling of a small bell, and the dull sound produced by striking with a mallet a queer-looking piece of wood, which has been made hollow by abstracting the inside material in a very skillful manner. When worshiping, the abbot stands directly in front of the idols, and the priests are ranged in rows on each side.

We have now noticed at considerable length the principal buildings. On each side of these are other edifices. Some are small temples, where a private enterprise seems to be carried on by priests in the way of sight-seeing and fortune-telling. In one we were shown one of *Budh's teeth.* There, sure enough, it is, confined in a strong box, with iron bars in front, through which the faithful and the heretic alike view the sacred relic. I was amused with this sight. The Chinese are a matter-of-fact people, and always like to receive full value for their money. The priests have fully met their wishes in this respect; for while for the sight they abstract a few cash from the Chinaman's pocket, they compensate him by showing an *enormous tooth.* I should think this molar might better have suited the jaw of a mastodon than of Budh. It is about eight inches long, with proportionate size.

There is also a library containing a large collection of Budhistic books. I had made arrangements for examining it, but the sudden illness of one of our party hastened our return, and thus defeated my plans in this respect.

"Do you wish to see the recluse?" asked the priests, as they pointed toward the apartment where the man was confined. The recluse is a man perhaps thirty years of age, and sits in a small room lighted from the roof. There is a small hole in the wall, through which, by removing the cover, visitors look to see him. He has been shut up in this cell for perhaps two years, and expects to remain one or two years longer. Theoretically he sees no one, converses with no one, and thinks only of Budh and the future state. I had supposed he was a priest, but was told he was not. "Why, then," I inquired, "is he here?" The story is that, from great honor and affluence, his family had been reduced to the most distressing poverty; and now, forsaking all earthly things, he had sought refuge here.

"But how does he employ himself? has he no books to read?"

"O yes," they replied, "he reads the doctrines of Budh."

"To what," I asked, "does he aspire?"

"Absorption into Budh," was the reply

And this, I thought, is Budhism. Look on this man! Disease has not weakened his system; God has not cursed him; around him is a world of suffering, calling loudly for help; and yet, in the full vigor of manhood, he betrays his high trust, flies from those who look imploringly for assistance, and here buries himself in indolent comfort and seclusion. Pitiable man! Again, this man has a family, possibly aged parents, looking to him for aid; a wife and helpless children dependent for bread on his exertions. In the days of prosperity he shared their joys, but now, when the hour of stern trial comes, he, the husband, the son, the parent, abandons them to the cold charities of the world. I thought of other and higher duties: God has given him being, talents, influence, and a field for usefulness; but, alas! he knows nothing of all this. The light of the Gospel has never shone upon him. It was saddening to think of his going into eternity surrounded and stupified by such deplorable ignorance, and with a heavy heart I turned away.

The attention of every visitor at the temple is arrested by the ceaseless tolling of the great bell. It is placed in a cupola, elevated perhaps fourteen feet from the ground, on the right of the first open court. The bell is large, and has a fine deep tone. It is fastened in a permanent frame. A piece of hard wood, about three feet long and two inches in diameter, is horizontally suspended by ropes, the one end of the stick being within a few inches of the rim of the bell. To the other end a rope is attached, which passes through the floor down to the ground. By pulling this rope the wood is drawn against the bell, and rebounds with the slackening of the rope, preparatory to another stroke. The tolling goes on almost incessantly, and frequently with intervals of only thirty seconds between the strokes. To my mind there was something very impressive in the deep, measured tones of this bell. I listened to the sounds as fainter and fainter they echoed around the rocks "far up the height," and then I thought of the many seasons of wild excitement and startling changes through which the world has passed, while here in this mountain solitude the flight of each hour, frequently the flight of each minute, has been noted by these sounds.

Just below the temple buildings is a large artificial pond for fish. As none of them are ever caught or killed intentionally, they attain to great age. It is a favorite amusement with the Chinese visitors to throw cakes on the water, and watch the fish contending for the prizes.

There is a fountain of most excellent water situated in a deep glen about half a mile below the temple. The water is conveyed for some distance along the side of the mountain in stone troughs, and finally issues from the mouth of a stone dragon. There is a story told about this fountain. In former times the stream came leaping down a rocky glen near to the monastery; but the sound of the water having greatly annoyed a student who frequently visited the place, he constructed an artificial channel, which conducted the water around the spur of the mountain to the glen where it now forms this delightful fountain. A small temple has been erected beside the fountain. Apartments for the priests who officiate in the temple, and a light structure covering the water, are placed along side. Innumerable inscriptions have been engraved on the large rocks near the spring. A prospect house has been built on a spur east of the fountain, which affords a splendid view of the river winding far below, the plain of Fuhchau studded with groves, and villages, and abrupt hills, the dark jagged mountains in the distance, while southward the eye looks out on the great wide ocean.

A few words now as to the scenery around the monastery. Directly in front, south, the wooded ravine slopes down to the river; on the right sweeps round a spur of the mountain, covered with pines and huge bowlders of granite; a spur covered with the giant camphor-tree, the slender bamboo, the quivering aspen, and a dense undergrowth, runs down on the left; while immediately behind shoots up the high Kushan Peak. On the right, left, and rear the view is shut in by the peak and spurs just referred to; but to the south, opening up through a vista of trees, the prospect stretches far and broadly away. The peak just behind the monastery presents a grand appearance. Its form is conical, the top attaining an elevation several hundred feet above the level of the monastery. The sides are destitute of trees, and dark, precipitous rocks, lined with white streaks, made by rain torrents, throw a somber shade over many a yawning chasm below. A growth of wild grass obtains in places a meager support from the thin soil formed by the disintegration of the granite rock. In the ravines which pass down from the summit the soil has been collected from the barren cliffs around, and many a family is cheered and nourished by the harvests gathered there.

Seen in the light of closing day, the aspect of the peak is singularly impressive. Around the temples where you stand the long shadows of evening are falling; the deep silence of the hour is unbroken, save by the solemn tolling of the bell, which, indeed, from its regularity, seems only to increase it; but on the broad bosom of the peak a clear, mellowing light is shining, and one can see the rustic guiding his plow along the dizzy heights. A thin carpet of grass, the grain waving in the ravines, impart a beautiful greenness and freshness to the scene. The air seems to wanton with the frowning cliffs; not a sound strikes the ear; the shadows ascend the mountain still higher; a brilliant glow, like a crown of glory, decks the top of the peak for a few minutes, then fades away, and the mountain, with vast yet graceful outlines, lies darkly painted against the ruddy heavens.

The cemetery is situated in a grove of pines, perhaps three fourths of a mile from the monastery, near the road leading to the city. It is on a declivity with a southern outlook. There is a stone platform about forty feet square, raised perhaps nine feet from the ground. You mount to this terrace by a flight of stone steps. Beneath this terrace is the final receptacle for the jars containing the ashes of the deceased priests. To this gloomy vault the entrance is effected by removing part of the wall on the right of the steps. This is done only at long intervals, when the large stone urn on the terrace has been filled with these relics. This stone urn stands near the center of the terrace, and is capable of containing the ashes of perhaps thirty priests. When a priest dies, the body is burned and the ashes put into a jar, which, after being sealed, is placed in this large urn. Here the jars remain till the urn is full, when the vault below is opened and the jars placed in it.

The site for the cemetery has been well chosen; the scenery is suited to excite solemn thoughts; and as I sat there in the shadow of those old pines, my mind was busy with saddening yet profitable reflections. O how different is this from the cemeteries in a Christian land! For these I heard no voice from heaven saying, "Write, Blessed are the dead who die in the Lord!" All, all is dark. "The sharp malady of life" is past; but where the victory, the crown, the glory? Reader, to thee also must come the last mortal struggle. God grant that in that solemn hour the Saviour may be with thee!

I have now noticed the most prominent features of this celebrated place, as they presented themselves to my mind. An interesting thought occurred to me during one of my walks over the temple grounds. As I observed the healthiness of the location, its proximity to a great city, the high literary character of that city, and its relation to this mighty empire, it stood before my mind in the form of a delightful possibility that upon the ruins of these heathen temples there shall rise a noble structure for the Christian education of ingenuous native youth; that this lovely spot shall be a fountain for religion and learning, from which shall flow out over these lands holiness and knowledge; and that the chimes of other bells shall

"Ring in the valiant man and free,
The larger heart, the kindlier hand;
Ring out the darkness of the land,
Ring in the Christ that is to be."

CHAPTER VIII.

CHARACTER OF THE CHINESE.

PUBLIC opinion throughout Christendom underrates, we think, the intellectual capacity of the Chinese. What we have already written in the course of this work indicates for them no mean position, intellectually, in the great family of man. Instead of predicating stupidity of the Chinese because of certain apparent incongruities and absurdities in their character, or because of the few unworthy representatives of the Chinese race who find their way to western countries, it would be more judicious to reserve judgment on the subject till we obtained more full and accurate knowledge of their character. It is entirely probable that a more intimate acquaintance with them and the difficulties through which they had to force their way, would excite our cordial sympathy and admiration. It is certainly highly creditable to them that as a nation they can point to a history and character such as are presented by their authentic records and by the patent facts of their civilization; and if under all the disadvantages, and against the fearful odds with which hitherto they have struggled, they have been able to accomplish so much, what may we not expect from them when the light of the Gospel shall shine upon them, and shall lead them forth into the joyous freedom of the sons of God.

The Chinese mind is eminently quick, shrewd, and practical. It has an intuitive logic of rare vigor and certainty. Admit the premises in the argument of a Chinese, and his conclusion is generally inevitable. In their processes of ratiocination the defect is usually in the premises. Owing to their meager knowledge of many subjects they frequently assume things to be true which are not true, and hence the logical structure they rear on such a basis topples and falls the moment you point out the error. As business men they are remarkably energetic, efficient, and adroit. The foreign merchant, whether European or American, who goes to China for business purposes, finds it necessary to avail himself of all the helps and safeguards which his own judgment or the principles of trade suggest in order to protect himself; and it not infrequently happens that after all his precautionary efforts he is overreached by his unscrupulous competitor. The yankee must rise early in the morning and keep wide awake all day if he expects to get to windward of a Chinaman before nightfall.

The *permanence* of Chinese institutions is worthy of notice in this connection. It is a significant and singular fact that, from the earliest period of their authentic history to the present time, the Chinese have preserved intact and inviolate every important feature and principle of their government and civilization. The successive irruptions of northern barbarians have neither abrogated nor essentially modified

Chinese institutions. The conquering races who have overrun those fertile plains have stood abashed in the presence of a superior civilization; and after subduing the empire, they have invariably adopted its government, laws, civilization, and language. Similar results have followed all efforts to introduce foreign religions into China. Budhism, Judaism, Nestorianism, and Mohammedanism have all lost much of their peculiar spirit, and many of their external features, when brought into contact with Chinese mind, succumbing apparently to its rigid immobility and inherent force. Romanism has won its way in China by subterfuges and compromises of the most questionable character, and even jesuitical casuistry and chicanery are almost overmatched in the struggle. Protestant Christianity has now entered the field, and a great cloud of witnesses watch the issue of its conflict with this, the oldest form of heathenism the world has ever seen.

Paradoxical though it may seem to some of our readers, we proceed to state that the Chinese have long been a colonizing people. They have colonized along the sea-board of Asia, from the Sea of Ochotsk to the Bay of Bengal. The Japanese are an offshoot from China. The islands off the coast of China, and many of those in the East Indian Archipelago, have been colonized by the Chinese; and in nearly every kingdom of eastern peninsular Asia they are found in large and influential communities. It is a noticeable fact that whenever the Chinese colonize among a heathen people, their superior civilization gives them at once a decided advantage over the native population. By their intelligence, industry, and capacity for business they almost monopolize all the important and highly remunerative departments of labor; commerce passes into their hands, and they become the chief factors, the leading spirits in the native communities where they live. A year or two since a missionary in the Micronesian Islands was walking along the beach of one of the islands and found there a shipwrecked mariner, whose dress was strange to him, and with whose language he was utterly unacquainted. Through the natives of the island he ascertained that the stranger was a Japanese, whose vessel having been injured by a storm and rendered unmanageable, was drifted southward by the great oceanic current, until some of its fragments, bearing the sailor referred to, were stranded on the shore of the island. Following up the train of thought suggested by this incident, the missionary ascertained from the natives of the Micronesian Islands that similar incidents were of not infrequent occurrence, that every few years one or more of the people from those northern latitudes would be drifted on their shores; "and indeed," said they to the missionary, "*our ancestors came from that northern region.*" The incident is certainly most interesting and suggestive; possibly it throws light on the question as to the origin of the tribes found in the islands of the South Seas. Any one familiar with the features of the North American Indian, who will look into the face of a Chinese, cannot fail to observe a striking resemblance between them. Whence came our North American Indians? They neither dropped from the clouds, nor sprang, like the oaks, from the earth. Is it not, at least, plausible that they came from the continent of Asia, the old homestead of the human race, by the way of Behring's Strait? If this supposition should prove to be correct, we must conclude that China furnished the pioneers who first looked on the magnificent scenery of the western continent.

Within the last few years the Chinese have migrated in large numbers to Australia, Havana, the western coast of South America, and California. We have a vivid recollection of the excitement along the southern sea-board of China produced by the intelligence from the California gold-diggings. Thousands of the Chinese at once decided to seek their fortunes in the land of gold. They chartered foreign vessels to transport them, but in a short time the entire fleet of available vessels was taken up, and thousands of eager emigrants were left waiting for a passage. Unable to charter ships as rapidly as they desired, the Chinese proceeded to buy up the old hulks which were used by foreigners as offices or stores, and after fitting them up with masts, rigging, and sails, they employed a foreign commander and crew, and then, trusting themselves to these unseaworthy crafts, sailed away for California.

This brief sketch of Chinese character would be imperfect without a reference to some of its defects. The vices of the Chinese are those peculiar to all Orientalists who, deficient in physical strength, endeavor to accomplish their ends by cunning, thus substituting duplicity for force. The art of deceiving, is well-nigh universally studied and practiced in China. Deception pervades all classes of society and characterizes every department of business. The popular sentiment, indeed, regards it as an accomplishment rather than as a vice. The man who gains his end by deception is applauded for his sagacity and esteemed a person of ability; while he who would lose it by adhering to downright honesty is certain to be ridiculed as a dolt, destitute alike of native talent and business tact. We might almost designate cheating as the rule of business in China. It is only when his own interest imperatively demands honesty that you can expect a Chinese to act with fairness in a business transaction. When urged to embrace the Gospel, the first objection with business men invariably is: "Cheating is essential to success in trade; I really cannot succeed without it. Were I to confine myself to the truth I should starve." Lying seems to be universal. Everybody lies; parents to children and children to parents; masters to servants and servants to masters; sellers to buyers and buyers to sellers; subjects to government and government to subjects. A man's word is never taken in business affairs; no tradesman will consider any arrangement or contract binding unless what is called "bargain money" has been tendered and accepted; and no agreement is considered valid until it is written out and signed by the parties in the presence of witnesses. In the administration of government you meet with the most unscrupulous mendacity. The people lie to the constable, the constable to the squire, the squire to the sheriff, the sheriff to the governor, the governor to the privy council, and the privy council to the emperor. We might truthfully designate the entire system of government administration in China one stupendous lie. This rule of lying works both ways. If a stream of lies passes through the arteries of the political system to the emperor, at least an equal veinous supply of the same commodity is thrown out from the emperor and his advisers to permeate the entire body politic.

In the early days of foreign residence at Fuhchau, the Chinese authorities compelled the English consul to live in most uncomfortable quarters in a very ineligible situation. The consul protested against the arrangement as inconvenient, oppressive, and absolutely outrageous, but the Chinese authorities were incorrigible. To all his remonstrances and appeals they invariably replied: "You must remain where you are; we cannot possibly find a better place for you." The consul was an energetic man, and not easily turned aside from his purpose, so he began to explore the city to find a more suitable position for his residence. Within the city walls there is a beautiful hill called Ushih-shan, and as the consul passed over it one day in the course of his rambles, he found there some half-occupied temple buildings, and he determined, if possible, to procure one of them for his accommodation. He accordingly intimated his wishes to the authorities; but they replied that it was utterly out of the question for him to live within the city walls, that the hill where he proposed to live could never be used for private residences, and they quoted statutes and historical precedents innumerable to fortify their position, closing the argument with the remark: "The people are unwilling, and therefore it must not be." All negotiations having failed, and finding his health suffering in the miserable quarters to which he was confined, the consul, after much deliberation, finally concluded to take the matter into his own hands. Summoning a posse of marines from an English man-of-war then lying in the river near Fuhchau, he made preparations for taking possession of one of the temple-buildings on Ushih-shan. The morning of the eventful day at length dawned upon him, and, after dispatching his goods, he mounted his sedan and, escorted by the marines, started for the city. The cavalcade moved quickly along the street, the people opening a passage for it, and then staring with a kind of bewildered astonishment as it passed. Finally they entered the south gate of the city, and began to approach the hill. "Now comes the tug of war," thought the consul as, turning into a broad gateway, he found himself within the limits of the temple grounds. Judge of his surprise and embarrassment when, looking up through the trees, he saw the temple occupied by the Chinese officials, heard shrill voices giving out loud orders in rapid succession, and observed soldiers and lictors moving round the building in evident excitement. What was to be done? To retreat would be utter disgrace; to go forward might result in bloodshed. Controlled more by excitement than by reason, he determined to go on, and dismounting from his sedan, he began to ascend the steps toward the temple. His approach seemed to increase the stir within and around the temple. Lictors in flaming jackets were rushing hither and thither, mandarins in splendid robes were bustling about, venting vollies of rapid orders to which no one seemed to give attention, and to increase the uproar, just as the consul came in full view of the main entrance to the building vollies of rattling fire-crackers were discharged, and a bevy of gongs set up a most unearthly clanging and banging until it seemed as though pandemonium itself had broken loose. Utterly confounded by the scene, the consul still advanced, his vision filled with anything but agreeable images, when just as he entered the building a company of brilliantly costumed officials sallied forth from a side chamber, and, with indescribable bowings and scrapings, proceeded to welcome him to his new residence. This unexpected denouement was well-nigh fatal to the gravity of our hero, but, resolutely maintaining his dignity, he proceeded to reciprocate their compliments. Passing through an open court, they ushered him into the main hall of the temple, where, to his utter astonishment, he beheld a splendid entertainment spread out, and official dignitaries flitting about apparently anxious to do him honor. The transition was so sudden that for a time it seemed more like a dream than reality; but, gradually regaining his self-possession, he was proceeding to congratulate himself on the success of his dashing policy when one of the mandarins interrupted the sweet flow of his thoughts with, "What a splendid place this is! How far superior to the quarters you left! and, by the way, *why in the world did you stay so long in that inconvenient and excessively disagreeable place?*"

As another illustration of this trait in Chinese character, the following narrative, which I wrote at the time the incident occurred, is here introduced. The sketch was written in Fuhchau.

I was surprised and grieved, a few days since, to learn that a young man who was a candidate for baptism in our mission had suddenly died of cholera. His death occurred some weeks since, but I did not hear of it at the time. This young man had been coming to us for four years, and during most of the time was a candidate for baptism. His education was respectable, and his character fair, in the estimation of the Chinese. There was, however, one serious defect in him. Whether it was, as I sometimes inclined to believe, a constitutional defect, or whether it was that his ingenuousness disclosed frankly what other Chinese seek to conceal from our notice, I never could fully satisfy myself; but this feature in his character painfully impressed all the missionaries who became acquainted with him. He seemed to be almost totally deficient in what may be termed conscientiousness. He would lie, and that, too, when it was evidently from constitutional bias, or vicious habit, rather than from any definite purpose or wish to deceive. I labored with him long and, I think, faithfully to aid him in remedying the evil, and I have good reason to believe that he sincerely desired reformation. During the past year he very frequently attended our inquiry meeting, and I thought he was gradually receiving light and power from on high. He usually spoke in these meetings, and often with an earnest frankness that stirred our sympathies. The last time he was present at our inquiry meeting I was deeply impressed by the simplicity of his experience and the unusual solemnity of his manner. I felt then that he was not far from the kingdom of God. So strong was this impression on my mind that I spoke of it to the other members of our mission. The following Sunday I looked for him in the public congregation, but his seat was vacant. I was disappointed and sad, fearing I had been deceived. I spoke of him to our native members, and they stated that, as he lived some three miles from the church, he might have been detained by the heat of the weather or by the sickness of his aged mother, who was in feeble health. Day after day passed without any tidings from him, and I began to fear he had become discouraged in his efforts to become a Christian. One of the native brethren went to his house, and, to our sorrow, ascertained that he had died some three weeks before. His mother gave the particulars of his death, and I here put them on record.

The last appearance of the young man at our inquiry meeting was on Friday afternoon. He reached home that evening about dark, and was taken sick during the night. He sank rapidly, but retained his consciousness. Through Saturday and Saturday night he lay in a very critical state. On Sunday morning he seemed to revive somewhat, and said to his mother: "To-day is the Sabbath; how I should like to go to worship in the *Ching Sing*

Tong," (Church of the True God.) He spoke of his wish and purpose to be a Christian, and then, as he felt his end approaching, he said to his mother: "If I die, send word at once to the missionaries." And thus, on that beautiful Sabbath morning, with his thoughts fixed on the blessed Saviour and his heart longing for the courts of the Lord's house, this young man passed away. It is probable, from what I learned as to the *time* of his death, that just as we were engaged in the opening exercises of public worship in the church he was passing—whither, O whither? Thou knowest, O Saviour! Thy name was upon his lips as he went down into the cold waters, and before his vision there passed "the Lord's house" and "the worshiping congregation" as the last of earth. What of heaven? Did any light from that glorious land shine on his mind when the darkness of the grave was thickening around him? Did any scenes of beauty arise before him? Did any music from the worship around the throne fall upon his ear? Thou knowest, O Saviour! this is enough. In eternity it may be found that the published statistics of the results of missionary labor indicate only a small fraction of the aggregate amount of good accomplished.

Passing one day over the great bridge at Fuhchau, I stopped at one of the stalls which then lined one side of the bridge, to purchase a few articles. To my surprise the prices named by the shopman were evidently about what a native would pay for the same articles. The Chinese who stood looking on, and the shopmen in the adjacent stalls, seemed utterly confounded by this public deviation from the system of cheating foreigners, which forms so prominent a feature of Chinese mercantile tactics. Presently an excited neighbor of the same craft thrust his head into the stall and indignantly called out to the man with whom I was dealing:

"What makes you sell so cheap? Why don't you cheat the foreigner?"

With an expression of countenance at once doleful and ludicrous, the crest-fallen shopman turned to the crowd and whined out:

"There is nothing to be gained by lying to this foreigner; he talks our own language."

While on this topic I may remark that the Chinese are disposed to consider it something wonderful that foreigners are able to acquire the correct and fluent use of their language. After preaching on one occasion at one of our chapels, a company of loquacious Chinese remained to converse with me, and very soon the inquiry was started:

"How is it that while we, the Chinese, cannot learn to speak foreign languages, foreigners are able to acquire ours?"

The question called forth an animated discussion, and a number of theories were propounded to account for and explain the phenomenon. At length an elderly gentleman, of astonishing volubility, volunteered an explanation which was greeted by the crowd as entirely satisfactory. "The truth is," said the orator, "the tongue of these foreigners resembles the tongue of a parrot or mocking-bird; it has a kind of pivotic position in the mouth, and hence both ends are available in talking. Besides," he continued, "there is a certain ligature under the tongue which is always cut by foreigners in infancy, thus increasing the flexibility of the organ to an astonishing degree."

It seemed downright cruelty to mar the effect of this speech on the minds of the delighted auditory, but, under the circumstances, I felt constrained to state that though the theory just propounded might be ingenious and plausible, it was unfortunately opposed by all the facts in the case. Notwithstanding this disclaimer, the crowd were evidently determined to stand by their orator, thinking perhaps with the adroit Frenchman, that if the facts were opposed to the theory, *it was so much the worse for the facts.*

Thieving is another characteristic propensity of the Chinese, and the thieves of China are probably as expert and dexterous as any in the world. The thieves are divided into separate and distinct gangs, each known by the kind of instruments employed in its operations, so that wherever a theft has been committed, an examination of the *modus operandi* will show which gang has done the deed. In its detective police arrangements the government acts on the principle, "Send a thief to catch a thief;" and hence in many of the government offices you find the official "thief-catcher," a person of energy and cunning, who, for a material consideration, has consented to stop stealing on his own account, and henceforth employs his talents in ferreting out and arresting thieves on behalf of the government. A foreign ship captain was once dining at the table of a foreign merchant in

China, when the conversation turned to this subject, and a number of illustrative anecdotes were recited by members of the company. Among the incidents narrated was one in which it happened that the burglar had entered the room where the occupant was sleeping, and had stolen the laid off clothing of the sleeper without disturbing his slumbers. The captain received this story with staunch incredulity, and declared with emphasis that he defied any person to enter a room where he was sleeping without awaking him.

"Why," said the gentleman at whose table he was dining, "there is a Chinese thief in this city who can steal the sheet on which you are sleeping without awaking you."

"Impossible!" cried the indignant captain; and certainly the assertion did seem to savor strongly of exaggeration. The merchant, however, was in earnest about the matter, and it was finally agreed that the captain should spend a few nights in a designated room of the merchant's house, just to test the matter. In accordance with the arrangement, the thief was informed of the circumstances of the case, and was assured that if caught on the premises during the time specified no harm should come to him. The captain occupied the room one or two nights, and nothing transpired to disturb his repose. The succeeding night, about two hours past midnight, the thief approached the window of the room in which the captain slept, and finding all quiet within, cautiously made his entrance. It was a hot summer night, and the sleeper, in his night-clothes, lay about the middle of the bed, having his person only partially covered by a thin counterpane. Softly approaching the bedside, the thief proceeded to remove the counterpane, and then addressing himself to the sheet on which the unconscious sleeper was lying, he began in the gentlest manner to fold it up in narrow plies, lengthwise, advancing slowly toward his person. In a few minutes the last fold of the sheet came close up against the form of the sleeper. And now came the most difficult part of the performance. It was comparatively easy to fold up that part of the sheet not in immediate contact with the captain's person; but how is it possible to get the sheet from under him without disturbing his repose? Taking a straw in his hand, the thief passed round to the other side of the bed, and softly uncovering the sleeper's side, proceeded gently to tickle him with the straw. Instantly the sleeper begins to squirm and shrink, and after a few seconds rolls heavily over, away from the persecuting straw, and quite off the coveted sheet, thus leaving the prize to be gathered up and carried off in triumph by the thief. Next morning, when the captain awoke from his refreshing sleep, to his utter surprise and amazement, behold! the sheet was gone! when, and whither, he had not the slightest conception.

Licentiousness is another prominent trait in the character of the Chinese. Its corrupting and debasing influences pervade all classes of society. Forms of this vice which in other lands skulk in dark places, or appear only in the midnight orgies of the bacchanalian revelers, in China blanch not at the light of noonday; are pictured, in shop fronts and in other modes, to the eyes of the thousands who throng the streets; or flaunting their gaudy blandishments, the living embodiments of this lust find ready access to the precincts of the family, the forum, and the temple. Saddening evidences of the almost universal prevalence of this vice are everywhere apparent among the Chinese, and the Christian prays and longs for the glorious day when a pure morality and a pure language shall supplant the vices which now fester in Chinese society.

Opium smoking in China is a vice whose magnitude and baneful effects can scarcely be exaggerated. Facts innumerable, and patent to every observer, stamp it one of the most pernicious and destructive vices of human society. Dr. Smith, of Penang, who had every opportunity for a thorough examination of the subject, says: "The baneful effects of this habit on the human constitution are particularly displayed by stupor, forgetfulness, general deterioration of all the mental faculties, emaciation, debility, sallow complexion, lividness of the lips and eyelids, languor, and lack-lüster of eye, and appetite either destroyed or depraved." A Chinese writer says: "It exhausts the animal spirits, impedes the regular performance of business, wastes the flesh and blood, dissipates every kind of property, renders the person ill-favored, promotes obscenity, discloses secrets, violates the laws, attacks the vitals, and destroys life." Dr. Williams, referring to the progress of the habit, says: "The thirst and burning sensation in the throat which the wretched sufferer feels, only to be removed by a repetition of the dose, proves one of the strongest links in the chain which drags him to his ruin. At this stage of the habit his case is almost hopeless. If the pipe be delayed too long, vertigo, complete prostration, and discharge of water from the eyes ensue; if entirely withheld, coldness and aching pains are felt over the body, an obstinate diarrhea supervenes, and death closes the scene. The disastrous effects of the drug upon the constitution seem to be somewhat delayed or modified by the quantity of nourishing food the person can procure; and consequently it is among the poor, who can least afford the pipe, and still less the injury done to their energies, that the destruction of life is the greatest. The evils suffered and crimes committed by the desperate victims of the opium pipe are dreadful and multiplied. Theft, arson, murder, and suicide are perpetrated in order to obtain it or escape its effects. Some try to break off the fatal habit by taking a tincture of the opium dirt, gradually diminishing its strength until it is left off entirely; others mix opium with tobacco, and smoke the compound in a less and less proportion, until tobacco alone remains. The general belief is that the vice can be overcome without fatal results, if the person firmly resolve to forsake it, and keep away from sight and smell of the pipe, laboring as much as his strength will allow in the open air, until he recovers his spirits, and no longer feels a longing for it. Few, very few, however, ever emancipate themselves from the tyrannous habit which enslaves them. They are able to resist its insidious effects until the habit has become strong, and the resolution to break it off is generally delayed until their chains are forged, and deliverance felt to be hopeless. The resolution in their case has, alas, none of the awful motives to enforce its observance which a knowledge of the Bible would give it. The heathen dieth in his ignorance!

"Opium is often employed to commit suicide by swallowing it in spite when displeased with others, or to escape from death, oppression, or other evils. The missionary physicians are often called upon to rescue persons who have taken a dose and been found before life is gone, and the number of these applications painfully show how lightly the Chinese esteem life. A comparison is sometimes drawn between the opium-smoker and drunkard, and the former averred to be less injured by the habit; but the balance is struck between two terrible evils, both of which end in the loss of health, property, mind, influence, and life. Opium imparts no benefit to the smoker, impairs his bodily vigor, beclouds his mind, and unfits him for his station in society; he is miserable without it, and at last dies by what he lives upon. The manufacture is beyond the country, so that every cent paid for the drug is carried abroad, and misery in every shape of poverty, disease, and dementation left in its stead, attended with mere transitory pleasure while the pipe is in the mouth. Fully one hundred millions of dollars have oozed out of China within the last fifty years for this article alone, and its productive capital decreased fully twice that sum."

CHAPTER IX.

CITY OF FUHCHAU.

THE city of Fuhchau is the center of the missions of the Methodist Episcopal Church in China. It is the capital of the Fuh-kien province, belongs to the first class of Chinese cities, and contains a population of about six hundred thousand. It has long been a celebrated city among the Chinese, and its beautiful scenery has often inspired the genius of native poets, one of whom seeks to express his admiration in highly wrought hyperbole, beginning

> "Ten thousand miles around Fuhchau
> Spread out the terraced hills."

The city has been considered one of the strong military posts of the empire; and its inhabitants have always enjoyed a high reputation for literary attainments and commercial activity. In the early history of foreign intercourse with China attention was directed to Fuhchau as an important commercial entrepot. In 1668 an agent of the English East India Company reported to the Court of Directors: "Hokchue (the local pronunciation for Fuhchau) will be a place of great resort, affording all China commodities, as tutanag, silk, raw and wrought,

City of Fuhchau.

gold, China-root, tea, etc.; for which must be carried broadcloth, lead, amber, pepper, coral, sandal-wood, red-wood, incense, cacha, [cassia,] putchuk, etc. In 1681 the Company ordered their establishments at Formosa and Amoy to be withdrawn, with a view to opening trade at Canton and Fuhchau." These early efforts were unsuccessful, and it was not till 1853 that foreign commerce was fully opened at Fuhchau.

The city is situated in the northern portion of an amphitheater about twenty miles in diameter, formed by the circling ranges of high mountains. The surface of this amphitheater is diversified by wooded knolls and occasional hills of considerable altitude, some of which the husbandman has cultivated to the summit, while others present to the eye immense masses of granite, relieved by intervening patches of sparse vegetation. The Min River enters the amphitheater from the northwest, through a narrow mountain pass, and flows, with a winding stream, out to the sea through a somewhat similar pass in the southeast. On the banks of this picturesque stream stands the city of Fuhchau; the portion within the walls and the greater part of the suburbs occupying and stretching away from the north bank, while the south bank is covered with a straggling suburb extending some three miles nearly parallel to the river. The general aspect of the city is pleasing. The monotony of dark roofs and dingy walls is relieved by a few picturesque hills and a plentiful supply of banians, whose perennial greenness imparts an air of freshness and beauty to the scene.

Fuhchau furnishes a fair specimen of Chinese provincial cities. The city proper is surrounded by a substantial wall, built compactly of brick, and resting on a foundation of granite. The wall is about twenty feet high and ten feet thick, surmounted by a parapet five feet high with bastions at regular intervals. The gateways are of great size and strength, and so constructed that a small force in charge of them could hold at bay almost any number of attacking troops. The public buildings comprise government offices, temples, and colleges, or halls for the literary examinations. The government offices comprise those of the viceroy, Tartar-general, governor, treasurer, judge, commissioners of rice and salt, prefect, district magistrates, etc. These buildings are one story high, constructed of wood with the aid of lath and plaster, cover an immense area, and are inclosed by a high fire-proof wall. The open courts, which form prominent features of these vast compounds, are ornamented with flowers and shrubbery and shaded with fine old trees. The buildings are constructed of very perishable materials; the workmanship is usually clumsy and tawdry, while, owing to the plan of the edifice, the rooms are almost invariably deficient in light, ventilation, and comfort.

Temples abound both within and without the wall of the city. Of those within the city wall the more prominent are the Confucian temple, the imperial temple, the *Tai-seng* temple, the temple of the city king, and the temples crowning the two hills called *Ushih-shan* and *U-shan.* The Confucian temple was built about eight years ago, and is a fine-looking edifice; most of the other temples are dirty, gloomy, and dilapidated structures. Outside the city wall there is what foreigners designate the "Ningpo Temple." It stands in the suburb, on the south side of the river, not far from the foreign residences, and is really a handsome edifice. It is dedicated to the goddess of seamen, and is more largely patronized than any other temple in the city. Two tall pagodas, each having nine stories, stand just within the south gate of the city, and are connected with two Budhist temples. One of them is called the "White Pagoda," and the other the "Black Stone Pagoda." They are both old, and the former is so much injured that no person is allowed to ascend it.

The Provincial College, or Literary Examination Hall, situated in the northern part of the city proper, is an immense open compound, filled with rows of low compartments for domiciling the students during the examinations, and is surrounded by a high and thick wall. An avenue about twelve feet wide runs nearly north and south through the center of the compound, extending from the main and only entrance to the opposite side, where are the apartments fitted up for the examining committees and official visitors. At right angles to this central avenue, on each side, branch off rows of compartments or cells in which the students are incarcerated during the examinations. These rows of cells are separated from each other by brick walls about ten feet high, with a space about two feet wide between the wall and the fronts of the cells to furnish the means of communication with the central avenue. These cells are about two and a half feet deep, four feet wide, and eight feet high, and are covered with a shed-roof to protect the occupant from the weather; but as the entire front of each cell is left open, the poor students must suffer terribly from the sun and rain; and it is not surprising that at every examination some of the candidates die from exposure and excitement. It is estimated that from eight to ten thousand students can be accommodated at one time in this compound or college. The other examination halls are somewhat similar to the one we have just described, though much smaller and less substantially built.

The city is laid out with some degree of regularity, the streets in many cases running parallel to each other, or crossing each other at right angles. The principal street, called *Nanka*, that is, South-street, divides the city into two nearly equal portions, and runs from the south gate almost to the north gate of the city. This is a well-paved and (for China) wide street, and being the great business thoroughfare of the city, where all the best stores are located, it presents a fine appearance. The western portion of the city is largely taken up with the residences of retired officers, or other persons of wealth and influence. Some of these mansions are fitted up in a style that indicates considerable refinement of taste and artistic skill. A portion of the eastern division of the city, comprising about one-eighth of the area within the city wall, is the Tartar quarter, and is occupied by the Tartar garrison of the city. These Tartars are soldiers in the pay of the government, and are not allowed to engage in trade or intermarry with the Chinese. In general they lead an idle, listless life, and are sadly addicted to opium-smoking and other vices, fully confirming the truth of the old adage that "an idle man's brain is the devil's workshop." The execution ground is just outside the north gate, and the military parade ground immediately outside the south gate of the city.

The extra-mural population is almost equal to that within the city wall, and comprises large suburbs outside the principal gates of the city. Of these suburbs, the largest and most important one extends from the south gate to the river, and is called *Nantai*, or southern suburb. Its population stretches some three miles from the south gate to the river, covers most densely a small island in the river; and then, on the south side of the river, spreads out into another narrow suburb some three miles in length. The approach from the south to the city of Fuhchau is very impressive. For six miles, before reaching the gate of the city, the traveler passes along an almost unbroken street, lined on both sides with shops and residences, and filled with a bustling and vociferating crowd. This southern suburb is the great center of trade, both native and foreign, in Fuhchau; and it is here, in close proximity to the river, that foreigners have erected their business hongs and most of their residences. The southern bank of the river opposite the city swells up into a pretty eminence, and foreigners have succeeded in obtaining a large part of it for their private dwellings and offices. This picturesque hill, the great temple hill on the northern bank of the river, the two stone bridges, and the winding river with its fleet of boats and junks, are the more prominent features of the scenery in this part of the city. The bridges are rude but substantial structures, built of granite. There is at this point in the river an island called *Changchau*, or *Tongchin*, in the local dialect, which forms the connecting link between the two bridges. The bridge over the northern division of the river is called, in popular language, "the great bridge," to distinguish it from the smaller one over the southern division of the river; but the title on the façade, spanning the entrance to the bridge, is the grandiloquent designation, "Bridge of Ten Thousand Ages." It is composed of twenty-six spans, each span measuring some twenty feet. The piers are built strongly of large blocks of granite, and then the spans are formed by laying from pier to pier large blocks of granite about three feet wide and deep, and some twenty-three feet long. These blocks are placed side by side, forming a surface about eight feet wide, extending the entire length of the bridge. On this solid foundation are placed, transversely, thin slabs of granite, which form the road for travelers, and on each side of the bridge is constructed a stone balustrade some two feet high. The other bridge connects Changchau to the south side of the river. It is similar in construction and appearance to the great bridge, though much shorter, comprising only nine spans. The Chinese call it the Chongseng Bridge, deriving the title from the local name of the ward at the southern extremity of the bridge.

The boat population of Fuhchau constitutes a large and interesting class of society. The shoal water on both sides of the river, above and below the bridges, furnishes excellent anchorage, and is covered with immense fleets of all varieties of river craft. The larger boats are used for transporting merchandise to and from the interior of the country, or for discharging the cargoes of the salt and rice junks entering the port of Fuhchau, while the smaller craft are engaged in ferrying and fishing. The sea-going junks anchor below the bridges, and at this point the river is frequently crowded with them. The trade of Fuhchau embraces tea, lumber, rice, salt, sugar, charcoal, paper, sea-weed, camphor, and other commodities.

The climate of Fuhchau will compare favorably with that of any other part of China. In summer the mercury rises to about 98° Fahrenheit, and the lowest point reached in winter is 32°. It should be observed, however, that, owing to the humidity of the atmosphere in China, the same degree of temperature, whether of heat or cold, is more oppressive than in the United States. From May to the first of October the weather is warm, at times oppressively so, and foreigners generally suffer from it considerably in the loss of appetite, and the consequent prostration of physical strength. During this period, however, the extreme heat is occasionally modified by the rains, which fall copiously for days together. These rains occur most generally in May or June, about the time of the annual freshet in the river, which inundates a large portion of the suburbs of the city. From October to the middle or close of April the atmosphere is usually clear, dry, and, at times, bracing. One could scarcely desire more agreeable weather than Fuhchau affords during this season of the year. Its cool, refreshing atmosphere exerts a most salutary influence on the system prostrated by the continued heat of the preceding summer.

The people of Fuhchau are characterized, in the main, by energy and perseverance, accompanied by an independent free and easy kind of address, which frequently degenerates into coarse vulgarity and offensive impudence. Such we have found to be their deportment toward each other as well as toward foreigners. As compared with the Chinese in other parts of the empire with whom we have become acquainted, the Fuhchauans appear to exhibit more of the rough, manly, outspoken traits of character, and less of the cunning, servile, and sycophantic traits. The native Chinese hauteur is strikingly apparent among the people of this city, and this characteristic is perhaps due quite as much to the fact of their never having felt the terrible effects of foreign military power, as to their constitutional temperament. The Fuhchauans, in fact, cherish most cordially and sincerely a very exalted conception of their own importance, both collectively and individually. It would seem, indeed, that they are not singular in entertaining this opinion, for certain facts with which we have become acquainted show that the government cherishes a similar estimate of their character. During the negotiations immediately preceding the formation of the Nankin Treaty between Great Britain and China in 1842–3, it was observed that the Chinese officials were exceedingly reluctant to include Fuhchau in the list of cities to be thrown open to foreign intercourse, and it was only by the most energetic perseverance that the English plenipotentiary succeeded in carrying the point. The subsequent policy pursued by the Chinese authorities at Fuhchau indicated their determination to prevent, if possible, the growth of a foreign trade at that city, and for nearly ten years their policy was almost completely successful. In 1853, when the movements of the insurgents in the southern provinces of the empire were cutting off the revenue derived by the imperial government from the tea duties at Canton, the government authorities at Fuhchau took measures for opening a foreign trade at that city. The trade thus commenced sprang at once into a vigorous existence, and has developed rapidly, so that now Fuhchau is one of the most important points connected with foreign commerce in China. Its proximity to the black tea-producing districts enables the foreign merchant to purchase his teas here at a lower price than at any other port in China, and he is able also at the opening of each season to lay down the new teas in London, New York, or elsewhere, about a month in advance of shipments from any other port in China.

In 1847 the committee appointed for this purpose by the Missionary Society of the Methodist Episcopal Church, after a protracted and prayerful examination of the subject according to the information then in their possession, decided that the Fuh-kien province, on the coast of China, was the appropriate field for the China mission of our Church; and we are happy to corroborate the wisdom of this selection by subsequent facts, and by the experience of our mission in the prosecution of its work among the Chinese. Of the eighteen provinces of China proper six are situated on its eastern sea-board, and furnish to Protestant Churches their *points d'appui* for the evangelization of the empire. Of these six maritime provinces four have been entered and partially occupied by American Protestant Missions. In the Canton province missions have been established at Canton, and more recently at Swatow; in the Fuh-kien province at Fuhchau and Amoy; in the Cheh-kiang province at Ningpo, and in the Kiangsi province at Shanghai. The American Board has missions at Canton, Fuhchau, and Shanghai; the Presbyterian Board at Ningpo, Canton, and Shanghai; the Baptists (North) at Hongkong and Ningpo; Baptists (South) at Shanghai and Canton. The remaining four American societies have concentrated their operations at one point, the Protestant Episcopal Board and Methodist Episcopal Church, South, at Shanghai, the Dutch Reformed Board at Amoy, and the Methodist Episcopal Church at Fuhchau. From this statement it appears that there has not yet been a formal assignment of Chinese territory to any societies, with a view to its efficient occupancy and evangelization by them; and yet we can discover the informal initiation of the general features of such an arrangement.

Four of the eight societies referred to have already concentrated their forces at one central point; and we think it probable that in the progress of the work the other societies will adopt a similar plan. We are not solicitous, however, with reference to the formal initiation of the above arrangement; whether or not it goes into effect, we conceive that the present tacit distribution of territory will form, in the main, the basis for future operations in China.

Taking the Fuh-kien province, then, as the starting point for our operations in China, the expansion of our work will necessarily be westward. Eastward is the sea, northward we trench on the territory occupied by the Ningpo missions, southward we enter the appropriate sphere of the Amoy missions; so that, if we grow at all, we are shut up to a westward development. The field thus indicated contains the provinces of Fuh-kien, Kiangsi, Hunan, and Szchuen, and forms a belt some three hundred miles wide, stretching through the central portion of China from its eastern sea-board to Thibet. It contains an area of 313,000 square miles, and a population of 74,000,000. Its climate is mild and salubrious, its internal resources apparently inexhaustible, and its people remarkable in China for their intelligence and enterprise. Foreigners have called Fuh-kien the "New England," and the Fuh-kienese the "Yankees" of China. Such is the interesting and inviting field providentially assigned to the Methodist Episcopal Church, and to aid in the evangelization of which she is now called upon to send out and support missionaries.

Fuhchau, the capital of Fuh-kien, has hitherto been the center of our operations in China, and its advantages in this respect are probably as many and great as those of any other city on the coast of China. Its foreign commerce brings it into direct and easy communication with the home Churches, while its native trade opens up channels of intercourse with the interior of the country. Our mission here is gradually coming into possession of the buildings and other appliances necessary for a great center of missionary operations. The Church is not to expect, in all the mission fields she may enter, precisely the same encouragements. In some fields it would seem that the work of preparation had been already performed, and that the missionary has only to gather in the harvest. In others the harvest so rapidly follows the seedtime that the voices of the sowers mingle with the songs of the reapers. But there are other fields where the giant oaks must be felled, the tangled undergrowth torn away, the soil broken up, the seed sown, and then the husbandman wait through long months of sunshine and storm for the reward of his toil. At Athens Paul was confronted by the caviling Stoic and Epicurean, at Lystra he was hailed as a god, at Ephesus he was set upon by an infuriated mob; while at Antioch, where the disciples were first called Christians, he, with Barnabas, tarried a whole year, assembling with the Church and teaching much people. Some of the Indian tribes of North America, where our own missionaries have labored, and the Karens of India, where our Baptist brethren have preached the Gospel with such success, furnish instances of fields white unto the harvest, while the efforts of the Moravians in Greenland, and of the English and American missionaries in the South Pacific, in parts of India, and in China, give us examples of earnest, faithful labor, and patient, persevering waiting for the desired result.

He who knows somewhat of the vastness of the work to be done in China will be neither discouraged nor surprised to find that its day of preparation is long and toilsome. The immense population of the empire, the vast extent of territory over which this population is diffused, the antiquity and power of their political and literary institutions, the interminable network of superstitions which trammels their minds, and their written language, with its unnumbered spoken dialects, all these circumstances combine to present to the Church an array of difficulties which nothing but the most implicit faith in God's word, and the most prompt and hearty obedience to his commands, can overcome.

It is important that we recognize the greatness of the work to be done in China, if we would have our efforts for its accomplishment wisely directed and efficiently sustained. Let the Church then bear in mind that it now seeks to change the religious faith and crush the religious institutions of *one third of the human race;* that it proposes to strike down before their eyes the objects endeared to them by a thousand associations; that it hastens to tear from their hearts the hopes and aspirations which their depraved natures and corrupt faith have ever nourished and shielded; that it wages a war of extermination against idolatry, not sparing even that most insidious and attractive form of it embodied in ancestral worship; that it introduces to them a religious system of which they are almost totally ignorant, and the simplicity and purity of whose doctrines must necessarily excite the sternest opposition from their previously formed habits and their depraved natures; and that these doctrines are preached to them by foreigners, with whom, in consequence of a difficult language and dissimilar tastes and feelings, they cannot fully sympathize: these are some of the circumstances which suggest to the Church that the work before her in China is of no ordinary magnitude and difficulty.

What then? With the outlines of this immense field, and the greatness of the work opening up and extending before us, shall we sit down in despondency, and suffer the enemy still to enjoy undisturbed dominion in China? or shall we gird ourselves to the mighty struggle, and claim this empire for our Lord and Master, demanding for him the homage, obedience, and love of every heart? It is high time for us to consider this subject, to rise to the height of the grand argument. China at this hour demands from the Church tenfold more of men and means than she receives; and it is almost certain that within the next decadal period these demands will increase a hundredfold. The cycle of wondrous events has already commenced in China. The first throes of the approaching conflict have shaken her giant frame. It would seem that the Gospel is about to renew its youth, preparatory to the accomplishment of glorious results in this old, storied land. The age of heroism, of battle and conquest, may again return to the Church. There are indications that the Gospel is already arresting the attention of the Chinese in an extraordinary degree. The Sacred Scriptures circulated throughout the empire have opened the eyes and interested the hearts of thousands. A great movement is now going forward, and who can tell how soon other *mines* may be sprung under the shattered structure of heathenism as it now exists in China?

The following table, showing the names and terms of service of all the missionaries connected with this mission to the present time, is appropriately introduced here, and will prove, we trust, interesting and acceptable to the reader:

NAMES.	Sailed from U. S. A.	Died in China.	Died in U. S. A.	Left the Mission.
Rev. M. C. White	1847	....	....	1854
Rev. J. D. Collins	1847	....	1852	1851
Mrs. J. I. White	1847	1848	....	....
Rev. H. Hickok	1847	....	....	1849
Rev. R. S. Maclay [1]	1847	....	....	....
Mrs. E. G. Hickok	1847	....	....	1849
Miss H. C. Sperry [2]	1850	....	....	....
Rev. I. W. Wiley, M.D.	1851	....	....	1854
Rev. J. Colder	1851	....	....	1854
Mrs. F. J. Wiley	1851	1853	....	....
Mrs. E. C. Colder	1851	....	1858	1854
Miss M. Seely [3]	1851	....	....	1854
Rev. E. Wentworth, D.D.	1855	....	....	....
Rev. O. Gibson	1855	....	....	....
Mrs. A. M. Wentworth	1855	1855	....	....
Mrs. E. C. Gibson	1855	....	....	....
Rev. S. L. Baldwin	1858	....	....	1861
Mrs. N. M. Baldwin	1858	....	1861 [4]	....
Miss B. Woolston	1858	....	....	....
Miss S. E. Woolston	1858	....	....	....
Miss P. E. Potter [5]	1858	....	....	....
Rev. C. R. Martin	1859	....	....	....
Mrs. Martin	1859	....	....	....
Rev. N. Sites	1861	....	....	....
Mrs. Sites	1861	....	....	....

1 Visited U. S. A. with his family, 1860. 2 Married to R. S. Maclay, 1850.
3 Married to M. C. White, 1851. 4 At sea, off the United States coast, March, 16.
5 Married to E. Wentworth, D.D., 1859.

CHAPTER X.

BUILDINGS, LAND-TENURE, ETC.

INTIMATELY connected with the practical operation of a Christian mission in heathen lands, there is a large amount of what may be called civil engineering. The work of evangelizing the heathen would be much simplified, both in theory and practice, if the missionary could devote himself exclusively to preaching the Gospel. Actual experience in this enterprise, however, has shown that the duties of the foreign missionary are numerous and varied, and that his qualifications should be composite rather than simple, his talents painstaking rather than brilliant. Transferred from the known influences of a home atmosphere to the unknown tendencies of a foreign climate, from the refined comforts of Christian civilization to the rugged exigencies of, at best, semi-barbarism, the missionary, on entering the foreign field, finds himself confronted with necessities at once multifarious and imperative. One of his first and most urgent wants is a place of residence for himself and family. There is, perhaps, no heathen people in whose houses it would be safe or prudent for the foreign missionary to reside. In the selection of sites for dwelling-houses, churches, school-houses, etc.; in preparing plans, drawing up contracts, choosing materials for the buildings, and in superintending their erection, he will find ample opportunity for the exercise of all the business talent and knowledge he may possess.

In Fuhchau the Chinese houses generally are only one story high, built of wood, with lath and plaster, and covered with tiles. The houses of the lower classes, stores, shops, etc., open directly on the street, and frequently the entire front is thrown open during the day, but closed again at night. The house is lighted through openings in the front and rear, furnished, in many instances, with wooden shutters to close against the wind and rain. The houses have neither chimneys nor ceiling, and frequently have only earthen floors. Thus constructed, these buildings are low, dark, hot, filthy, and necessarily unhealthy. The houses of the higher classes are superior, in some respects, to those we have just described, and yet they are rude, uncomfortable, gloomy structures. They are built between two high walls, and have, in front and rear, open courts inclosed by a continuation of the high side walls of the premises. These open courts are paved with smooth, flat stones, and in most cases have a well, protected by a stone curb, in the center or corner. They are frequently ornamented with shrubbery, flowers, and artificial rocks and poles. Occasionally, on each side of the court, as you enter from the street, you will see a row of low rooms placed against the side wall, with roofs sloping inwards, and extending from the front wall to the main building. Passing through this court you enter the central room of the house, having a room of similar width, but less depth, immediately in the rear of it. On each side of the central room is another room of similar depth, but narrower, and having also in their rear a room corresponding to the one behind the central room. The rear court is similar to the one in front, though generally it is smaller and less tastefully fitted up. Large mansions sometimes comprise a series of houses with intervening courts, such as we have described, extending back from the street, and formed into one general compound by a high wall surrounding the entire premises.

The principal building materials used in Fuhchau are wood, brick, tiles, stone, lime, etc. The wood most generally employed is a kind of pine or cedar. It is easily worked, light, and durable. There are varieties of hard wood much used for costly work, but they are not employed to any considerable extent in house-building. This pine or cedar is very abundant at Fuhchau, and can be obtained at reasonable prices. It is cut from the mountains in the interior of China, and is floated in rafts down the Min to Fuhchau. Lumber is an important item in the native export trade of this city, and large quantities of it are annually shipped to the northern ports of China. Bricks are abundant and of good quality. One kind is of a light, ashy color; another kind is made from a reddish soil, and when burnt is very similar, in color, to the red brick used in the United States. These bricks can be procured in any quantity, and of any size or quality. In order to insure a good quality, however, it is necessary to have a written contract with either the merchant or manufacturer, specifying the exact kind of brick desired. The bricks in common use among the Chinese are of an inferior quality. They are burnt about ten miles from Fuhchau, in kilns similar to those used in America. There is also a flat kind of brick, measuring about fourteen inches square by one inch thick. It is red, well burnt, and much used in facing cooking ranges, paving bathing rooms, and for covering terraces or flat-roofed houses. The tiles are made at the places where the bricks are burnt. They are prepared with a kind of earth which, when burnt thoroughly, is of a pale ashy color. The tile is about nine inches square, always a little narrower at one end than at the other, and about one quarter of an inch thick. Its form is oval, so that when laid in a row they form a kind of trough. When well laid on, they make a safe and durable roof. Their weight is the great difficulty to be overcome in adapting them to foreign use, where large chambers, parlors, and audience-rooms, as in churches, are desired. It is sometimes difficult to construct a self-supporting roof sufficiently strong to resist the pressure of the tiles required to cover it. Granite is the kind of stone used for building purposes. It is quarried from the mountains on the banks of the Min, about fifteen miles below Fuhchau. The quality is excellent, the price moderate, and the supply apparently inexhaustible. It is cut with hammer and chisel from the solid rock in blocks of size and shape to suit purchasers, is then moved carefully down the side of the mountain and placed on strong boats for transportation to Fuhchau. Their lime is prepared from the shells of oysters, clams, muscles, and other bivalves, whose flesh is eaten by the Chinese. These shells are burnt in large kilns, and produce an excellent quality of lime, suitable for mortar, cement, plaster, whitewash, etc. It is almost impossible, however, to obtain the lime in a pure state, as the adulteration of it by the admixture of a kind of white earth is generally practiced by the Chinese. This system of adulteration is carried on so skillfully and persistently that it is difficult, without the application of scientific tests, to detect the imposition; and after a few indignant protests against the cheat, the purchaser gradually subsides into a stoical indifference on the subject, and seeks to indemnify himself by beating down the prices to the lowest possible figure.

The title by which foreigners hold property in China deserves at least a passing notice in this connection. Until within a comparatively recent period the imperial government of China affected contemptously to ignore even the presence of foreigners within its dominions, and persistently withheld from them all civil immunities and political consideration. The war of 1842–3, however, between England and China effectually dissipated this illusion, and served to initiate for the Chinese government a more just and magnanimous policy with regard to foreign intercourse. By the treaty formed at the close of that war China ceded to England the island of Hongkong; and in subsequent negotiations grants of land at Shanghai, Amoy, and other ports, were made to certain foreign governments for the use of their subjects or citizens, who thus derived the title to the land they obtained, from their respective governments.

At Fuhchau no land was set apart by the Chinese government for foreign occupancy, and we accordingly proceeded to obtain situations wherever they were offered in desirable positions. Our first lots were procured by the payment of an annual rent, but this arrangement was not entirely satisfactory to us, and we soon sought to procure more reliable titles for them. At the outset, however, we were confronted by a most formidable difficulty. In China there are neither mesne lords nor allodial proprietors of the soil; all Chinese landowners hold their lands directly from the emperor, who is regarded as the great landlord of the empire. In accordance with this view, the Chinese government conceived that it would be unlawful to sell, that is, in their judgment, alienate any portion of the territory of China to a foreigner. After a protracted discussion of the subject, it was finally arranged that whenever a foreigner obtained landed property from a Chinese, the Chinese landlord should give him a perpetual lease of the property, for and in consideration of a specified sum of money, which he accepts as the value or price of said property. This perpetual lease is regarded as, in all respects, equivalent to a purchase. In thus leasing his property to a foreigner, the Chinese landlord transfers to the lessee all the old deeds and other papers belonging to the property, and then writes for him, in triplicate, a new deed or article of perpetual lease, which, having been duly sealed by both the Chinese officer and foreign consul, becomes the valid title for the property. One copy of this triplicate is deposited with the Chinese government, another with the consul of the country to which the purchaser belongs, and the third is held by the purchaser.

The following is a translation of the title-deed by which we hold one of our lots in Fuhchau, and is a fair specimen of such documents:

Article of perpetual lease, showing—That Tieu Nang, holding a plat of land which he purchased in the twenty-eighth year of the emperor Tau-Kwang, situated in the Tienang ward, Mirror Hill vicinity, and bounded *west* by the premises of W. S. Sloan, Esq., *east*, including the ground below the embankment, by the wall of the Tienang temple, *south* by the old wall of the lot, and *north* by Mr. Maclay's premises; everything concerning said lot being clear, he now voluntarily transfers it on perpetual lease to the American teacher, R. S. Maclay, and others, for the purposes of erecting buildings and living thereon. He receives this day as the price of said land the sum of six hundred dollars.

Everything on said lot is at the disposal of the aforesaid Mr. Maclay and others, and he may cut down the fruit trees on it, or allow them to remain, just as he pleases.

After paying for the land, Mr. Maclay shall never pay any more money for the land, and the landlord *Nang* shall never bring up any other matters. But should the title prove to be defective, or should it appear that the property has been sold to other parties, and persons come forward to dispute, then *Nang* shall settle the matter, and it shall not concern Mr. Maclay.

In witness whereof, this deed of perpetual lease, in three forms, is prepared.

(Signed) TIEU NANG, Landlord.
SAH-HUAH LYNG, Witness.

Hienfung, fifth year and second month.
[A. D., April, 1855.]

In the foregoing deed or lease we notice:

1. The full value of the land is paid down at once by the foreigner to the Chinese landlord.

2. In consequence of receiving the stipulated value of his land, the Chinese landlord disclaims "*forever*" all title to said land, and all right to any other payment of money upon it.

3. He also pledges himself to guarantee to the foreigner a valid and clear title to said land, or land and buildings thereon erected.

The legal charges in procuring this lease are: 1. The consular fee, ten dollars, for stamping each deed. In our case this charge has not been made. 2. A per centage of about eight per cent. on the purchase money, to be paid to the Chinese government *when the land purchased is occupied by buildings.* This per centage is paid by the purchaser. Thus far, I believe, no foreigner here has paid this per centage; but, as it is the custom among the Chinese, I see no reason why foreigners should refuse to pay it if requested to do so. This charge would affect only our purchase of the chapel lot at Iongtau; possibly also the chapel lot in Chong-seng; but our other lots being unoccupied land, are free from this charge.

When cultivated land is purchased the government receives annually its tax in kind, as formerly, unless the foreigner compounds with the government by paying down at once a specified sum. The lots we have purchased in the olive orchard are cultivated land; but the Chinese landlord compounded with the government many years ago, so that there is no ground tax on them.

As a matter of *economy*, we all greatly prefer to hold property by perpetual lease. The prices we have paid for our lots would pay the annual rents accruing on them only from *four* to *seven* years.

The mission now holds by perpetual lease all its property in Fuhchau, except the land in the lot I occupy. This we hope to get in a year or two, and then we shall have all the land we shall need for dwelling houses for many years.

The annexed schedule of prices will indicate the value of land in Fuhchau at the time these lots were purchased. It is necessary to add that recently the price of lots suitable for foreign residence has largely increased:

1. For a very desirable building lot, situated just back of the premises I occupy, measuring about one hundred and twenty by two hundred and forty feet, and sufficient for two dwelling houses, the mission paid six hundred dollars.

2. For a chapel lot situated on the main street leading to the south gate of the city, and measuring

Changchau Island—First Methodist Episcopal Mission Premises.

about sixty-six by one hundred and forty-five feet, the mission paid four hundred dollars.

3. For the lot on which Dr. Wentworth's house now stands, measuring one hundred and twenty by one hundred and seventy feet, the mission paid three hundred and fifty dollars.

4. For the chapel lot just in front of the premises I occupy, measuring sixty-two by one hundred and forty feet, the mission paid one hundred and fifty-four dollars fifteen cents.

5. For the lot on which Messrs. Russell & Co.'s house stands we are to pay three hundred and fifty dollars. This lot is two hundred and fifty feet deep, with a front of ninety feet, and a rear of forty.

The first building fitted up by the mission in Fuhchau for a place of residence was an old Chinese house, one story high, and surrounded by high walls. The house stood on the island called Changchau, and during the annual flood in the river, which occurs in May or June, the water would rise about two feet above its floor. To adapt the place to foreign occupancy, it consequently became necessary to add another story to the building, and transfer the residence for the family from the lower to the upper floor, using the rooms on the lower floor for store-rooms, kitchen, and servants' apartments. The house was raised by splicing the posts, occasionally inserting a new one to reach the entire heighth of the building, putting down a second floor, setting up new partitions, and relaying the roof.

The engraving shows the upper or west end of the Changchau island. The house on the left was formerly owned by the Methodist Episcopal mission. The two houses on the right were built by the American Board mission. All this property has now passed into other hands, the missions having obtained more eligible situations elsewhere.

The first house built from the ground by the mission stands on Mirror Hill, and is a light frame structure, with lath and plaster walls and partitions. The mission decided to erect these cheap buildings because, at that time, from the temper and policy of the Chinese authorities at Fuhchau, it seemed very doubtful whether they would permit us to remain there for any considerable length of time, and also because at that early day we were not fully prepared to decide as to the best kind of house for that climate. Subsequent experience in the climate convinced us that as a general rule it is best to erect, wherever practicable, substantial brick buildings for dwelling houses, church edifices, etc. The original outlay of money for these buildings is much greater than for the frame houses to which we have referred; but for this there is more than ample compensation in the greater durability of the houses, in the comparatively small expense they entail on the mission in the way of annual repairs, and in the increased comfort and security of their occupants. In Fuhchau the winters are very mild, and there is scarcely any frost, so that in preparing the foundation for a house it is not necessary to dig deep trenches to get beyond the influence of frost. In low situations it is necessary to drive wooden piles, from five to ten feet long, in the ground wherever a wall is to be built. Flat stones about three feet long are then

First Dwelling-House built by the Mission.

laid down over the piles, the stones being placed transversely to the line of the wall, and on these stones the foundation of the house is built. The foundation is always of stone, rising at least one foot above the surface of the ground, or, in cases of inequality of surface, until the foundation is about one foot above the highest part of the ground. In high situations, where the ground is dry and hard, the flat stones are sufficient, and on these alone the foundation is built. Two kinds of stone wall are used for foundations: the one of long, smoothly-dressed stones, laid in right lines, and presenting a handsome appearance; the other of a kind of cobble-stone, so laid as to form acute angles, and presenting an appearance singular and not unsightly. In building this cobble-stone kind of wall, it is necessary to begin with a wide base, and contract the sides as you ascend. No mortar is used in this cobble-stone work. The mason selects the best stones for the sides, the handsomest being placed on the outside, and then the middle of the wall is filled up with the refuse. In building the other kind of wall, the mason forms a kind of box with side and cross stones, and then fills up this vacuum with any coarse stones, thrown in without any regard to beauty or order. The surface and exterior edges of the side stones are cut and smoothed into perfectly straight lines, and are fitted to each other with great exactness. In this kind of work a kind of cement, formed from lime, oil, and hemp, is used to supply any defects in the facing stones. Bricks are laid in a mortar made from a reddish kind of earth, with the admixture of lime. For plastering walls, partitions, etc., the first coat is generally a rough preparation of earth, cut straw, and lime; the second coat is a mixture of river mud and sawdust; and this is immediately followed by the third and last coat, which is a composition of the best lime and white paper. This produces a beautifully white surface, if the materials are of good quality, and the work properly executed. Tiles, such as we have already described, are universally employed in covering roofs. The tiles are laid on a flooring of thin boards nailed over the lathing of the roof, and are placed in rows running up and down the sides of the roof. The tiles are laid on this flooring without any mortar or cement except at the eaves, ends, and comb of the roof, where mortar is employed to protect the tiles from the action of the wind and rains. In covering a roof, the first work is to make the comb; and in doing this, tiles, brick, and mortar are employed. A bed of soft earth is made along the comb of the roof; on this a thin layer of single tiles is laid, then another layer of earth, followed by another of tiles, until the comb has attained a sufficient height, when it is surmounted by one or two layers of brick, and then entirely covered with plaster, either white or colored. The ends of the roof are then formed in a somewhat similar manner, though with less expenditure of materials and labor. These preliminaries completed, the tile-layers proceed with the body of the roof. Commencing at the eaves, the tiles are laid in parallel rows, from two or three to four inches apart, up to the comb of the roof. In these rows the tiles overlap each other, so that each tile presents only about three inches of its surface to the

Methodist Episcopal Mission Compound.

weather. The first rows are laid directly on the boards of the roof, with the *concave* side of the tile placed upward, and the rows being, as already stated, from three to four inches apart. These narrow spaces between the rows are then covered by upper rows of tiles, the tiles overlapping each other as in the lower rows, but having their *convex* surface turned upward. To protect these tiles against the force of the winds, their edges are covered with a lime mortar, and single bricks are set in cement on the top, at intervals of about four feet.

In the accompanying picture the mission compound crowns the summit and slope of the hill on the south side of the river. It contains six dwelling-houses, only four of which, however, appear in the above cut. Beginning at the left side of the picture you have the corner of a house belonging to a foreign merchant. Passing to the right you have (1) a low bungalow occupied by Rev. R. S. Maclay; (2) a two-storied house by a flagstaff, formerly the United States consulate, but now belonging to our mission, and occupied by Rev. S. L. Baldwin; (3) a two-storied house now forming the Chinese portion of the Waugh Female Academy. Immediately to the right of this, in the background underneath a flagstaff, is the British consulate. Then we have (4) the residence of the Rev. Dr. Wentworth. On the extreme right is a portion of the residence of another foreign merchant. The edifice was subsequently removed, and its place is now filled by a very pretty and substantial building for the Church of England service.

CHAPTER XI.

TRIP INTO THE COUNTRY.

On the 4th of January, 1849, in company with the late Rev. J. D. Collins, I started on a trip of exploration up the Min River. A small Chinese boat, rowed by four stout Chinese, sufficed for ourselves and traveling equipage. We felt great interest in the proposed excursion as it was our first attempt to explore a portion of China on which, so far as we knew, no foreigner had ever looked. Our plan was to wear our own costume, make no effort at concealment or deception, distribute Christian books, talk to the people, and advance as far into the country as the authorities would allow, or as we might deem desirable. It was moreover highly gratifying to us to think of escaping even temporarily from the persistent surveillance to which we had been subjected for nearly a year by the Chinese in Fuhchau. Availing ourselves of the flood tide we commenced the voyage, and were soon passing through the fleets of boats anchored in the river. On our right rises a bold hill covered with pines and banians, through whose thick foliage peer out at intervals the cottage of the peasant and the more pretentious temple edifice. Looking to the right, as the boat sweeps along, the eye falls on a vast extent of slate-colored roofs, relieved by the foliage of the overspreading evergreens which constitute so attractive a feature in Fuhchau scenery. Beyond, and overlooking this portion of the city, stands the great temple hill, with its altar, sward, and trees, where at sunset the people meet for recreation and amusement; while still farther to the northward you trace the outlines of the towering mountains which for centuries have beleaguered this old city.

The course of the river, as we ascend, is quite circuitous, at one time trending away southward, and then suddenly deflecting to an almost due northerly point. The channel, too, we found to be of very unequal depth, our boat sometimes passing over places where a frigate might float, and then suddenly thumping its keel on one of the sandbars which cross the river in all possible directions. About six miles above Fuhchau we came to the "upper bridge," a stone structure similar to those at the city, which we have already described. The water rushes through its spans with great velocity, and it is only at or near the top of the tide that boats can go through with safety. A small village stands near the end of the bridge on the right bank, and a petty officer is stationed here to look after the river traffic. Fearing the officer might prevent our going any farther, the boatmen advised us to conceal ourselves under the cover of the boat; but we preferred a seat on the forward deck, where all could see us, and accordingly directed the men to pull away at their oars and answer promptly when hailed from the shore. The policemen soon saw us, and our approach evidently produced considerable excitement. Lictors were seen hurrying hither and thither through the motley crowd that had assembled to gaze at the foreigners. We could distinctly hear the jargon of their voices, while our ears were saluted by successive vollies of ejaculations and objurgations designed for our benefit.

"Where are you from?" at length shouted a stentorian voice from the shore.

"From Fuhchau," answered our man at the rudder.

"What cargo have you?"

"No cargo; we are chartered by two foreigners for a trip up the river."

Then followed an earnest and noisy colloquy among the police on shore, and we waited with much interest for the result. Meanwhile our boat was moving forward, and while the air was ringing with the vociferations of the excited lictors, we passed the village, and stood on our course. We soon entered a beautiful pass formed by sparsely wooded hills, which sloped down to the water's edge. A well-beaten foot-path ran along the hills on the right, and as there were houses or people in sight we could not resist the temptation to take a run on the hills. For the first time since entering China we now experienced a sensation of relief from Chinese curiosity, and were conscious of a kind of home feeling. To our mutual surprise and amusement, we soon found ourselves running and leaping over the hills, indulging in all sorts of impromptu peripatetics and calisthenics.

Toward nightfall we anchored near a sandy beach, about five miles above the upper bridge. The valley of the Min is here some ten miles wide, with alluvial savannas stretching from both banks of the river, away to the dark mountains, whose rugged outlines are limned against the sky. Our anchorage was a retired, quiet spot, the nearest village was a mile distant from us, and after our evening repast we landed for a moonlight stroll along the beach. I shall not readily forget the scene or the emotions it excited. At our feet lay the broad river, whose waters had flowed directly from the interior of this great and, to foreigners, almost unknown country; around us were rice farms, fruit-orchards, groves, villages, and the graves of those who

"Sleep the sleep that knows no waking;"

while, flashing out like brilliant stars through the night air, we could discern the lights of Chinese dwellings, within whose frail walls thousands of the natives were now chatting over their evening meal, totally unconscious that in such close proximity to their ancient homesteads two strangers from the western ocean were quietly rambling, to enjoy their beautiful scenery, and the balmy air of their eastern sky.

Before day-break next morning we resumed our voyage, and throughout the day the general course of the river, as we ascended, continued about from southeast to northwest. Some six miles above our last night's anchorage the mountains, becoming more lofty and precipitous, again closed in upon the river, leaving only a narrow valley, varying from one to five miles in width. The river banks are skirted with orchards of the orange, olive, pumalo, pomegranate, tallow, lichi, lungan, and other fruit trees, interspersed with fields of luxuriant sugar-cane, and copses of tasteful bamboo. Early in the forenoon our attention was attracted by an object floating in the water near the shore. Rapacious birds were hovering around it, while one and another in rapid succession would alight on it and drive their beaks into it. We had heard of female infanticide among the Chinese, but had never seen positive proof that they were guilty of the horrible practice. The terrible idea at once flashed upon our minds that the object before us was the body of some cast-away infant, which the birds were now tearing to pieces. I confess to a sickening sensation as the dreadful truth fastened on my mind. "What is that?" we inquired of the boatmen, as we pointed to the object which had arrested our attention. They shook their heads, and for a while seemed unwilling to answer our question, but finally answered: "A cast-away infant." The birds slowly retired as we approached, and on coming up to the object our worst fears were realized. There, lashed to a small bundle of straw, were the mutilated and loathsome remains of a tender infant. Half of the face and one side with the entrails were eaten away, but the rest of the body was perfect. "Let us bury it," we involuntarily exclaimed; and digging with our hands and a few pieces of boards a deep hole in the sand, we committed the disfigured corpse to the rest and protection of the best grave we could then provide for it. Out boatmen utterly refused to assist us. They sat in the boat scarcely venturing to look at us while engaged in our mournful task. Smoothing the surface of the grave, and breathing a prayer for the besotted inhabitants of this dark land, we turned away from the spot with saddened hearts, and resumed our voyage. During the forenoon we landed for a walk along the shore. We passed through fields and groves and villages, startling the people by our unexpected appearance among them, and exciting the wrath of troops of yelping curs, both "mongrel, puppy, whelp, and hound," who kept the air ringing with their protracted concerts of canine music.

We passed large fields of sugar-cane, and a little below *Min-ching* we came to a sugar factory in active operation. The building was a frail wooden structure, covered with thatch, and one story high. It was surrounded with innumerable stacks of ripe cane ready for the sugar-making process. The interior of the building was occupied by the mill for bruising the cane, the vats or reservoirs for the juice, the kettles for boiling it, etc. The mill was quite similar to those used in the United States for bruising apples in the cider-making process. Bullocks were employed in turning the mill, and the machinery, though simple in conception and clumsy in construction, seemed efficient in action. The press was constructed on the lever principle in a most primitive stage of development. The expressed juice is conveyed to vats sunk in the earth, and then by successive processes of filtration and boiling is converted into sugar. The factory we examined prepared only the coarser qualities of sugar; but in other parts of the Fuh-kien province there are extensive factories which produce white sugar, loaf sugar, and a rock candy, which is a superior article of sugar. Bidding good-by to the workmen, who had kindly allowed us to watch their operations, we passed through some villages and climbed some beautiful hills, followed by a few energetic boys, who observed our proceedings with great interest. Descending the slope of the last hill, we unexpectedly found ourselves on the outskirts of a large village called *Min-ching*, where there is a resident government officer. It had been our wish and purpose to approach this place as quietly as possible, hoping in this way to pass without being noticed from the shore; but our forenoon ramble completely spoiled this arrangement. Our appearance in the villages and on the hills along the river had been heralded far and wide, so that when we approached *Min-ching* we met the entire population pouring out to see us. It was too late to undo the mischief, and all we could now hope for was to escape from the gathering crowds by stepping quickly into our boat and pulling out into the stream.

"You have spoiled everything," said our boatmen despondingly as the boat moved away from the shore; and we felt sure our voyage would terminate at this point. The people were evidently excited, crowds gathered on the bank of the river to look at us, and the activity of the police, discernible by their costume, showed us that the mandarin was aware of our approach. The crowds beckoned and called to our boatmen to stop, but no attention was paid to them; and as we received no official intimation to suspend our voyage, we kept on our course, and began to flatter ourselves that possibly we might still be allowed to go forward. We were now right abreast of the mandarin's office, when *whirr*, *boom*, *clang*, *bang*, went the drums and gongs, and hundreds of hands were vibrating most rapidly in the air, beckoning to the shore.

"What shall we do?" inquired the boatmen.

"Obey orders," we replied.

As we approached the shore we observed an official personage moving down to meet us. Directing our men to answer truthfully all official inquiries, we supplied ourselves with some of our Christian books and tracts, and, retaining our position on the forward deck of the boat, awaited the issue. As we drew up to the landing the crowd subsided into a state of quiet expectancy, and the official personage, to whom we have already referred, stepped forward with becoming dignity and grace to interrogate us. The bank was somewhat steep, the soil was rather moist, and just as his excellency was about taking his final position preparatory to commencing his oration, an unfortunate misstep precipitated his entire length into the mud. The collapse was terrible, and a roar of laughter burst from the crowd. Unabashed by the untoward accident, the plucky officer was instantly on his feet again, and sternly commanding silence, while the attending lictors cleaned the mud from his soiled robes, he proceeded to catechize our boatmen:

"Where are you from?" was the first inquiry.

"From Fuhchau," replied our boatmen, with an unusual degree of assurance.

"Where are you going?"

"Up the river, to distribute books. These are foreign teachers, and it is their custom to travel through the country, talking to the people and distributing books."

At this point we interjected a few words explanatory of our character and operations.

"How long will you be gone?" inquired the officer, evidently disposed to favor our enterprise. We gave him all the desired information, and he promptly responded: "Very well, continue your trip, and report yourselves here on your return."

Delighted with this unexpected issue of the affair, and anxious to avail ourselves of so good an opportunity to commend the Gospel to one in authority, we ventured a few remarks about the doctrines of Jesus, and begged his honor to accept some of our books. He received them with studied propriety of manner, and then, desiring to make us some present in return, he took some oranges out of a man's basket near at hand and handed them to us.

"Those oranges are mine! those oranges are mine!" vociferated a rough-looking customer, rushing forward to rescue his property.

"Silence! silence!" shouted the lictors, flourishing their whips, and arresting the progress of the excited proprietor of the oranges. But the man refused to be satisfied.

"The oranges are mine!" he continued to vociferate, while his supple, eel-like gyrations of body seemed to defy the combined manipulations of the police.

Thinking to settle the dispute, we proposed to return the oranges; but this plan of compromise was totally inadmissible.

"Silence! silence!" shouted the lictors for the thousandth time, "the officer will pay you for your oranges."

"Pay me now! pay me now!" screamed the shrewd rustic, well knowing that instant payment was his only hope. Scores of dirty hands forthwith plunged into scores of dirtier pockets, and after an energetic search among tobacco-boxes and other etceteras of a Chinaman's pockets, the combined proceeds of the operation, amounting to a few tens of most villanous looking *cash*, were handed over to the man for his fruit. Thankful for our unexpected deliverance we resumed our trip, amused and instructed by the scene we had just witnessed.

During the remainder of the day we continued slowly to ascend the river, occasionally landing for a short walk on shore. The scenery becomes more impressive and grand as we advance, and the channel of the river gradually contracts, the water generally flowing with a strong current over a pebbly or rocky bottom. The valley of the river becomes narrow and circuitous, though the general direction as we ascend continues to be about northwest. The villages to-day are smaller and less numerous, and the population more sparse than yesterday. The people, though intensely anxious to examine our persons and clothes, behaved with great propriety, and treated us courteously. Our books were eagerly received, and a good degree of attention was paid to our statements concerning the doctrines of the Gospel. Walking along the shore toward sunset, we entered a most quiet and beautiful place. It was a small cove or recess, extending back from the river to the massive rocks forming the base of the mountain, whose summit rose, with a rapid ascent, to an elevation of perhaps fifteen hundred feet. A luxuriant growth of fruit trees throws a dim religious light over this Arcadian scene. The overspreading foliage forms beautiful arbors, and the upright trunks, arranged in parallel lines, seem to constitute long-drawn aisles in this stupendous and unique forest-temple. Coming abruptly round a rocky point, we found ourselves entering this almost enchanted spot, and impressed, awed by the solemnity of the scene, we instinctively removed our hats and stood bareheaded, and for some moments silent, beneath the boughs of those stately trees. Years have passed away since that hour, and yet the memory of that scene is as vivid and fresh as though it were but a day since I looked upon it. Beckoning to our boatmen to wait for us, we retired to the side of a high rock, and there reverently kneeling together we united in humble, fervent prayer. Rising from our knees, we paced for some minutes the aisles of this natural temple, and conversed of that glorious period when China, clothed and in her right mind, shall be found sitting at the feet of Jesus. Shortly after nightfall we anchored, unobserved, close under a high cliff that overhung the river. Our situation as we lay there, in the deepening shades of evening, on the waters of that strange river, and in close proximity to a constant stream of native boats passing up and down, was well calculated to impress the mind and excite the emotions. Weary as we were from the exertions and excitement of the day, it was well on toward midnight before we could compose ourselves to sleep.

Sunrise next morning disclosed to us a scene of rare beauty and splendor. Our boat lay in a bight of the river, which presented the appearance of a mountain lake. The shores were fringed with beautiful foliage; beyond, the mountain acclivities were adorned with fruit-orchards and pretty cottages, while upward and away rise successive ranges of grand old mountains. The effect of the sun's first rays on those dizzy peaks was singularly pleasing, as point after point received the golden light and, beaconlike, flashed up into the morning sky. We thought of Coleridge's "Hymn to the Sun" in the Vale of Chamouny, and could readily conceive the effect of that magnificent Alpine scenery on his exuberant imagination.

We continued to ascend the river during this, the third day of our trip. The prominent features of the scenery are similar to those described yesterday. Some of the mountains rise at least three thousand feet above the level of the river. The villages are small, and seem to rest on a very precarious foundation, perched on the precipitous sides of the mountains. As the population was apparently sparse, we walked for hours on the shore and were courteously treated by the people. Our boatmen, however, began to grow timid and suspicious as we advanced. Their excited imaginations filled every hamlet with thieves and outlaws, and transformed every pass or defile on the river into rendezvous for bloodthirsty pirates. Early in the afternoon we came in sight of Sui Këu, a town built at the foot of the rapids, about sixty miles from Fuhchau. At this place there is a government officer, and all boats are closely examined. Having now ascended the river farther than we dared to anticipate at the commencement of our trip, and not having supplies for an extension of our excursion, we decided to terminate our upward voyage at this point.

While making arrangements for descending the river, our attention was directed to a very high mountain on the left bank, and we determined to climb to its summit in order to obtain a view of the surrounding country. An unexpected difficulty met us at the outset and well-nigh defeated the enterprise. No one was able or willing to give us any assistance in ascending the mountain. The Chinese declared there was no path in that direction, and when we urged them to act as our guides they stared at us in blank amazement and shook their heads.

"Why we have never been there!" they exclaimed; "nobody dares to ascend that peak, and no amount of money could induce us to attempt it."

Our prospect seemed sufficiently discouraging, but we resolved to start alone and go as far as we could. Noticing a wood-cutter's path leading in the desired direction, we at once struck into it and commenced the ascent. Our task was more difficult than we had expected. The path was both steep and slippery, and at times it seemed almost impossible for us to advance. Still we pressed forward, and after half an hour's exertion found ourselves on the summit of the first spur of the mountain. Here our path left us, turning quite away from our course. While deliberating as to our farther advance, the sound of a woodman's ax fell on our ear, and off we started in that direction to seek for a guide, or at least for information. Making our way over rocks and through a dense, tangled undergrowth, we finally came upon the wood-choppers. The first one we came to was an old man, and it would be utterly impossible to describe the look of wild amazement with which he gazed at us as we came splurging through the fern and bushes. There he stood with uplifted ax, apparently unable to move or speak. We addressed him with the usual Chinese compliments, and proceeded to state the occasion of our abrupt appearance in such a place.

"Why, you speak our language!" was the first exclamation that burst from his lips.

"Yes," we replied, "we have been studying it for a year."

"And where are you from?" he continued, looking as though he fancied we must have dropped from the clouds.

"From Fuhchau," we replied.

"Come! come!" he shouted to one of his companions at a little distance from him; "come quickly and see the foreigners!"

"Will you not show us the way to the top of the mountain?" we inquired.

"Never was there in my life," he replied; and neither persuasion nor money could induce him or his companion to go with us. We then determined to make another effort with our own resources. "Aim for the clearing directly ahead, and avoid the precipice on the left," were the parting words of the wood-choppers as we left them to resume our ascent. Emerging from the forest, we came to the clearing referred to, and then proceeded in a direct line toward the summit. Our course brought us along the edge of precipices, and over sharp peaks where the head would grow dizzy, and I was compelled, in self-defense, to shut my eyes and feel my way along in the wake of my stronger nerved friend. After an hour's exhausting labor we reached the summit, and never shall I forget the scene that there opened before us. Far as the eye could sweep in all directions it resembled the pictures of an Arctic sea, with mountains like icebergs swelling or splintering up everywhere. The clouds were floating round us, and just to the south of us there stood a majestic mountain whose sides at our altitude were wrapt in clouds, and whose summit, bathed in a soft sunlight, seemed to be nearly as far above us as we were above the river which flowed at our feet. Descending the mountain, we commenced our return trip, and next day arrived safely at Fuhchau.

CHAPTER XII.

PREACHING AND CHURCHES.

THE first and great effort of the missionary, on reaching his field of labor in China is to acquire, as rapidly and perfectly as possible, the power to communicate orally with the people. The possession of this power places him at once on high vantage ground with reference to the native population. It goes far toward shielding him from the impositions which natives are so ready to practice upon foreigners, gives him free access to the people, and invests him with a prestige and influence which prove invaluable to him in the prosecution of his work. The Chinese are fond of listening to public discourse. One everywhere meets with restaurants, in connection with which you almost invariably find the public audience room, where the lecturer holds forth to the people on topics of popular interest. This custom supplied at once the precedent and type for the Christian congregation and pulpit, and we proceeded immediately to avail ourselves of the suggestion. Our first chapels were ordinary Chinese houses, which, by a little scrubbing, painting, joinery, and efforts at improved lighting and ventilation, were, after a fashion, adapted to our purposes.

Soon after its organization in 1847, the mission recommended to the Board of Managers at New York the erection of a substantial church edifice in Fuhchau. The board cordially approved the suggestion, and the Methodist Churches of New York, Brooklyn, and Williamsburgh generously contributed the sum of five thousand dollars for the accomplishment of the desired object. The mission succeeded in purchasing a plat of land on one of the chief thoroughfares of the city outside the walls, and there, toward the close of 1855, began to lay the foundations of a solid Christian church building. The erection of this structure constitutes an era in the history of the mission. The event convinced the Chinese that we expected to remain permanently in Fuhchau, that we believed the Gospel would triumph over all opposition in that city, and that consequently the mendacious slanders of their officers against us, to the effect that we were to be tolerated at Fuhchau only for a brief period, and that the Gospel could never enter China, were utterly without foundation. The blessing of God was promptly vouchsafed to the enterprise; for scarcely had we completed this edifice of brick and stone, when the Holy Spirit began to furnish "living stones" for the spiritual temple of the Almighty in Fuhchau. The accompanying drawing will give some idea of this interesting building.

The position of this church is admirable. It stands on the main street leading to the south gate of the city. Within a few steps of it is a very large tea-pavilion, or restaurant, where travelers stop for refreshment. On one side of the church, distant per-

Iongtau Church.

haps three quarters of a mile, lies the city within the wall, containing a population of about four hundred thousand. On the other side of the church, and at about the same distance, lies the immense southern suburb of the city, stretching to and beyond the river, and containing a population of about three hundred thousand. The only direct communication between this vast suburb and the city within the wall, is by the street which passes in front of our church. From morning till night this street is thronged with people, and by simply opening our church doors we can usually obtain a congregation at any hour of the day.

The building is of a very substantial character. The foundation is of stone, and is raised five feet, to avoid the annual flood that submerges the greater part of Fuhchau. Upon this solid foundation the edifice rests. It measures thirty-eight feet wide by seventy-six deep, and has twenty feet between the floor and the ceiling. The building contains a vestibule, measuring ten feet deep by thirty-four wide, in the clear; an audience-room, forty-seven feet by thirty-four, with twenty feet height of ceiling; and (back of the audience-room) four rooms, two on the lower floor, measuring respectively twenty-one feet by twelve, and thirteen feet by twelve; and two on the second floor of similar dimensions. The ceiling of the lower rooms is twelve feet high, and of the upper rooms it is ten feet high. The walls are of brick, the outer walls being two feet thick, the inner one eighteen inches. The side and rear walls are built of common brick, and plastered white inside and gray outside. The front is built with handsome red brick, neatly painted and whitelined. Each side of the building has six high windows, measuring in the clear ten feet by four feet four inches. Of these windows two open into the vestibule, (one on each side,) eight open into the audience-room, (four on each side,) and two open into the rear lower rooms. The upper rooms are lighted by two smaller windows in the sides, directly over the large ones in the lower rooms, and by two windows in the rear of the building.

The front of the building presents an imposing appearance. As the floor of the church is five feet above the street, it was necessary for us to provide a flight of steps for entering the church, and thus the front wall of the building was placed back eight feet from the street, making a pretty court between the street and the church. In order to make the street front as wide as possible, we built on each side, from the corner of the church front to the street, a wall flaring outward six feet, thus making the street front fifty feet, whereas the church front is only thirty-eight feet wide. For the present we have put up a neat wooden railing, ten feet high, on the street front, in the middle of which is a gateway eight feet wide, opposite to the flight of steps by which you ascend to the entrance of the church. This little court we have sodded on each side of the stone steps, and its greensward adds much to the beauty of the building.

There is only one opening in the front wall of the church. This is the door-way, measuring eight feet wide and eleven high. The door-jams flare outward, and are faced by a pilaster on each side. On these two pilasters rests a pretty wooden façade or entablature, spanning the door-way, and painted white. On each side of this door-way are two large pilasters rising from the stone foundation and reaching an elevation of twenty feet. These four pilasters also are built of the red brick which compose the entire front surface of the wall; they project about two inches from the wall, and measure three and a half feet at the base. The brick work rises only to the top of the pilasters; above this point there is a wooden façade or entablature similar in design (but of course on a larger scale) to the one over the door-way. It also is painted white. This façade conceals the gable of the roof, and rises a foot above the comb of the roof. A pretty cupola, about thirteen feet high, rises from the front part of the roof, and in it we have placed our bell, which was cast to our order in the city of Fuhchau. The bell is suspended from the ceiling of the cupola, and is rung by pulling quickly against the outer rim a wooden billet suspended by ropes. The bell weighs three hundred and thirty-three and a half pounds, and, with the hangings, cost twenty-four and a half dollars. The tone of the bell is soft and pleasing. The sound, however, is not loud, and it cannot be heard beyond a very limited circle.

The audience room is neatly fitted up with pulpit, altar, and seats, and will contain about three hundred persons at one time. The seats and the entire interior woodwork of the building are of a mahogany color; the exterior woodwork, except the cupola and part of the front, is of the same color. There are two aisles, each three and a half feet wide, and communicating with the vestibule by two doors each four feet four inches wide by nine feet high. The vestibule is paved with stone, the audience-room is floored with plank two inches thick, and the rear rooms with plank one and a half inch thick.

The accompanying drawing presents the interior of the church at Iongtau.

We have named the church "Ching Sing Tong," that is, "Church of the True God." A tablet of handsome porphyry, four by one and a half feet, is inserted perpendicularly in the wall, just over the front door-way, and on it are carved the three Chinese characters representing the name of the church. The letters are gilded, and being large they present a fine appearance, and are read daily by thousands of Chinese who pass along the street.

The entire cost of the church, including price of land, four hundred dollars, and cost of walling it in, two hundred and eighty dollars, is under two thousand six hundred dollars.

The church was dedicated on Sunday, August 3, 1856, the exercises commencing about a quarter past nine o'clock A. M. The church was filled with an orderly and attentive congregation of Chinese. All the teachers, scholars, and servants connected with the three missions in this city were present. We were also favored with the presence of Revs. C. C. Baldwin, J. Doolittle, and C. Hartwell, of the American Board Mission; and of Rev. Mr. M'Caw and

Interior of the Church at longtau.

Rev. Mr. Fearnley of the Church of England Mission. We were also gratified to notice several members of the foreign mercantile community present on the occasion.

In the chapel at Iongtau the congregations are of a floating, miscellaneous character. The doors of the chapel are thrown open as an invitation to come in, and generally the room is soon filled with people. The smith comes from his anvil, the tradesman from his shop, the cake-vender enters boldly with his tray on his head, the rustic marches up the aisle with his poultry on his shoulders, the cooly lays down his burden at the door, and all take their positions, either sitting or standing, to hear what the foreigner has to say.

The preacher commences, and perhaps his first sentence elicits from some one of his auditors a rather loudly expressed approval or dissent. Disregarding, or, perhaps, hurriedly chiding the objector, the speaker goes on with his remarks. Presently one or more spring to their feet and move to another part of the chapel, or, muttering some words, (usually not very complimentary to the speaker,) retire from the congregation. While this winnowing process is going on the preacher continues his discourse, and sometimes is gratified to observe that a goodly number are sitting quietly and listening attentively to what he is saying. Encouraged by this attention, the preacher grows more anxious to impart to them a knowledge of "the truth as it is in Jesus;" his enunciation, at first faltering, becomes more distinct and confident, his manner waxes more earnest, one and another of his restless auditors become quiet, the idlers about the door gradually draw toward the pulpit, and, amid general stillness and attention on the part of the congregation, the preacher closes his discourse, feeling in his heart that it is blessed to sow beside even these waters; and that "he that goeth forth and weepeth, bearing precious seed, shall doubtless come again with rejoicing, bringing his sheaves with him."

Dr. Wentworth writes: "It is exceedingly trying to be in the midst of a heathen people, and see them going on in the practice of all manner of superstitions, without being able to tell them fully the folly of their courses. If we begin, the newly acquired words and accents halt and falter upon our foreign tongues, and provoke derision rather than produce conviction or turn attention to the truth. At our August mission meeting we resolved to keep our chapels open every day, and, 'preach or no preach,' to go to the pulpits, and from *thence* distribute books and make the best effort we could to talk to the people of 'Jesus and the resurrection.' In accordance with this resolve I repaired, on the afternoon of the first of September, to our little wayside synagogue at Chong Seng, with something like the trepidation I used to feel in approaching a school-house congregation in the days of my exhortership. The door was shut and the sexton 'gone to dinner.' I placed my back against the outer gates of the chapel, and a crowd instantly gathered, choking up the narrow street and impeding all passage. 'Are you going to preach?' 'Are you going to preach?' was the cry from all quarters. 'Not much; I do not understand enough of the language to make a regular sermon.' And then followed the usual shower of questions suggested by the curiosity and allowed by the impertinent and tiresome courtesy of this inquisitive people: 'How old are you?' 'How long have you been here?' 'Where do you live?' 'Are you American or English?' 'Do you come here to buy tea?' and the like.

"One offered me fruit; another, tobacco and a a pipe; another, a couple of papers of the vile betel-nut to chew; another, a stool to sit upon; another, to break open the door; another, to go for the sexton There was no end to their kindness. Among others a young man living near our new church paused to ask me if I 'had been to dinner,' the Chinese 'How do you do?' I told him I was glad to see him so decently dressed and looking so well. The last time I saw him, some weeks since, his clothes hung about him in filthy and disgusting tatters, and his countenance wore the ghastly hue and expression of the confirmed opium-smoker. He replied: 'I had no money; I dress well when I can get the means.' I told him I fancied he smoked opium and was idle. The crowd said, 'Yes, he smokes opium, and is idle.' He denied it vigorously. I told him if he worked he would get means, and if he had means he could clothe himself well, if he did not squander his earnings in a fatal indulgence. This was my first sermon in Chinese. My auditor bade me 'sit quietly,' the Chinese 'good-by,' (I was standing withal,) and went his way.

Gratified and encouraged by the successful completion of our church edifice at Iongtau, the mission next proceeded to purchase an eligible site for a church in the ward in which the majority of our houses are situated, the situation being just in front of the lot I occupy. When we purchased this lot it was not our intention to proceed at once to erect upon it a church edifice, though we all felt the importance of having such a building at the earliest possible date. In conversation, however, with some of the foreign residents at this port, it was proposed that our mission erect on this lot a church edifice containing two audience rooms, one being for Chinese, the other for English worship. In view of the increasing foreign community in this city, it was felt to be important to provide at once a place for public religious worship in the English language, and our mercantile friends offered to place at the service of our mission one thousand dollars to aid in erecting the building. Under these circumstances we decided to erect the church, availing ourselves of the subscription tendered to us by the foreign community in Fuhchau, which in the end amounted to the handsome sum of thirteen hundred dollars.

The Chinese portion of this church edifice in the Tienang (that is, Heavenly-rest) ward, was dedicated to the worship and service of God on Sunday, October 18, 1856. The Rev. Messrs. Peet, Doolittle, and Hartwell, of the American Board Mission in this city, united with us in conducting the services. The building is a neat and substantial struc-

English and Chinese Church at Tienang.

ture of brick, resting on a stone foundation. The outer face of the walls is of red brick, lined with white. A very pretty wooden finish, painted white, runs round the entire building, underneath the eaves of the roof, and imparts to it a fine appearance.

The interior of the audience-room is twenty-five feet by thirty-four, height of ceiling twenty feet. A vestibule eight feet deep extends across the front of the building, faced by four wooden columns, fluted and painted white. The windows are ten feet high by four and a half wide.

The pulpit, altar, and seats are of hard wood, varnished. An aisle three feet wide passes up the middle of the audience-room. The building stands immediately in front of the premises I occupy, and abuts on our new road leading from the street to the foreign residences on the hill. The situation is quiet and accessible.

We regard this as our normal church. In it we conduct public religious worship in a formal manner, thus furnishing to this people at once a model for worship, and an answer to their ever-iterated interrogatory, "How do you worship Jesus?" We hold public religious service in this church every Sunday morning at nine o'clock, and we hope to be able, before a great while, to have two services in it on Sunday.

On Sunday, the 28th of December, 1856, we dedicated the English portion of our Tienang church edifice. The services on the occasion were conducted by the Rev. Dr. Wentworth, who delivered, from

14

1 Kings ix, 3, a most appropriate and able discourse to a highly gratified audience. This church is designed for public worship in the English language. The foreign community here have very generously aided in its erection, and we devoutly pray that it may prove to be a perpetual blessing to them. It is the first Christian church ever erected in this ancient city for the worship of God in the English language. It is opened twice every Sunday for public worship, and we transferred to it the English Sunday service we had hitherto held in private houses.

We cannot be sufficiently grateful to God for bringing us into the possession of these beautiful churches. It would be difficult, indeed, to exaggerate the importance of these sacred edifices in connection with our work. The church at Iongtau fully meets our expectations, and we believe that the Tienang church also will be an invaluable acquisition to our mission. For myself, I cannot express the solid satisfaction these churches afford me. After years of desultory and wearing toil in the alleys, dark rooms, waysides, and places of public resort in this city, I feel it a glorious privilege now to stand up in these noble buildings, and tell to these erring heathen the story of the cross. I feel, indeed, as if our mission had only commenced efficiently to deliver its message to this people. Not that I believe we, as a mission, have been derelict as to our duty in the past. I am satisfied that, according to our ability and opportunities, we have from the first borne a faithful and unfaltering testimony against the sins of this people. But when I compare our past disadvantages with our present facilities for making known the truth as it is in Jesus, I cannot repress the jubilant feelings excited by the contrast. I fancy at times that the light, the long expected, blessed light, is now breaking upon this dark land. I find my heart thrilling with emotions which indicate victory rather than stern, protracted conflict. I am not singular in this experience; it is participated in by every member of the mission. We all breathe more freely, and tread with a firmer step to the solemn music of our life-labor, as we look on these sacred structures.

The annual report for 1857 says: "We continue to make the public preaching of the Gospel our distinguishing work; and in this department of our labors we have derived incalculable advantage and comfort from the noble church edifices which the liberality of the friends of missions at home enabled us to erect the previous year. Our congregations in them have been uniformly orderly and respectful. Not one instance of disorderly conduct has occurred in these congregations during the year. We note this fact as furnishing ground for great encouragement. What people are induced to respect, we may suppose they will finally imitate; and we are convinced that these orderly religious exercises are doing much to prepare the way for the general introduction of Christianity in Fuhchau. The seed, we believe, is now falling into good soil, and we are earnestly praying and looking for the glorious harvest. We have three public services every Sunday in these churches, and generally two other services during the week."

On Sunday, July 14, 1857, we baptized our first convert in connection with our mission. The convert's name is *Ting Ang.* He was forty-seven years of age, and had a wife and five children. His home was within a few minutes' walk of the viceroy's palace in the city of Fuhchau. He stated that about two years before his conversion he began to drop in at our Iongtau chapel to hear what the foreigner had to say. This happened as he was passing in and out of the city on business, and it seems that he was interested in what he heard. He obtained some of our books, and perused them. Subsequently he began to call in at our boys' day-school in the ward where we live, and not long afterward the teacher of the boys' school brought him to our Sunday morning service in the *Tienang* church. This was our first acquaintance with the man, and we at once invited him to attend the weekly inquiry meeting which we had just established on Friday afternoon. He continued to attend the inquiry meeting, and we were much pleased with his deportment. He was not familiar with the written character, and could not read very well, but he at once commenced the Commandments and Apostles' Creed, and soon he was able to read and explain them quite correctly. We instructed him carefully in the doctrines of Christianity, and he expressed his fixed purpose to live according to its principles. He commenced private and family prayer, and frequently spoke of the delight he felt in the service of God.

One day Brother Gibson and I called to see him at his house. Our visit was unexpected to him, but he received us very cordially. On entering the house we were pleased to notice on the table a number of Christian books, which, it was evident, he had been reading. We looked in vain for any traces of idolatry, and we felt thankful that from at least one house in this city the idols had been cast out. Some six weeks before our visit the man had brought out and given to us all his household gods, and one object of the present call was to ascertain whether he had really cast away his idols. Our examination fully satisfied Brother Gibson and myself on this point. We conversed with his family, and found that they understood and approved of the course he intended to pursue. After conversing some time I read a part of the fifth chapter of Matthew's Gospel, and prayed with them. It was not without emotion that I thus offered prayer, for the *first* time, in a Chinese house within the walls of this proud city, and that, too, almost under the shadow of the viceroy's palace. The man continued to attend our meeting, gave us every evidence of a sincere determination to lead a Christian life, and after a rigid examination our mission decided that he was, in our judgment, a proper subject for baptism. The ordinance was administered in the Tienang church, in the presence of the congregation, at the afternoon service. After suitable introductory remarks, explanatory of the nature both of Baptism and the Lord's Supper, the candidate was requested to stand up and repeat, in an audible voice, the Commandments and Baptismal Covenant. I then explained them, sentence by sentence, the candidate audibly expressing his cordial belief in them, and his determination faithfully to keep and obey them. I then proceed to baptize him, sprinkling the water on his head while he kneeled at the altar. After his baptism he united in the celebration of the Lord's Supper with the members of our mission, and the Rev. Mr. M'Caw, of the Church of England mission, who was present on the occasion.

Since his baptism the convert has given us great satisfaction by his meek, confiding spirit, and his consistent conduct. We cannot but feel that his heart has been changed by the Holy Spirit, and that he is indeed a new creature. We would earnestly solicit for this our Chinese brother an interest in the prayers of God's people.

On the 18th of October, 1857, the wife of Brother Ting Ang and two of their younger children were admitted to the ordinance of baptism. About the same time Brother *Ting Ing Ko*, the Fuhchau youth whom the Rev. Mr. Colder took to America and educated for some years, returned to Fuhchau, and having presented his certificate of church-membership, given him by Mr. Colder, we judged it proper to receive him, and he accordingly became a member of our infant Church. The annual report of the Mission for 1858 states:

"We would refer with profound gratitude to the outpouring of the Holy Spirit upon this people which we have witnessed in connection with our labors during the past year. Since the date of our last annual report we have baptized thirteen adults and three infants. All the adults remain with us in Church fellowship, and give encouraging evidence that they have indeed become the children of God through faith in our Lord Jesus Christ. On the seventh of August, 1858, we organized our first class of Chinese converts in this city. The class is attached to the Iongtau appointment, and now has fifteen members. Rev. Otis Gibson takes charge of the class for the present, with Brother Hu Po Mi as assistant leader. Three stewards were appointed, of whom two are Chinese. Arrangements were made for class-meetings, quarterly meetings, monthly collections for the poor, and quarterly collections for the support of the Gospel. A Sunday-school was organized for the children of Church members and others. The school is conducted by our native members, and at the present time contains seven pupils.

"Brief notices of some of our converts may perhaps be interesting to the friends of the China mission. I note them in the order of baptism:

"1. *Hu Po Mi*, aged 31. He has a good common education, is a soldier by profession, has taken the lowest military degree, and is entitled to hold office in the army. Baptized January 17, 1858, he has given us much satisfaction by his humility, zeal, courage, and desire for a thorough knowledge of the Bible. He is a fluent speaker, and has rendered us efficient aid in the public preaching of the Gospel. His wife also has been baptized and received into the Church.

"2. *Ngu Teng Hai*, aged 37. He is a scribe by profession, and has been connected with missionaries three or four years. His education is respectable, and he possesses some ability as a public speaker. He was baptized March 21, 1858, and renders us important help in public preaching. His mother, aged sixty-nine years, has also been baptized and received into the Church.

"3. *Wong Cheng Kuong*, aged 50. He is a common day laborer, but has sufficient knowledge of the written character to enable him, with a little study, to read our books. He was baptized March 21, 1858, and exhibits good evidence of the genuineness of his conversion.

"4. *Hu Ngieng Seu*, aged 57. He is the father of Hu Po Mi, is a man of more than ordinary talent, has a common education, and has filled some inferior offices in the government service. He has attended our preaching for nine years, and has treated us with uniform courtesy. During the past four years he became more frequent and regular in his attendance on our preaching. It was evident the Holy Spirit was striving with him, and many prayers were offered for him. About a year ago his eldest son became interested in Christianity, and the father encouraged him, saying: 'Go forward, and I will follow.' May 9, 1858, he, together with his wife and two younger sons, was admitted to baptism.

"5. *Wong Tai Hung*, aged 35. He belongs to the literary class, and is our first convert from this influential body. He has been connected with the missionaries nearly eleven years as a teacher, first, of the Rev. J. D. Collins, of our mission; then, and for a much longer time, of the Rev. J. Doolittle, of the

American Board Mission in Fuhchau. During all these years he had the respect and confidence of all who knew him, though he remained a proud and persistent idolator. It seemed as though nothing could subdue the pride of his heart. Even after his mind opened to receive, one by one, the cardinal truths of Christianity, his pride still seemed to present an insuperable barrier to his conversion. But grace triumphed at last; his proud heart yielded, and after counting the cost he publicly announced his purpose to become a Christian, and on September 10, 1858, he was baptized and received into the Church.

"It may be profitable to notice more particularly this work of grace. We select a few points for brief reference:

"1. The outpouring of the Spirit was preceded by months of the most pointed and earnest preaching we could bring to bear upon our public congregations, accompanied by the most direct and persevering exhortations in private. The work seemed to commence in the hearts of the missionaries, the Holy Ghost filling them with great searchings of heart and with intense yearnings for the salvation of this people.

"2. The work, in its inception and progress, was unaccompanied by any extraordinary manifestations. So gradually and quietly has it gone forward, that at times we fancied it had ceased, and were gratefully surprised when new inquirers came to us seeking religious instruction and advice.

"3. We think it a noteworthy fact that so large a proportion of the converts are of mature years, while some are even in advanced age. There are those who affect to consider the conversion of aged and adult heathen as impracticable, if not impossible. We have cherished the opposite belief, and have received according to our faith.

"4. The growth of the converts in Christian knowledge and grace has been very gratifying. So marked in many cases has this been, that the converts refer to it with astonishment. Whether we kept the candidates on a long course of training, or, as in one or two cases, admitted them into the Church after a shorter trial, the result is the same. We think it would be difficult to find converts who surpass those of our mission in their desire for a thorough knowledge of the blessed Bible. This has greatly encouraged us.

"5. Another trait in the character of our converts is their boldness in confessing Christ before the world. This, under God, we attribute partly to the character of the Fuhchau Chinese, who all seem to be naturally eloquent, but mainly to our system of training. Our entire operations are public, our inquiries are public, our baptisms are public, and we aim at training every one of the converts to do something toward the spread of the Gospel."

The Report for 1860 says:

"The principal facts of our operations during the year may be presented very briefly. We have seven appointments in our regular work. During the year we have baptized thirty-eight adults, and nine infants; total, forty-seven. Three probationers have been dropped, and one Church member has died in the faith. Our native membership, including probationers, is forty-nine, showing an increase of thirty-six during the year. In our mission class there are seven members (wives of missionaries and teachers in our girl's school) whose names are not elsewhere reported in the statistics of the Methodist Episcopal Church, and hence we have deemed it proper to report them in this connection. This gives us fifty-six as the membership of this mission at this date.

"Appointments in the regular work:

"1. *Iongtau.*—This appointment is on an important thoroughfare a short distance outside the south gate of the city. We have an excellent church edifice at this point, the first building of the kind ever erected in this city, and worth to us $2,500. The class at this appointment contains eighteen members, all of whom seem to be sincerely trying to 'follow the Lamb whithersoever he goeth.' One of the brethren is a licensed exhorter in the service of the mission, and gives himself to the work of preaching the Gospel. Two others are much exercised in mind with reference to engaging in the same blessed work; and during the year, after working in their shops all the secular days of the week, they have devoted their Sundays to preaching the word both in the city and in the country villages. There is a Sunday-school connected with this appointment, and it has been attended by the adult membership as well as by their children.

"2. *Tienang.*—This appointment is in the ward where our mission compound is situated. It has an excellent church edifice, and a class of nine members. This class has been organized during the past year, and is doing as well perhaps as could be expected. All the members give good evidence of the genuineness of their conversion to Christianity, and appear to be making encouraging progress in the knowledge and practice of the Gospel. One of the members of this class, a licensed exhorter in the Church, died September 21, 1859. His end was very peaceful and satisfactory. He had been one of our most laborious and efficient helpers, and his death is a heavy stroke upon us. We are hoping to organize a Sunday-school at this appointment.

"3. *City.*—This appointment is in the western part of the city, within the wall. One of our members lived there, and through his influence we rented a small building for a chapel. The front part of the house we use as a chapel, and the rear portion is occupied by the family in charge of the premises. We have not ventured to change the form of the house, and our services are conducted in a quiet way, so as not to excite the apprehensions of the people of the neighborhood. Thus far we have not had any difficulty in visiting the place and holding our meetings. The room is usually filled whenever we preach there, and the people seem interested in our message to them. We have not yet organized a class at this appointment, but shall do so as soon as possible. We consider the appointment a very important one, and look to it with great interest as the commencement of a glorious work in this proud heathen city.

"4. *Ato.*—This is another appointment that has come under our care during the past year. It is in a populous suburb of this city, and is situated about half a mile southeast from our mission compound. The place had been for some years under the care of our brethren of the American Board mission here. They built a neat little chapel, and kept up regular preaching in it. These brethren are now concentrating their mission on the northern bank of the Min, and accordingly transferred this chapel to our mission. We hope to occupy efficiently, and look for God's blessing on our labors. The chapel is worth $275. Annual ground rent, $18.

"5. *Kuaninchang.*—(Goddess of Mercy's Well.) This appointment also has been transferred to our mission during the past year by our brethren of the American Board mission. It is a small chapel quite close to our mission compound, and is useful as a place for meeting the people and distributing books. The building is worth about $60. Annual ground rent, $10.

"6. *To-cheng.*—(Peach Farm.) This is our first country appointment, and has a class of thirteen members. Our meetings at this place have been held in a private house, and we are much encouraged by the deportment of all who have united with us here in Church-fellowship. The neighborhood in which this appointment is located is sparsely inhabited, and yet if the good work spreads among the people we could soon have a large congregation at this place. We are laboring and praying in faith for the accomplishment of this object."

The expansion of our work into the country westward from Fuhchau, constitutes an important and auspicious era in the history of our mission in China.

The success of the Gospel among the more ingenuous rustics in country towns and hamlets gave a most opportune and powerful impetus to our faith and zeal. It furnished, also, to the Chinese a striking illustration of the Gospel's power, and a most intelligible indication of our plans and expectations as missionaries among them. The village in which the Ngu-kang parsonage is situated is perhaps twelve miles west of Fuhchau.

The accompanying cut represents the residence of the first native Methodist circuit preacher sent forth in China. The ends and back are built of pounded mud, the front of boards and plaster. It has no floors but the bare ground. The left hand door opens into a room probably ten by fifteen feet, where we have often slept on a few raised boards with a billet of wood for a pillow. The center room, the grand reception hall, or guest room, of every Chinese house, is about twenty feet square, with a dirt floor, and once furnished with a high altar and huge pictures of grim household gods; it is now hung around with large sheets, or charts, containing the Ten Commandments, and extracts from the Old and New Testaments. Here we assemble every Sunday at two o'clock for service—preaching and class-meeting; and here, every evening in the week, our new circuit preacher catechises and teaches the poor ignorant natives the Scriptures of divine truth. You must not imagine that our preacher has all this grand house to himself. He has only one room, entering by the right hand door of the house, and over it is a low, smoky loft, which

Kgu Kang Parsonage.

we intend to paper or whitewash, and furnish with a bedstead, chair, and table for our own convenience hereafter. At the right is the cook-shed, always full of choking, blinding smoke, as the Chinese seem to prefer sore eyes to chimneys. We have had some pleasant times in the Ngu-kang parsonage, and hope it may be one of the centers from which light and truth shall radiate far and near upon the minds of this dark people.

The Annual Report for this mission, dated September 30, 1860, and prepared by the Rev. Dr. Wentworth, makes the following showing:

MISSIONARIES.

Revs. Robert S. Maclay, Superintendent, Erastus Wentworth, D.D., Otis Gibson, Stephen L. Baldwin, Carlos R. Martin, Nathan Sites.

ASSISTANT MISSIONARIES.

Mrs. Henrietta C. Maclay, Mrs. Phebe E. Wentworth, Mrs. Eliza C. Gibson, Mrs. Nellie M. Baldwin, Mrs. Mary E. Martin, Mrs. ——— Sites, Miss Beulah Woolston, Miss Sallie H. Woolston.

NATIVE HELPERS.

Hu Po Mi, exhorter, and teacher of girls' school.

Uong Tai Kung, exhorter, and teacher of boys' school.

Uong Kiu Taik, exhorter, stationed at Pavilion Church.

Hu Iong Mi, exhorter, stationed at Ngu-kang.

Tang Ieu Kong, exhorter, stationed in the city.

Ting Seng Mi, exhorter, stationed at Ato Chapel.

PREMISES.

Our mission will soon have six substantial and comfortable dwelling-houses and a church in the same general inclosure or "compound," bounded on the south by the open country, across which we get the sea-breezes; east and west by the foreign community, and north by the city and suburbs of Fuhchau, with its living masses of idolaters. It seems quite providential that our mission secured so reasonably such valuable premises, as it is now next to impossible to get building lots here on any terms.

APPOINTMENTS.

The "Church of the True God," at the Tea Pavilion, has been opened for preaching every Sabbath, and nearly every day in the year. Extra meetings were held at New Year's, and during the cool weather evening services were kept up quite regularly. Class number one meets here every Sunday after the morning service, and consists of sixteen members, one of whom, an old man, "died in peace" on the 15th of August last.

"Heavenly Rest Church" is opened every Sunday at nine o'clock and two o'clock for divine service in Chinese, and at eleven and five for English. Class number two meets here immediately after the nine o'clock preaching, and consists of ten members.

The chapel in the city, and the two in the southern suburb, have been opened as often as the health and strength of the brethren would permit.

COUNTRY APPOINTMENTS.

Class number three, consisting of thirteen members, meets at Koi-Hung every Sunday morning. This appointment is visited by a native pastor every Sunday, and by one of the missionaries once in two weeks. The brethren are growing in grace and in the knowledge of God.

Ngu-kang.—Brother Hu Iong Mi was stationed here by Brother Gibson at the beginning of the year, and the result has been most favorable. Men, women, and children are learning to read, and sing, and pray with the greatest avidity. A hamlet of ignorant and degraded idolaters is being converted into a civilized and Christianized community, observing the Christian Sabbath, abstaining from the miserable vices of their countrymen, and walking carefully before the Lord. The class at this place consists of fifteen members. Both these appointments have asked for aid in building suitable chapels for public worship. We intend to assist them during the coming year in the erection of places of worship. A couple of plain Christian synagogues will serve to distinguish these simple-minded disciples from the masses of idolaters who worship in the costly temples with which the country is everywhere supplied.

NATIVE CONTRIBUTIONS.

Quarterly collections for the poor, and class penny collections, have been successfully instituted among the members during the past year.

PERSECUTION.

Brother Tang was apprehended by the authorities a month since and imprisoned, for assisting in renting a chapel in the city by the English Church mission. The English and American consuls promptly applied to the prefect for his release, which was speedily effected by the former threatening to stop payment of the duties on exports in case the man was not set free. The gentry have hitherto succeeded in preventing access to the city except in the way of street-preaching. What the victories of the British at Tien-tsin will do for us remains to be seen.

PRESS.

Funds have been provided for the establishment of a printing office with Chinese and English type; the Chinese type to be obtained in China, and the English type, press, and cases to be sent from America. We have good hope that this establishment will be in operation speedily. The object is chiefly to print the Holy Scriptures in the colloquial language of the province; also books of instruction for the mission, and tracts and religious books ere long. This printing establishment will be a great addition to the ability of our mission.

STEADY INCREASE.

Brother Gibson has baptized ten adults and fourteen infants during the year. This is a respectable increase; but the most encouraging feature is that our converts increase in grace and knowledge as fast as they do in numbers.

SUMMARY.

Missionaries	6
Assistants	7
Native Helpers	6
Churches in Fuhchau	2
Other preaching places in city and country	5
Baptisms: Adults, 62; Children, 26	88
Died in the faith, males	3
Dropped, for various causes	5
Present adult membership	54
Increase in adult membership this year	10
Sunday-school	1
Teachers	6
Scholars	30
Members in English Class	8
Pupils in Boys' Boarding School	17
Pupils in Girls' Boarding School	8
Scholars in Girls' Day School	8
Foundlings in Asylum	18

MISSIONARY SUBSCRIPTIONS.

James Dick, Esq.	$10 00
Mrs. E. Wentworth	5 00
Rev. O. Gibson	5 00
Rev. S. L. Baldwin	5 00
Rev. C. R. Martin	5 00
Miss B. Woolston	5 00
Dr. H. B. Gibson	10 00
W. Gregory, Esq.	5 00
W. C. M'Cue, Esq.	5 00
E. G. Hedge, Esq.	10 00
G. F. Weller, Esq.	10 00
Thomas Dunn, Esq.	10 00
J. H. Nichols, Esq.	20 00
A. B. Neilson, Esq.	25 00
Lieutenant Beaumont, U. S. N.	5 00
Mr. Higgs	1 00
W. H. Medhurst, Esq., H. B. M. Consul	10 00
W. H. Chapman, Esq.	20 00
Rev. B. W. Gorham, through Rev. S. L. Baldwin	25 00
Total	$191 00

SUBSCRIPTIONS FOR FOUNDLING ASYLUM.

W. S. Sloan, Esq.	$25 00
D. O. Clark, Esq.	20 00
M. G. Moore, Esq.	5 00
G. F. Weller, Esq.	10 00
G. W. Schwemann, Esq.	5 00
H. King, Esq	5 00
A. B. Neilson, Jr., Esq.	10 00
John Odell, Esq.	5 00
Thomas Dunn, Esq.	5 00
E. G. Hedge, Esq.	5 00
W. H. Green, Esq.	10 00
William Brand, Esq.	5 00
John O. Lent, Esq.	5 00
John Forster, Esq.	20 00
H. Lowcock, Esq.	5 00
Thomas K. Ashton, Esq.	10 00
Arthur Smith, Esq.	20 00
Thomas Smith, Esq,	10 00
D. N. Bottlewalla, Esq.	5 00
Jairaz, Fazul & Co,	10 00
W. H. Chapman, Esq.	5 00
George Wordsworth, Esq.	5 00
Thomas L. Larken, Esq.	10 00
Total	$215 00

CHAPTER XIII.

SCHOOLS.

ORDINARY day schools for Chinese boys, under native teachers and supervised by missionaries, were instituted at the commencement of the mission. As the mission advanced, however, and entered more fully on the work of public preaching, these schools were gradually suspended, and, with the approval of the Missionary Society of our Church, the educational interests of the mission were concentrated into a boarding school, organized November 26, 1856.

Despairing of immediate reinforcement, and anxious to make the most efficient use of the facilities and disposable force on hand, the mission resolved to authorize Brother Gibson to open a boys' school, as the basis of a future academy, in the house purchased of Russell & Co. for a girls' school and seminary, believing there would be ample time to build an establishment for the reception of female teachers while awaiting their arrival. The house is spacious. It is built of wood, and one of the first specimens of houses erected by carpenters uneducated in Western modes. The lot is ample, and now furnishes a good site for a substantial brick house, and academy attached, which are occupied by the Waugh Female Seminary.

Brother Gibson proposed to take sixteen or twenty boys as boarders, under his immediate supervision, and provide them with Christian education. The American Board Mission had a most flourishing school of this kind, and a large proportion of the scholars are now exemplary and efficient members of their Church in Fuhchau.

The premises represented by the opposite cut, purchased by our mission from Messrs. Russell & Co., being well-suited for accommodating a class of Chinese boys, the mission cordially approved of Brother Gibson's plan for a select boarding-school, and authorized him to make the arrangements necessary for effecting the desired object. Boys from twelve to eighteen years of age, who give evidence of talent, are received into the school, on a written agreement signed by their parent or guardian, for a term varying from four to six years. While the boy is with us we furnish him board, clothes, books, and room accommodations; our object being to give him a Christian home. If, after a fair trial, any boy fails to meet our expectations, we are at liberty to return him to his friends; but if, at any time, a boy is removed from the school against our wishes, then his parent or guardian shall pay the mission for his board, clothing, etc., while he was in the school.

The Bible is the prominent text-book in the school, and our object will be to imbue the minds of the scholars with its sacred principles. We shall also avail ourselves of all the appliances within our reach for imparting to their minds such knowledge of the natural sciences as may tend to elevate their thoughts,

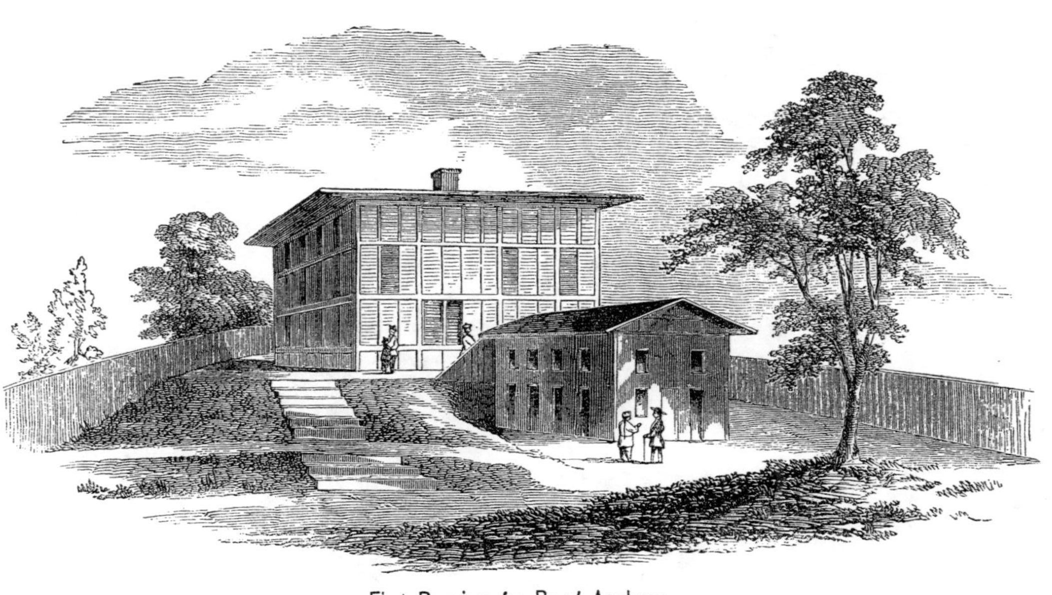

First Premises for Boys' Academy.

and prepare them to conceive more worthily of Him to whom we direct them as the only proper object of religious adoration. In this school we desire to train a class of gifted Chinese youth, who shall be lights amid this appalling darkness. We wish to make it a Christian Propaganda, from which shall go forth holy young men, with apostolic zeal and courage, to preach Jesus through this vast empire.

The following letter from the Rev. S. L. Baldwin, of the Methodist Episcopal mission at Fuhchau, will give the reader a pleasant impression of the school:

"Last Saturday evening ten of the boys belonging to Brother Gibson's school gave us a call. Mrs. Baldwin invited them into the parlor, whereupon they all took off their shoes, and leaving them on the verandah, came in with noiseless tread. They first examined with great interest some pictures which were hanging about the walls; one which attracted considerable attention was 'the death-bed of Wesley.' I tried to explain to them that he was the 'head man' of the Methodist Episcopal Church, and that when he was dying he exclaimed: 'The best of all is, God is with us!' After making a pretty thorough examination of the room, they got together in a group, and seemed to be talking pretty earnestly about something, and finally one of the little boys came up to me in a very respectful manner, and asked if *Sinaniong* (Mrs. Baldwin) would make some music for them. She gladly consented, and took her place at the melodeon, around which the boys arranged themselves in a semicircle, and listened with great attention while she sang and played one or two pieces. She then proposed to give them a lesson in singing, and spent some time in practicing them on the 'the scale,' first taking each boy separately, and then all together. Most of them have good voices, and sound the notes quite as readily as a class of boys at home. They closed their part of the exercises by singing a Chinese hymn set to the tune of Balerma. These boys are in fact the life and soul of our singing at the Tienang church, and I think it would be well to take them all over to Iong-tau occasionally, to give the brethren and fathers there a few lessons, and prevent such a merciless slaughter of Old Hundred as takes place there every Sunday.

"I brought out a quantity of daguerreotypes for the boys to inspect, and I assure you they underwent a careful scrutiny. Many questions were asked about the manner in which they were made, but I found my present knowledge of Chinese entirely inadequate to an explanation of the process of daguerreotyping. When all their comments were ended, and the likenesses put up, a very earnest request was made for a 'little more music,' which was readily complied with. The boys then expressed their thanks, and requested us, according to the Chinese rules of politeness, to 'take a seat,' whereupon I advised them to 'walk slowly,' and they took their departure in an orderly manner.

"Having thus given you a Saturday evening scene, let me describe a missionary's Sunday in Fuhchau. Brother Maclay has gone to our country appointment, where he enjoyed the luxury of sleeping on a

Chinese table last night, and will preach two or three times to-day, hold class, and give instruction and answer questions in an inquiry meeting. Dr. Wentworth goes to Iongtau, where he will preach twice, and hold class. At nine A. M. I repair to Tienang church, and listen to a sermon preached by Brother Gibson from John x, 9: 'I am the door,' etc. I do not understand enough of the language to get a connected idea of the sermon, though I often catch a word, and occasionally a whole sentence. But I know it is a good sermon, because the words come out earnestly and rapidly, as though the speaker had something at heart for which he wished to find expression; and the audience are all looking eagerly at him. As he proceeds with the subject his voice becomes more tender, and his eyes begin to moisten, and something in his throat seems to keep back the words he would utter; and then my heart feels that it is a good sermon, and sends up a prayer that the darkened souls about me may enter in by 'the door' into the kingdom of our God."

The following report for the boys' boarding-school connected with this mission is furnished by the Rev. Otis Gibson, principal of the school, and is dated September 30, 1857:

"The boarding-school which I was authorized to establish was opened November 26, 1856, with four scholars, and has been in constant operation since. Twelve boys in all have been in the school, two of whom have been dismissed. One, *Chun Huah*, was dismissed for incapacity soon after the school was opened; the other, *Pin Kuong*, was sent away this morning for continued misconduct, especially wrangling and fighting. *Pin Kuong* was the most troublesome boy in the school. He had been in the school from the first, is sixteen years of age, has acquitted himself well in his studies, but is of a quarrelsome, overbearing disposition. I trust the example thus made of him will prove a wholesome lesson to the other boys.

"There are now ten boys left in the school. Four of them are committed to us for a term of six years, three of them for five years, two who clothe themselves, and had previously been a long time in the Rev. Mr. Peet's school, for four years, and one lately received for eight years.

"The boy Neng Sicu, son of Brother Ting, has continued to give satisfaction, and I now recommend him to the mission as a suitable boy to be educated by the bounty of Sister Hill, of New Haven, Connecticut. It will be necessary that the boy retain his Chinese name among the Chinese; but the Board and Mrs. Hill will hereafter know him as Samuel Agur Judson, according to Sister Hill's request.

"The general deportment of the boys has been good. I think I may safely say that their general behavior and progress in study would be creditable to boys of the same age in our own more favored land. One class have committed to memory the Catechism of our Church, (excepting proof-texts,) the Catechism prepared by the Rev. Mr. Baldwin, some ten chapters of Matthew's Gospel, and more than half the primary geography and astronomy. They have also studied Chinese literature half of each day.

They not only commit to memory, but are made to understand everything they go over. I am both surprised and pleased at the success which has attended this the first year's experiment of a boarding-school."

I take much pleasure in bearing testimony to the zeal and ability exhibited by Brother Gibson in the management of this school, and I cannot doubt as to the blessed results of such judicious and faithful labors. The school has become already an interesting and important branch of our operations, and we have an abiding confidence that it will accomplish great good. The report of the principal for the year 1859 says:

"In addition to my regular share of the labors of our general work, I have given all the time and attention I could spare to the boys' boarding-school under my charge. The new school-house has been erected at an expense of $500. It contains a small cook-room, dining-room, school-room, and sixteen sleeping-rooms, each room intended to accommodate two boys. One of these rooms is used as a store and clothes room, one is occupied by the school-teacher, and one by my personal teacher, leaving accommodations for twenty-six boys. During the past year I have received four new boys into the school, and have dismissed two, one for inefficiency, and one for continued vicious conduct. The present number in attendance is fourteen.

"The total current expenses from September 30, 1858, to September 30, 1859, is $350, or an average of $25 for each boy. This includes teacher's salary, cook's wages, books, stationary, beds, board, and clothing for the boys. By making wholesale purchases of rice I have succeeded in reducing the cost of board, and some presents of cast-off clothing from gentlemen of the foreign community have reduced the expense of clothing.

"The oldest boy, Ing Kuang, has been received into the Church, and is, I believe, a consistent and growing Christian. Two others who were candidates for baptism failed to give permanent satisfaction as to their fitness, and consequently their baptism is indefinitely postponed. In their studies the boys have made commendable progress, and for the most part have been regular and orderly. In several instances, however, I have been obliged to resort to very severe discipline, and the proper use of the rod has not been without a salutary effect. Chinese boys need a master no less than American boys of the same age. The school continues to commend itself to us as an efficient auxiliary in our great work of evangelizing this strangely idolatrous people."

Brother Gibson's usually robust health was somewhat impaired during our recent hot weather, and referring to this topic, he writes: "It was an affliction for me to be obliged to accept a discharge from regular duty during the months of July and August, on account of my health. I am now regaining my usual strength, and rejoice in the privilege of resuming my labors with increased energy. With the exception of the two months mentioned above, I have endeavored to bear my regular share in our laborious but glorious work, striving to be 'instant in season and out of season,' if by any means I might, through the blessing of God, be instrumental in saving some souls for whom Christ died."

The report for 1860 says:

"Since the date of our last annual report five new scholars have been received into the school, under the usual written agreement, for a term of years. One is in attendance on trial, one attends as a day scholar, four have been expelled from the school for constant bad conduct, leaving the present number in attendance seventeen. Of these fifteen are regular members of the school by written agreement. The other two are as yet simply day scholars.

"The total expenses of the school, including repairs of the house, boarding, clothing, and bedding for the boys, teacher's salary, and cook's wages, from September 30, 1859, to September 30, 1860, is $488 23, making an average of about $32 50 for each scholar. Last year the average was but $25. The increased price of all kinds of food and clothing fully accounts for the increased average expense.

"The boys have made commendable progress in all their studies. Especially is this the case with the class in geography and Scripture history. In their behavior the boys are quite orderly, and have caused me but little trouble during the past year. We have all been greatly rejoiced by the conversion and reception into the Church of Ing Sing, the second boy of the school. He has given satisfactory evidence of his sincerity, was baptized in September, and is a boy of much promise. One other lad, who at one time was an applicant for baptism, proved himself a base hypocrite, and became so notoriously bad that I felt compelled to dismiss him from the school. At present there are a number of the boys who seem quite serious, and who are in the custom of holding prayer-meetings in their own rooms.

"I am happy to believe that the school commends itself to the brethren of the mission as a promising and fruitful branch of our great work."

The mission, soon after its commencement, began to feel the importance of a school for the education of Chinese girls. Mrs. J. I. White was admirably qualified for initiating this enterprise, but, alas! she finished her course on earth before her burning zeal could develop her long cherished plans on this subject. During the autumn of 1850 a small frame building, plastered within and without, was erected on the rear portion of the lot occupied by Mr. Maclay; and about the first of January, 1851, a day school for Chinese girls was commenced in it under the care of Mrs. Maclay. The cost of the house was fifty-five dollars. The scholars lived at home, but took their dinners at the school.

The success of this Christian enterprise was quite gratifying, and its influence upon the Chinese of the vicinity entirely salutary. The average daily attendance at the school was about fifteen scholars, and the progress of the little pupils was very encouraging. The school was continued, with occasional interruptions, till the summer of 1856, when, in consequence of Mrs. Maclay's inability to attend to its supervision, it was temporarily suspended. It was resumed early in 1857, under the joint supervision of

First House for Girls' School.

Mrs. Gibson and Mrs. Maclay, and the annual report of the mission for that year says:

"Mrs. Maclay and Mrs. Gibson have devoted a portion of their time to the day school for girls. We think these unassuming labors are not unacceptable to the Lord of the harvest, and we feel assured that the good fruit will hereafter appear. About thirty girls have been connected with the school during the year. The course of study in these day schools is not so extensive or thorough as in the boarding-school. The day scholars do not generally remain long in the school, and we think it best to confine them mainly to the sacred Scriptures, and to books prepared by missionaries."

During 1858 the school was suspended, with a view to the organization of a boarding-school for Chinese girls under the care of Miss Beulah Woolston and Miss Sallie H. Woolston, of New Jersey. Temporary provision was made for the school in the mission building formerly occupied by the boarding-school for Chinese boys under the care of the Rev. Otis Gibson. To provide suitable buildings for the girls' seminary an appeal on the subject was addressed to the Female China Missionary Society of Baltimore, and with the most praiseworthy zeal this society contributed a large portion of the funds required for the purpose.

The Rev. Dr. Wentworth prepared, in behalf of the mission, an appeal on this subject, in which he says:

"This noble enterprise has been taken in hand by the Baltimore Female Missionary Society, and generously indorsed by the Board. It is a work of some magnitude, and will require time for its completion. It is not yet too late to second the movement by additional facts drawn from the soil where it is proposed to erect so appropriate and durable a monument to the memory of a great and good man, distinguished by his fidelity to the Church and his zeal for the cause of missions.

"1. The low estimate in which females are held in China, and their consequent debased condition, are the first facts to which we would call attention in our appeal for means with which to elevate their social position. In five cases out of ten the birth of a female infant is regarded as a calamity. I am often asked the singular question, 'Which *sex* do you prefer in your country, male or female?' The reply, 'It makes no difference; we are thankful for such as Providence sends,' is received with a shake of the head or a smile of incredulity, and the invariable rejoinder, 'Boys are a blessed godsend, but girls are a curse and a nuisance.' Nor are the Chinese backward in using the readiest means to rid themselves of the thankless charge. A family in good circumstances will tolerate two or three daughters; but the poorer classes destroy them without compunction and without ceremony. Fathers and midwives believe themselves to be doing a meritorious act in quietly suppressing existence at its threshold by immersion in the nearest vessel of water, or exposure by night to the chance mercies of the public highways, with the surer hazards of cold and starvation. It would chill the blood of tender-hearted Christian mothers to hear the tales told to our missionary ladies by their native nurses. All these women converse with levity and indifference on the subject of female infanticide until they come to learn that we regard the practice with horror, when they will deny or extenuate the offense, lest they should suffer in the good opinion of their foreign employers. One of our ladies questioned a woman in her employ as to its commonness, and was told that in the rural villages there was 'scarcely a house in which one or more had not been destroyed;' that 'one of the woman's near neighbors, out of a family of seven daughters, had destroyed five; that she herself had not committed the cruel deed, though she had borne three daughters and one son; 'the son was alive, but the demons [query, midwives?] had carried off all the girls!' It is a significant intimation of the commonness of the practice, that almost the only great public charity known in China is the native Female Foundling Hospital, found, it is believed, in every important city to which foreigners have access. Among the better classes female infants are freely given away to anybody who will bring them up; and these, in some parts of the empire, are reared for purposes to which death itself would be a preferable lot.

"2. But supposing the female escapes suffocation at birth, what is her condition as she grows up? In this province she is either a lady or a day laborer; a gilded recluse or a field-hand; destined to idleness, frivolus occupations, and jealous seclusion, or made to delve in the soil, tug at the oar, groan under burdens, and jostle, shout, and swear with the roughest and rudest in the crowded streets, thronged rivers, and choked market-places. Bad as it is, the condition of the Fuh-kien field-woman is in one respect better than that of the Fuh-kien lady. She enjoys freedom of locomotion. The lady is systematically crippled from infancy. It is not without infinite pain and distress that the foot is thus unnaturally cramped, swathed with cruel bandages, dwarfed, and distorted, that it may be compressed for life into a gilded slipper two inches in length. But the cramping of the female foot is a small misfortune compared with the more cruel cramping of the female mind. In a land of books not one Chinese female in ten can read, and then scarcely more than sufficient to repeat, parrotlike, characters of which she does not understand the meaning. Her education is restricted to the few brief years of girlhood that precede a marriage consummated as early as years and growth will possibly allow. She is betrothed by others to one whom she has never seen, and bought at a stipulated price by a lover who has his first view of her when, after being carried to his house in the marriage sedan, and the ceremony completed, she is finally unvailed in the presence of a lord and master with whom she is never to eat, never to appear in public, and never to share those delicate attentions which constitute the charm of life in civilized and Christian communities. If she belongs to the working class she is expected to share the outdoor labors of her better half, or perhaps to work for an idle rake who takes her wages as fast as earned, to pamper his own intemperance or gratify his own beastly desires. In her best estate the Chinese female is ignorant, confined, and despised. Christianity alone will elevate her to her true and deserved position among the women of the earth. Christian schools, managed by Christian ladies, will have this elevating effect. Shall we have the means for establishing and maintaining such a school in our Fuhchau mission? Methinks if the heads and figures on the coins in your purses had tongues and vocal powers they would shout in chorus in the affirmative.

"3. The liberality of the merchants and other foreign residents of Fuhchau, English and American, has enabled us to establish in our mission a Foundling Asylum to rescue female infants from destruction. The native Christians assure us that so soon as its existence shall have become extensively known parents will hasten to avail themselves of so merciful an alternative in place of destroying their offspring, and that in a year or two we shall have as many applicants as we shall have room for, or know what to do with. This, in the suburbs of a city of six hundred thousand inhabitants, seems highly probable. All these female infants, doubtless as many as we shall be able to support, will grow up on our hands, and will be the property of the Methodist Episcopal Church. So long as they are infants they will remain, at our charge, in the hands of native nurses; but with the age of weaning it is desirable that they be also weaned, for a season at least, from all connection with heathendom. Our female boarding-school will necessarily have an 'infant department—a safe and convenient asylum in which to rear these rejected foundlings. Thirty or forty of these, grown up to girlhood, would of themselves constitute a female school of some magnitude. Will the Church, will the ladies of Christendom, provide the means for educating these adopted daughters, or shall they grow up in an atmosphere as thick with ignorance and darkness as that from which they have been providentially rescued.

"4. We want Christian wives for our Christian young men. We have already baptized and brought into the Church a number of single young men, but no single young women. All these youths will have to betake themselves to the Hittites for wives, or remain unmarried; and are in imminent danger of being drawn into or mixed up with the superstitions and idolatries inseparable from a Chinese wedding ceremony. The intermarriage of Christian converts with unbelievers has been a stupendous difficulty from the days of Paul until now. It is one of the most difficult things to manage connected with foreign missionary work. Female boarding schools, where females may be trained to Christianity, will alleviate the difficulty to a considerable extent, and, in connection with the orphan asylum, may ultimately do away with it altogether.

"5. Girls converted in Christian schools, and returning into the bosoms of heathen families, will carry with them the results of Christian instruction, and sow the seeds of Gospel truth in the minds of their children, and thus insensibly promote the spread of Gospel truth in quarters where no other influence could possibly be brought to bear. Christian school girls make Christian wives and Christian mothers. This it is that makes all Churches so anxious to get the educating of as many youth as possible within the influence of Bible truth. Chinese girls will form no exception to the general rule. The female heart is as religiously inclined in China as in any other quarter of the globe. Shall we leave it to be overrun with the weeds of iniquity, or shall we sow it with the seeds of virtue, and adorn it with flowers of celestial promise?

"6. The enterprise is already in hand. It is an eminently practicable enterprise. It has nothing prospective or visionary about it. It does not call for armies of missionaries to penetrate the interior, or for an annual expenditure in China of more missionary money than all the Methodist Church now raises for all missionary purposes. It is within the reach of small means, and entirely within the compass of female effort. Its success is assured by the success of similar operations in other parts of China. It is stimulated by the example of those heroic ladies who have in former years devoted their lives, accomplishments, and in some instances private fortunes, as well as personal labors, not without fruits, to the renovation of their own sex in this barbarous clime. It is encouraged by the success of the corresponding department in our mission. A flourishing boys' school has been in vigorous operation among us for more than a year past, with every prospect of usefulness and efficiency, as an auxiliary to the preaching of the Gospel among this people.

"We are just now completing premises for the accommodation of thirty boys, and the narrow quarters abandoned by the boys will suffice for a handful of girls for a year or so; but by the time our female teachers shall have learned a little of the language, and fitted themselves to teach through this medium, we shall need an academy building, with dormitories, class-rooms, and other apartments, sufficient for thirty or forty girls and their teachers, similar, on a smaller scale, to our conference academies at home. The Baltimore China Female Missionary Society have heroically taken it upon themselves to supply this lack. Will not the ladies of the entire connection come up to their help in this arduous enterprise? It is to be done by special contribution, and ought not to interfere with the regular missionary collections for the year. We feel intense interest in the scheme, but have endeavored to write calmly and dispassionately; and yet have desired to array before the female members of the Methodist Episcopal Church such substantial reasons for our appeal as should influence their judgments, and induce permanent interest rather than elicit a few flashes of sentiment, or a merely transient feeling, which would pass away without results, or substantial evidence, in the form of 'material aid,' that they appreciate the greatness of the cause to which we have thus briefly summoned their attention.

"I need not reiterate the arguments of former communications: the seclusion of Chinese women from male missionaries and the direct preaching of the Gospel; the impracticability of married women doing efficient missionary work and attending properly to their

Waugh Female Seminary.

own families at the same time; and the breadth of the field for the exercise of female teaching."

The accompanying picture will give some idea of the substantial, commodious, and handsome buildings provided for this most interesting and promising institution. But the Church should remember that the school is to be supported for years to come. Forty dollars a year will maintain a pupil in either of our schools. One lad in the boys' school is now kept by the liberality of a lady living in the United States. Are there not others who could support a China boy or a China girl in one of our boarding schools? Are there not classes of Sunday-school boys or Sunday-school girls which would undertake the yearly support of a little China boy or a little China girl in one of these schools? But above all, send with your contributions your prayers that God would bless these enterprises, for without his blessing they will prove none other than distinguished failures, while with his blessing they may be instrumental in bringing many into the ways of life.

Miss Woolston, who has charge of this interesting school, writes August 30, 1860:

"The boarding-school was commenced the 28th of last November. At that time the prospect of securing scholars was not favorable. A boarding-school for girls was a new thing to the natives of Fuhchau, and no one seemed willing to be the first to patronize it.

"The school opened with one little Chinese girl. She continued alone for eight days, when six others were added. In a short time four were taken home again. We have now in school ten little girls. These are all between seven and thirteen years of age, and nine of them are bound to the mission, three for five, four for six, and two for seven years. All these, excepting one, have unbound feet, though two others are considered as belonging to the small-footed class, and are to be dressed in that style. I speak of this because so much stress is laid on it by the Chinese.

"Our little girls are very interesting, and I think they are perfectly contended to be in school, separated from their homes. They delight very much to go home to make a visit, but are equally delighted to get back to school again. They seem to enjoy their studies, their play, their work, and their worship. They are very obedient, and it is rare that we are compelled to punish any one of them. They study the written character during the week, and on the Sabbath have a lesson in the colloquial.

"Many of the obstacles to obtaining scholars seem to be removed, and I think the school will be filled up as rapidly as will be well."

In a more recent letter from Miss Woolston, dated October 5, 1860, she says:

The girls' boarding school has been in progress ten months. During this time fifteen Chinese girls have been placed in school, only eight of whom now remain. Of those removed one was bound to the mission, and two others were considered secured. These last two were taken home on account of sickness, and it is doubtful whether they will be allowed to return.

"The oldest girl in school is thirteen, the youngest eight years old. They all are obedient, and seem quite contented to be from their homes.

"Through the week they study the Chinese written character, and on the Sabbath have a lesson in the colloquial.

"Two of the present number on first entering were exceedingly careless and stupid, but are now greatly improved.

"The girls already begin to receive some correct ideas of Christianity, and do not hesitate to say it is not only useless to worship idols, but very displeasing to the heavenly Father. Five of them are from idolatrous families.

"Hi-to, one of the youngest, paused one day in recitation to say that at her home there were two gods, which her father, mother, and brothers worshiped, and which she also used to worship; but now she did not wish to do so any more.

"Though the number of scholars is still small, the school is interesting, and in a promising condition."

CHAPTER XIV.

JOURNAL, TRANSLATIONS, ETC.

A FEW extracts from my journal will give the reader some idea of our life and labors during the earlier years of our operations at Fuhchau:

January 5, 1854. We are in the midst of many and conflicting rumors with regard to the movements of the insurgents. One day we hear that Pekin is about to be captured, and perhaps the very next day we are told that the insurgents have suffered an overwhelming defeat. An imperial proclamation has recently come down from Pekin stating that the "thieves" are nearly extirpated, that order will soon be restored in the disturbed provinces, that now all parties should be quiet and industrious, and, in view of the urgent wants of the emperor, that all should hasten with their money to fill the government's empty treasury. The good people of Fuhchau do not seem at all disposed to assist the emperor in this way; and the general impression here about the proclamation is that the emperor has stated what is not true in regard to the insurgents.

January 12. Distributing books in the city. Generally the people give me no serious annoyance in the performance of this difficult part of my work.

They are very eager to get our books, and sometimes embarrass me not a little; but usually I am able to select the persons to whom I wish to give books, and can refuse all others. To-day, however, a rude, boisterous young man rushed out of a public-house as I was passing, and pressing through the crowd, demanded a book in a vociferous manner. He followed me a short distance, giving me great annoyance; and finally seeing that I would not accede to his demand, he stepped behind me and with his hand gave me rather a heavy blow on the head. Having on a thick cap the blow did not affect me much, and turning round I saw the fellow making his escape as fast as he could along the street, frequently looking back over his shoulder as he ran. In true Chinese style, each man in the crowd proceeded to denounce most voluminously the unfortunate wight who was not present to defend himself, and then eagerly asked for books, saying, "We are good men, we would not strike you." Telling them, however, that I feared the people who suffered so bad a man to live among them could not themselves be very good, I declined giving them books and passed on, every few seconds hearing one and another of them say, "He speaks truly; it was very wrong to strike him," etc.

February 17. To-day, while distributing books at the door of the chapel, I observed a man who seemed to be greatly interested in what was going on. Some one said to him, "Why don't you take a book?" "I don't want any," was his curt reply. He seemed annoyed when any one looked at him steadily, and I became interested to ascrtain his character. Hearing me speak to the people while giving out the books, he gradually approached where I was standing. After listening for some time he touched my elbow, and drawing something from his bosom, he held it carefully covered in his hand, and opening his fingers a little asked me to look at it. I looked and saw that it was a portrait of one of the apostles, (St. Paul, I think,) nicely set into a gilt frame. He was much excited, and thrust it back quickly into his bosom, and asked me if I knew what it meant. I told him what it was, and that I supposed him to be a Roman Catholic. "Are you one?" he asked eagerly. "No," I replied, "our doctrines differ from yours." He appeared gratified with my noticing him, and taking a position at my side he proceeded to make sundry remarks to the people about our plan of operations, evincing a considerable degree of acquaintance with his subject.

December 2. Met a detachment of soldiers in the street as I was distributing books. They were on their way to the department of Fing-hua to join the imperial army under the lieutenant-governor of this province. As they straggled along the street I had a good opportunity for giving them some copies of our "Sermon on the Mount."

December 4. This morning I resumed our usual Sunday-school exercises in the girls' school-room. During the past summer they had been suspended in view of my absence, and now, with refreshed spirits, I felt it a great privilege again to address these scholars and teachers. I was pleased to find all our old scholars in their places, with the addition of a goodly number of new faces. There are now twenty little Chinese girls in the school. This is a greater number than we have ever had, and we feel much encouraged by it.

December 6. Chapel at Iongtau. We use the word chapel in an accommodated sense. In Fuhchau our chapels are generally one of the low, narrow, dark Chinese rooms, which, by a little extra scrubbing, paint, and efforts at light and ventilation, we manage to use as a place for meeting the people. The chapel at Iongtau is of this discription. Situated on one of the principal thoroughfares of the city, it affords us excellent facilities for coming in contact with large numbers of people. The people are generally disposed to hear what the missionary has to say, though, like many church-goers in America, they are fond of short sermons. During the hour I spend in the chapel there will sometimes be present two or three separate and distinct congregations, each one staying perhaps fifteen or twenty minutes. This grows out of the habits of the people. Our congregations are composed principally of the working classes of the population, and, while willing to hear us speak, the claims of their business prevent them from staying long. And with our feeble use of the language, and the crowds of people thronging past the chapel-door, this is no disadvantage, as it enables us to preach a short discourse to a larger number of hearers.

December 16. Three Luchuans came to my house to-day. One was the captain of one of the Luchuan junks now in this port. He was a shrewd man, and possessed more knowledge of foreign countries than any of the Chinese I have conversed with. A large map of the world was hanging in the room, and he at once recognized some of the countries upon it. The smallness of the English islands seemed to surprise him, while the broad territorial dimensions of the United States, comparing favorably with the eighteen provinces of China, seemed to demand his respect. After pointing out some of the larger countries, I showed them the little specks that designate Luchu. The great contrast evidently surprised them, and with a characteristic grunt they gathered closely around the map, as if to screen their kingdom from the rude gaze of foreigners. "Very large!" I said playfully, referring to Luchu. They smiled, and the captain touched his ear with his finger, saying in Chinese, "I understand." Finding them interested, I spent some time in pointing out to them on the map the various nations of the world, and adding such brief remarks as might convey to them some information about their character and mutual relations. I inquired about Dr. Bettelheim, but they manifested perfect ignorance on the subject. I then asked if any American ships of war had visited their country recently. They hesitated for some time, but finally stated that last summer some American war-ships had come to their country, and that one of the vessels still remained there. Before going away they seemed to grow more frank and confidential, and I could not but feel encouraged to hope that the Luchuans might soon come to entertain more correct views with regard to intercourse with foreigners.

December 19. News has been received that the insurgents have entered the Chih-li province, and are now within a few days' march of Pekin. It is said the tidings were communicated by a native of Fuh-chau, who fills a high office at Pekin, and who, in consequence of the imminent danger at the capital, has sent portraits of himself and wife to his kindred here, with some valedictory stanzas reciting the perils now threatening his sovereign, and announcing his determination of dying with him. If Pekin falls into the hands of the insurgents, it is highly probable this officer's anticipations will be realized so far as he is concerned; but I am inclined to think his friend, the emperor, considering "discretion the better part of valor," will make timely provision for his own safety by a swift retreat to the north.

December 29. Visited the city within the wall to-day, for the purpose of distributing books. I was surprised to find how easily I could pass along the streets and give books to such as appeared acquainted with the written character. I was careful, however, not to pass through the public thoroughfares, as in those places I would have been overpowered by the crowds. Selecting the most retired streets, and passing along rather quickly, riding occasionally in the sedan when a crowd would collect at any point, I was able to distribute over two hundred Gospels and about three hundred copies of the "Sermon on the Mount." Once a crowd of boys, to whom I was unwilling to give books, began to cry out after me. I immediately stepped into a shop and remarked to the shopkeeper that, as a citizen of that district, the officers would hold him responsible for any disturbance that might occur in the place. He at once apprehended my meaning, and obtained the services of an old man in the shop to settle the matter. Filled (at least apparently) with wrath, the old man poured out a perfect storm of rather highly seasoned epithets upon the poor boys, who appeared astounded at this sudden change in the aspect of affairs. The street was soon cleared; and, as I passed on, the tones of the old gentleman's voice kept ringing in my ears till I was quite out of the neighborhood.

1858. Our peaceable suburbs presented a scene of unusual uproar yesterday afternoon. A Canton man quarreled with a Fuhchau man in the street, and killed him on the spot. He was instantly seized by the mob, and, with his hands tied behind him, taken to the top of the hill back of the foreign hongs, and bound to a pine-tree. The wife of the deceased cooly took a nail, and drove it into the body, shoulders, breast, temples, and eyes of the writhing culprit, aided and abetted by a furious multitude in her bloody revenge. The man was just alive at sundown, several hours after. I saw the mangled body this morning. The head was a perfect mass of gore. The conduct of the woman is loudly applauded by the natives, who will doubtless erect a monument of granite to the memory of her virtuous indignation. The mandarins offered to take the offender into custody; but she resented their interference, and insisted upon her right, from immemorial custom, to avenge her husband's death, and boldly accused these sleek-faced officials, in the presence of the crowd, of taking bribes and letting the guilty go free. At home the Cantonites are the most insolent of any people in China to foreigners, and they carry that insolence with them to other parts. Brutal and bloody as this summary justice appears, it may do good, by holding the natural impudence of these proud southrons in check. There are two thousand of them here, greatly excited by this barbarous deed, and threatening revenge. A party of marines has been sent for, from H. B. M. ship-of-war Race-Horse, to protect foreign residents, in the event of an outbreak between them and the Fuhchauans.

A contributor to the "Fuhchau Courier" is responsible for the following. We are willing to attest its correctness:

"We were walking in the evening some time ago over the Consulate Hill, when our attention was attracted toward an old man seated by an open grave, and on going to the spot we found a coffin containing a man still alive, but breathing very heavily, placed already in the grave, with the lid lying just outside, ready to be put on as soon as the vital spark was extinct. The man in the coffin was dressed in usual costume, apparently not of the poorest sort. He looked ill, but it appeared to us that proper medical aid might have saved his life. In the morning we repaired to the spot and found the grave earthed up, and from the appearance of the ground the man must have died shortly after we saw him. The anecdote is curious, and may appear almost incredible. We believe those best versed in Chinese matters have not met with a circumstance so extraordinary as a man being positively put into his coffin and grave to die! The explanation may perhaps be, that the charges for carrying a live man are considerably less than for a dead one."

The Chinese are thoroughly persuaded of the existence of evil spirits. One day, as I was speaking about the demoniacs of the New Testament, a man probably forty-five years of age, and who lived some distance from the city, suddenly interrupted me by saying: "That is true; there are evil spirits;" and then he proceeded to tell us how, on certain occasions, these evil spirits had come to his house, and had given him great trouble. The Chinese present listened with much interest to the man's story, and appeared to assent to its truthfulness. Indeed, the man challenged any one to contradict him, and, pointing across the chapel to a young man who stood in the aisle, he said: "There is my son, who can vouch for the truth of what I say."

Brother Lo Ting, while preaching in the streets, was surrounded by a crowd of Chinese, who said: "You say you are not afraid of idols; we will now take you to a temple and you shall break one of the idols to pieces, and then we shall see whether it has not power to revenge itself." While they were hurrying him along with insults and derisive shouts, he said: "I do not fear your idols of wood and stone and mud, and will show you that I do not by smashing any number of them to pieces if you will give me a written agreement that I shall not be harmed by any man for so doing. I'll risk the gods, but I dare not risk you." The crowd dropped off and let him go. Brother Hu Iong-Mi, our first Chinese itinerant, stated that last Sunday, while in the country preaching to our little class of Church members, his heart sank within him to see the multitudes working in the fields in all directions where his message could not reach them. Soon a violent thunder shower came up and drove many of them into the house where he was preaching. He made them sit down, and for once he preached to a large congregation of them.

The following graphic sketch is from the pen of the Rev. Otis Gibson, of the Methodist Episcopal mission at Fuhchau:

"Brother Martin brought us a box from our friends, and I am sure some of your readers would have been amused could they have seen the performances when the box was opened. 1. A bonnet for Mrs. Gibson. Just the thing, how well it fits, what a beauty! I was wondering what I was to do for a bonnet, and here is one to hand, trimmings and all. 2. A dress pattern. Better than all my fears; thank God for friends. 3. 'What's that?' says Willie. 'Jacket and pants for you, my boy.' 'Just a fit.' 'How could they know that Willie was just so tall?' 'And here is a jacket and apron for Eddie.' On they go, and then such running and strutting and jumping. Eddie, who cannot run so fast as Willie, made up in screaming and laughing. He don't speak English, but he rattled off the Chinese like a native. His jacket was 'ching ho,' (first-rate); he was 'ting huang he,' (greatly delighted.) These new things were 'foe chay,' (a splendid affair,) and so they ran and jumped and crowed, and seemed to be as happy as children born in happy America."

We are indebted to the Rev. Justus Doolittle, of the American Board mission at Fuhchau, for the following interesting account of two of the methods employed by the Chinese of that city for ascertaining the will of the gods:

"PAH-LAH-TENG.—This expression denotes a very singular method (in some respects analogous to spirit-rapping, as practiced in the United States) of consulting some god, used either in a temple, or, more commonly, in a private house. It is usually performed in the evening, generally more as a matter of friendship and of favor to some one than as a way of earning money on the part of the operators. A present of food, or of something else, is often given them by the one who invites their assistance. Two performers are required besides the one who desires to inquire of the god. One of these takes his seat on a chair before the table on which incense and candles are burning, placed in front of the idol, or something which represents it. The other man seizes a pencil and draws a kind of charm on a piece of yellow paper. He then sets it on fire by one of the lighted candles, and, while burning, moves it gently up and down in front of the person seated. The object of this is to expel all defiling influences from him, and prepare his body to become the temporary residence of the god invoked. He now rises from the chair and receives from his companion a stick of lighted incense, which he clasps in both hands, and holds calmly before his breast, while he remains standing with his eyes closed and his back turned toward the table. The other person now begins to entwine the fingers of both his own hands together in a certain manner believed to be peculiarly pleasing to that particular god. He soon approaches the other one, and with a sudden motion throws his hands, with fingers thus interlocked, out toward his face, very much as though he was going to strike him. This motion separates the fingers, which he again interlaces in a similar manner, and which he again throws out toward him. This operation is repeated several times, being regarded as very efficacious in procuring a visit from the god. The person whose eyes are shut during this ceremony soon gives what is supposed to be unmistakable evidence of being possessed by some supernatural and invisible power. His body sways back and forth in an unusual manner. The stick of incense falls from his grasp, and he begins to step about with the peculiar stride, and assume the peculiar attitude and appearance belonging to the god. This is considered an infallible proof of the actual presence of the god in the body of the medium. Sometimes, however, it is said, some one of the attendants of the god comes in his stead, which is made evident by the medium assuming the attitude appropriate to such or such an attending spirit. If the individual on whose account the presence of the god is invoked insists on having the principal or master divinity himself come to consult, the medium after a short time usually assumes the manners belonging to the god invoked, as a token that he has arrived. The suppliant now advances, and with three sticks of lighted incense in his hands, bows down on his knees before the medium and begs him to be seated. After he has seated himself the suppliant states the object in regard to which he has sought an audience with the god. A conversation often ensues between the two parties on the subject, the one professing to give the information desired, and the other receiving it with reverence, humility, and gratitude. Sometimes, however, the god, using the mouth of the medium, gives the suppliant a sound scolding for invoking his aid to attain unworthy or unlawful ends, and sometimes he positively declines to communicate the desired information. At the close of the interview the medium apparently falls asleep for a few minutes. On awaking some tea is given him to drink, and he soon becomes himself again. It is said that very many adopt this method of learning the way to recover from sickness, and also to acquire knowledge to be used in a particular kind of gambling or lottery.

"KAUNG KI.—This phrase denotes a method of consulting the gods by means of a kind of pen, which traces the oracle on sand. The whole pen consists of two pieces of wood. The larger piece, which usually is between two and three feet long, is always made of willow, peach, or mulberry wood. Its shape is like a farmer's drag, or the capital letter V, being cut out of a very crooked branch, or a branch in connection with the trunk of the tree. The front end, or the point of this draglike stick, is usually, perhaps always, carved in imitation of the head of the Chinese dragon. A small piece of hard wood, of one of the three kinds above specified, about five or six inches long, is inserted under the front point, and at right angles to it, giving the whole utensil the general appearance of a very small drag having only one front tooth.

"When one wishes to consult a god by this means he makes his wish known to some one belonging to a society or company established for the purpose of facilitating such consultation. These societies are said to be numerous at Fuhchau. A table is placed immediately before the image of the god, or his representative. On this table, besides the candles and incense, are arranged some fresh flowers and some tea or wine; some mock-money is provided to be burnt at the proper time. In front of this table, and further from the idol, is placed another table, having upon it a wooden platter about three or four feet long by two feet wide, and several inches deep, which is nearly filled with dry sand. After the incense and the candles have been lighted the suppliant kneels down and states his request with the usual ceremonies. Having risen from his knees, some paper charms are set on fire, and, while burning, they are brandished over the pen, the sand, and the two persons who are to hold the pen, for the purpose of purifying them all. These men, standing with the table which has the platter of sand upon it between them, and with their backs to the idol, silently and reverently take hold of the draglike utensil, one at each side, in such a manner that the end of the tooth or the pen under its front point shall rest in the sand. A peculiar kind of charm is now lighted and placed in the censer standing on the table before the image, in order to purify it. Another is burned in some place near by, open or exposed to the direct light of the heavens. This is designed to cause the god to descend and enter the pen and deliver its oracles in writing. If he does not soon indicate his presence another charm is burned. His presence is manifested by a slow movement of the point of the pen tracing characters on the sand. After writing a line or two on the sand the movement ceases, and the characters there written are transferred to paper. After this, if the oracle is unfinished, another line is written, and so on till the pen entirely ceases its motion, which signifies that the spirit of the god has taken its departure from the pen. All that now remains to be done is to ascertain the meaning of the oracle, which not unfrequently is found to be a difficult task. Sometimes it is given in poetry, with allusions to ancient times and personages, or it is written in some ancient form of the Chinese character, not in common use at the present day, or in an abbreviated running hand. Sometimes the oracle, as in ancient times in Greece, has a double sense, or several ambiguous meanings. The suppliant has no resource but to get the best meaning he can from the coveted response of the idol he importuned. It is said that men of the literary class are more in the habit of appealing to the gods by the use of this method than others."

The following are given as specimens of Chinese proclamations. The first was issued soon after the foreign tea trade was opened at Fuhchau.

"*Wang*, President of the Board of War, Imperial Censor, Viceroy of the Fuh-kien and Cheh-kien Provinces, charged with military affairs, pay of the troops, salt department, etc., and *Lu*, Privy Counselor, Imperial Vice-censor, Lieutenant-governor of the Fuh-kien Province, etc., make this important and clear proclamation.

"With regard to the teas grown in the Fuh-kien province, it has been the custom for merchants from Kiangsi, Canton, and other provinces, to transport their funds, at the commencement of each tea season, by way of *Ho-keu*, into the tea region to purchase teas, and from thence the teas have been forwarded to the different provinces for sale. But in the third year of Hienfung, (1853,) in consequence of the irruption of the rebels into the Honan province, this route was broken up, so that the merchants could not pass that way. We therefore memorialized the throne, begging that the restrictions on trade at this port (Fuhchau) might be removed temporarily. Thus it has happened that the merchants now bring their funds to Fuhch'au; and from this point pass up into the tea region to purchase their teas, which they then bring to Fuhchau. There are, it is true, rapids and shoals in the up-river channel, but still the route is very plain and short in comparison with the routes to Shanghai and Canton. The difference in the difficulties of transportation is very great, and the transit charges by the Fuhchau route are much less than by the other routes. Besides, when the teas reach Fuhchau they can at once be packed and shipped for sea without paying duties at the custom-houses along the old routes. As a consequence, the duties on teas are rapidly diminishing, while the gains of the merchants have largely increased. In view of this depletion of the imperial revenue, we memorialized the throne, begging that custom-houses might be established at suitable points on the route to Fuhchau, thus replenishing the government treasury. To this memorial we have the imperial sanction, and accordingly we have appointed officers to take charge of the matter.

"Since all the people are nourished by the fruits of the emperor's soil, and their feet stand upon it; and whereas the present military expenses of the empire are very great, while the imperial revenue is much diminished, you, the people, would rejoice to aid his majesty with your contributions of money; how much more then should you cheerfully comply with the imperial commands, when they only require that, instead of the former transit duties on teas passing to Canton or Shanghai, where the route is lined with custom-houses, you now pay the prescribed duties in this province. And whether the duty now levied is a little more or less than the amount collected on the other routes, it is certain that, being relieved from the heavy charges for land or water carriage which you paid on the other routes, you still gain largely by the change. This is another instance of the imperial favor and is truly no trifling boon.

"We regard you all as possessing a correct moral sentiment, and believe you to be entirely unwilling to chaffer and banter with the government in the matter of its revenue. If you say that by paying this duty you are compelled to demand a higher price for your teas, you ought to remember that by selling your teas within the province producing them you avoid all the cost and risk of transporting them to distant ports, and thus, after all, you are able to offer your teas in Fuhchau at a lower figure than they can be purchased at any other port. Thus the purchasers of your teas do not suffer. Let there be no unwillingness or deception in this matter. Let all obey."

"*Hienfung*, fifth year, sixth moon, tenth day."
[July 23, 1855.]

During 1857 the currency of Fuhchau was in a most unsatisfactory state. The supply of copper cash, which is the circulating medium throughout the empire, was entirely inadequate to the demand; the government bank failed, and great distress prevailed among the people. The government authorities issued numerous proclamations on the subject, of one of which we offer the reader the following translation:

"*Wang*, President of the Board of War, Viceroy of the Fuh-kien and Cheh-kien provinces, makes this proclamation in reply to the memorial presented by —— of the —— district.

"The authorities of the Fuh-kien province established the government bank in Fuhchau to circulate, for general use, all the varieties of paper currency. It was conceived that as silver is scarce, this paper money might supply the deficiency, thus affording the people a medium of exchange for the transaction of business; and certainly, whether we consider the convenience of the people or the prosperity of the government, this plan is the best that can possibly be devised.

"When the Kiangsi thieves entered the Fuh-kien province the people of Fuhchau became greatly alarmed, and daily bought up the silver, in a clandestine manner, to hide it away, thus causing a sudden rise in its market value. Merchants also, when they brought rice to this city for sale, refused to take anything but silver for it; and the people, speculating as to the supply of food for the future, seemed actually to fear they should all starve sitting on their seats.

"Sincerely desirous of understanding the wants of the people, and anxious to save them, we issue orders with this proclamation to the provincial treasurer, directing him to transfer to the government bank a supply of silver for general circulation. Besides, we are arranging that the receipts of the custom-houses shall be used for purchasing rice to be sold to the people at a cheap rate. We have already arranged everything for meeting the demands of the present emergency.

"With regard to the scarcity of copper cash, we reply that an officer has been already sent to *Chehkien* to buy a large supply of copper for coining, and we have also ordered the government bank to commence at once the coining of a new supply of copper cash.

"As it regards your suggestions about 'deepening the moats, strengthening the walls, and stationing troops at all important points to protect the city,' we have to say that these matters belong entirely to us, and you need not waste your words about them.

"You state that 'the government bank paper does not circulate in the country; and that, when the people offer it to the government officials in payment of taxes, they will take it only at a discount of from *fifty* to *seventy* per cent., and that the traders all follow this precedent.' If these statements are correct, those parties are surely acting in a most detestable manner. We instantly command the treasurer to order all government officials to cease utterly this villainous practice of discounting the government paper. All officials who shall dare to offend in this matter we shall punish without the least leniency. Violate not this proclamation."

"*Hienfung*, seventh year, third moon, twenty-fourth day."
[May 16, 1857.)

The following extracts, from the recent letters of brethren connected with the Methodist Episcopal Mission in Fuhchau, will give the reader some idea of itinerant life in China.

Rev. Dr. Wentworth writes: "On last Sabbath it came my turn, in the two weeks' circuit plan, to go to the country appointment established a few weeks ago. On Saturday I took passage in a native boat up the river eight or ten miles, and then struck off on foot into the country five or six more. In a little gorge among the mountains lies a hamlet composed of a few farm-houses. Some of the occupants heard of Jesus and the new religion, came to Fuhchau, became inquirers, and invited us to their home in the country. It has resulted in a regular appointment, the baptism of seven or eight, and the waking up of a spirit of inquiry about the new doctrines that is spreading far and wide among the rural population. The people, men and women, were at work in the fields when I and my native exhorter arrived. They got us dinner about four o'clock. It was boiled rice served in bowls, with several kinds of stale fish, and greens for seasoning, coarse and unsavory fare to a foreign palate. I have dined on johnny cakes, cold and hot, overdone and underdone, without any other accompaniments than raw coffee or cold water, in the rocky districts of New England, the woods of northern New York, the prairies of Illinois, and the hither banks of the Mississippi. I thought such fare coarse, but there was an element of savoriness about it that does not pertain to the best cookery of the Chinese. Their highest culinary efforts are in the line of grease and garlic, and it needs a strong stomach and strong olfactory powers to satisfy hunger with their villainous preparations. I ate with chop-sticks, to the amusement of the brethren, who nevertheless were officiously kind in teaching me how to hold the instruments, and do away with my unchristian awkwardness in exercising the 'nimble boys.' What is the use of cutlery and plated forks, when a man can take his food into his mouth, without burning his fingers, with a couple of sticks that cost nothing compared with these expensive luxuries. What a demand there would be for steel and silver if the Celestials were to be so far Christianized as to eat with knives and forks like the rest of the world.

What an impulse would be given to the manufacture of cups and saucers, and spoons, and table linen and soap.

"At night I was laid on a board to sleep, but kept awake till after twelve o'clock by a discussion in the next room between my exhorter and a well-dressed intelligent gentleman, inquiring about the doctrines, but troubled about the fact if they were true, that his ancestors and parents had gone down to the grave and into the other world without the hope of salvation.

"At nine o'clock on Sunday morning the room was filled with a respectable and attentive congregation, who listened to a sermon, and all spoke in class-meeting at its conclusion. From this we went three or four miles to another settlement of newly baptized Christians, where we had another sermon, followed by a class and inquiry meeting. The sun was still high in the heavens, and I proposed that we go to the next village. We went to one where no foreigner had been before, and preached in the street to crowds.

"A popular objection and report among the natives is, that we give three dollars a month to those who will embrace our doctrines. Our exhorter repelled it with righteous vehemence. 'I,' said he, 'live in Fuhchau, at Iongtau. I invite all to come and see me at my house. I am a painter on glass, and support myself and family with the labors of my own hand, and preach on Sundays besides.'

"From thence we went to another village, and took our stand in a temple. I set one of the young converts to talk a while. The people were in the fields at work. So we sent out an appointment for evening, obtained some candles, lighted up the temple, and proceeded to hold Christian services right in the presence of the mud gods of Budhism. A large congregation gathered, and, as a preliminary exercise, both preacher and people stuck their long bamboo pipes into the candles, and then, puffing like locomotives, sat down under a cloud of smoke, and took their places to listen to the proclamation of the Gospel. At the conclusion of the services I answered questions for an hour touching foreigners and their ways and doctrines."

Rev. S. L. Baldwin also writes: "On Saturday, April 23, 1859, I accompanied Brother Gibson to our 'Peach Farm' appointment in the country, and united with our brethren there in various prayer-meetings, class-meetings, and more public services on that day and the Sabbath following. I was very much pleased with the serious deportment and earnest manner of the brethren there.

"On the seventeenth of May I repeated the Lord's Prayer for the first time at our Chinese family devotion.

"On the first of June I started on an expedition into the country, in company with Mr. Nichols, a pious young man from Boston, and Akaw, one of our native converts. We ascended the river Min in a boat to the distance of sixty miles, and reached Chuikan about two A. M. on June 2d. We rested in our boat until sunrise, and then traveled some eight or ten miles, when we halted under the shade of a large tree. Here we spent the heat of the day, the people gathering around us from all quarters, and receiving willingly Christian books and tracts which we presented them, and which were explained to some extent by Akaw. Toward evening we resumed our chairs, and traveled to Keukan, ten or twelve miles farther up the river. Here we secured rest for the night on a large covered boat at the beach. Akaw held conversations on Christianity with several of the boatmen during the evening, and in the morning we left them a supply of tracts. Crossing the river we made our way to Sangtau, a place which had never before been visited by foreigners. We rested during the day in a grove of camphor-trees just back of the village, and the whole population came out to see us, manifesting the greatest curiosity in regard to our appearance, clothing, etc. They were very civil, however, and listened attentively to a long talk from Akaw, who distributed a liberal supply of books among them. One old man invited him to his house, and talked with him for more than two hours about the Christian religion. On leaving this place we traveled to Nangkan, where we took a boat to Chuikan, and there rejoined our own boat.

"While ascending the hill at the latter place some boys threw stones at us, and called us '*huang-kiangs*,' which was the only instance of incivility we encountered during our absence.

"On Saturday, June 4th, we descended the river, stopping at the village at the 'upper bridge,' where we distributed a quantity of tracts, and reaching home in safety at six P. M. We trust that some of the seed thus scattered by the 'wayside' may yet spring up to the glory of God."

In further illustration of itinerant life in China we present another extract from a recent letter by the Rev. Dr. Wentworth:

"Yesterday, at half-past six o'clock, directly after dinner, I started on foot for Nanseu, a large village to the southwest of this that has been a few times visited by missionaries.

"Brother Ting went along to do the preaching. His son, my present table boy, went to act as steward for the wants of the outer man. My cooly, a great strapping fellow, went 'loaded to the keel' with books and tracts for distribution; and finally I went to attract the attention of the natives, and give them something on which to expend abuse.

"A heavy thunder shower was raging in the west as we started, and our course lay right into the teeth of it; nevertheless the sun was vailed in, and this was favorable; so we put out, thinking to run into any one of the numerous huts along the road in case we got caught by it. Six miles of vigorous walking brought us to the head of this island, near where you and I went with Mr. Clark three years ago. Here we took a boat, and steered away for our destination.

"It was manned by an old woman, a young man and his father, the young man's wife, and a sick boy. After sculling, and rowing, and poling, and sailing, and tacking until pitch dark, the storm, that had been long gathering, burst upon us in all the fury of wind and thunder, lightning and rain, when we were still about a mile distant from our landing-place. I tried to induce the Chinese to proceed. 'It was too dark,' 'the typhoon was upon them,' 'they must lie to.' So the boat went to anchor and the 'Celestials' to their suppers, which they ate as quietly as if riding at anchor in a smooth bay, instead of being tossed by the wild fury of the elements in savage commotion. As is often the case with thundergusts the first gust was the worst. The water came through the basket-roof of our boat like a cotton tabernacle at a camp-meeting.

"I covered myself with my sleeping blanket and kept dry. In an hour the gust had spent its principal fury, though the lightnings glared and thunders growled as fiercely as ever. The boatmen had finished their supper, and I persuaded them to resume their setting-poles that we might at least spend the rest of the night on terra-firma. In a few minutes I 'walked the plank' by a gleam of lightning, and clambered a crazy flight of steps up the bank to what seemed a temple on the hither shore.

"By the light of a pine stick our party proceeded to explore the interior. It was floorless, and tenanted by bats, and carpeted and curtained with no end of dirt and cobwebs. A couple of men had laid a door lengthwise, and laid themselves lengthwise upon it for the night. A stage occcupied one end for theatrical representations, and it was thought this was our only chance; but the men attempted to sweep it, and thereby raised a cloud of dust which rendered breathing impossible. 'Does no priest live here?' we asked. 'None.' 'Who keeps the temple?' 'A cooly sleeping over yonder.' 'Well, route him out; we must have his room.' And out he came, not well pleased at being disturbed in his slumbers, but set himself vigorously to work to put the filthy place in order. It was about ten feet square, with no floor. My bedstead was a door, the bed two yards of rush matting, and my pillow a pile of books. Brother Ting and his boy made a bed of another door in the same closet, and the cooly slept as he could catch it with the sexton outside. The rain continued, and paid its attentions to us in our beds, but did no serious damage. We slept soundly, and I was awake by daylight, and roused my forces for marching.

"Three miles travel across the paddy fields or rice flats, over stone-paved causeways worn as smooth as glass by the travel of unnumbered generations, brought us in sight of the village we were in quest of, beautifully situated at the foot of a hill crowned with pines, behind which rose a mountain in the shape of an inverted bowl, but jagged like crystalization from base to summit. It was a lovely spot, but all the romance vanished the moment we had crossed a substantial stone bridge, and entered the narrow, crowded, filthy Chinese streets.

"We instantly had a crowd at our heels, shouting 'whang-kiang,' 'foreign devil,' in all the tones and key-notes of human passion, surprise, astonishment, fear, pity, contempt, insolence, and bravado. We took our stand behind the counter of a respectable shop in the main street, an overwhelming crowd collected in front, blocking up the street, and rendering passage nearly impossible, when Brother Ting began to preach and peddle books at a cash or two apiece, a mere nominal value, not a hundredth part of what they cost. I put in a word now and then as I was able, though my rude brouge was more frequently assailed with shouts of laughter and mockery from the boys than otherwise. In a few minutes he had sold half his stock. Meanwhile my boy and the cooly got us breakfast in the book shop.

"I ate a plate of boiled rice with a Chinese porcelain spoon, and a slice or two of fried pork with my fingers; this, with a few native cakes, a bowl of tea, and a cut of watermelon, made a sumptuous repast, the whole of which cost ten cents.

"Removing hence, we took another stand on a covered stone bridge used as a market, and disposed of nearly all the remaining stock of books, Brother Ting 'preaching Jesus' all the time as fast as his tongue would wag, and as loud as he could halloo in the midst of a babel like that of Broadway or the polls of an American election—turbid waters in which to sow seed.

"Tired at last of the noise, and attracted by the beauty of the hill of pines, I bade my boy follow me, and started off at a round pace, hoping to get clear of the annoyances that beset us. We were soon out of town and climbing the beautiful hill, but with a crowd of a hundred men, women, and boys at our heels, and more than all, the hill itself was covered with grass and faggot gatherers, so that a head seemed to pop out from behind every tree and bush.

I returned to town in disgust, and ordered a retreat at once.

"In a short time we were once more on board our boat and on our own island, where the people are more accustomed to us, and a little more civil. Walking six miles in the sun opened the pores, and I reached home drenched in perspiration from head to heel. A bath, change of clothes, and a Christian dinner made all right again."

CHAPTER XV.

THE PEACH FARM.

THE influence of the gracious revival in Fuhchau soon extended to the country. Our young converts, filled with zeal for the cause of God, began to itinerate through the surrounding cities and towns, distributing Christian books and conversing with the people about the new doctrines. Brother Hu Po Mi was foremost in this corps of pioneers. He was admirably fitted for this work; possessing a fine personal appearance, a clear and forcible style of address, and a hearty Christian experience. In a secluded valley among the mountains, some fifteen miles northwest from Fuhchau, there is a straggling village containing perhaps sixty families. From a fancied resemblance of the valley at this point to a peach, the village has been named the "*Peach Farm.*" On the outskirts of the village stands an old farm-house occupied by the Li family. The ancestors of the family, about one hundred years ago, had lived in the Fing-hua prefecture, some forty miles southward from Fuhchau, and were acquainted with the Hu family, who also at that time lived in Fing-hua. These two families moved into the Fuhchau prefecture, Mr. Hu locating his family in Fuhchau city, and Mr. Li settling with his family in this quiet valley. For many years subsequent to this removal, the acquaintance between the two families was kept up by a mutual interchange of social courtesies and kind offices, but during the present generation this acquaintance had almost entirely ceased. When the Hu family became Christians, they soon visited the Li family, and urged them to seek salvation in the name of Jesus. Brother Hu Po Mi was active in this good work, and presented the subject with all the ardor of a young convert. His efforts were not fruitless; the younger members of the Li family began to attend our meetings in Fuhchau, and soon they presented themselves as candidates for Christian instruction and baptism. Encouraged by their manifest sincerity and earnestness, I resolved to visit them at their home in the valley, taking with me Brother Hu Po Mi as companion and guide. I shall not readily forget the incidents of this visit. February 10, 1859, we went on board a small native boat, and started up the river on our proposed trip. Having wind and tide in our favor we made good progress, passed under the "upper bridge" some six miles from Fuhchau, and soon landed at the salt-boat anchorage, three miles above the "upper bridge." Here we left the boat, and started on foot over the rice-fields for the Peach Farm. After walking about five miles through the most picturesque scenery, we reached the entrance to the valley. Crossing a bold spur of the mountain, our path led us along its side, with the thickly wooded heights above, and the quiet valley spread out at our feet below. I was charmed with the place. Its silence furnished such a grateful change from the jostling crowds of the thronged city and the vociferating boat population on the river, that I could almost fancy myself entering a new world, fresh from the plastic hand of the great Creator. The greatest width of the valley does not exceed half a mile, while in some places it contracts to a mere ravine. Human industry and skill have been busy, bringing under cultivation every foot of arable land, and, by terracing the mountain acclivities, extending the domain of agriculture to apparently inaccessible altitudes. A stream of water flows through the valley, and I was agreeably surprised to find on its bank a veritable water-power grist-mill in active operation. The machinery and building were of a rude character, but still all the essential elements of the mill were present, and the flour it turned out was of a fair quality for China. Farm-houses were sparsely scattered through the valley, some almost hidden by trees and others standing out boldly to view on elevated knolls, while light wreaths of smoke at the farther end of the valley indicated the position of the Peach Farm. It was about four o'clock in the afternoon when we arrived at the house of our friends on the outskirts of the Peach Farm. We found only the female members of the family at home; all the men and boys were out deer-stalking on the mountains. Toward nightfall the hunters returned, and it was really refreshing to observe their rustic habits and receive their cordial welcome. Notice of our arrival was circulated through the valley, the principal room of the house was arranged for preaching, and about dark the congregation began to assemble. Tea and tobacco were in constant requisition for some time after we commenced our exercises, the etiquette of the place demanding that each neighbor, on his arrival, should at once be waited on with these refreshments. We talked on notwithstanding these interruptions, and gradually the audience became quiet and attentive. Brother Hu and I spoke alternately, varying the exercises occasionally by a conversational episode, by a brief discussion of an objection started by some one in the congregation, or by calling on one of the candidates for baptism to tell his experience or lead in prayer. The scene was to me one of strange, exciting interest. It was a rare thing to see a foreigner in this retired valley, and the simple-minded rustics could scarcely credit their senses when they found themselves actually in the presence of a genuine "outsider." Their surprise was not diminished when they heard me address them in their own language, and tell them of God, and salvation, and heaven. After the numerous disappointments and rebuffs I had experienced in presenting the Gospel message to the Chinese, it was most cheering to feel that now I was under a Chinese roof where Jesus was an invited and honored guest, and that I was preaching to persons willing to accept the great salvation. It was past midnight when we retired; with me, however, sleep was out of the question. The scenes through which I had just passed kept whirling through my mind, till the cries of the early hunters and the light streaming in through the roof told me a new day had opened.

I spent part of the next day visiting the families of the neighborhood. Some of the people were bitterly opposed to the new doctrines, others seemed to be utterly indifferent on the subject of religion; while a few expressed an intelligent interest in the message I tried to deliver. I was gratified to find that in every family I visited there were some who had heard something about Christianity, and were able to state some of its prominent doctrines. In the Li family, where I was entertained during the visit, nine persons gave in their names as candidates for baptism. Encouraged by the promising state of things in the valley, we decided to take it into the regular work, and accordingly made an appointment for preaching every fortnight in the house of old Father Li.

The genuineness of the work thus auspiciously begun was soon put to the test. The enemy, so long in undisputed possession of this territory, had no idea of yielding without a struggle. A general alarm was sounded through the valley concerning the new doctrines, and earnest consultations were held as to the most effectual method of averting the apprehended danger. Some proposed to check the evil in the bud by entering in their courts of justice criminal charges against every Chinese who should embrace the new doctrines. The advocates of this plan stated that it had formerly been tried with great success against the Roman Catholics, and that it would certainly prove equally successful in the present case. At first the plan suggested met with great favor; but soon unexpected difficulties arose when they proceeded to act upon it. When these would-be prosecutors appeared at the government courts to enter their complaints they were told that the former modes of procedure against Christianity would not suit in these days, that foreigners now had treaties with the government of China, and that it was no uncommon thing at the present time for Chinese to become Christians. Foiled in this effort to check the spread of the new doctrines, they then proposed a more private plan of procedure, and soon our catechumens found all the heathen members of their respective families arrayed against them in bitter, persistent hostility, and employing every form of annoyance and intimidation to deter them from embracing Christianity. This plan also resulted in failure, and in a fit of desperation some *rowdies* of the neighborhood proposed *beating* the new doctrines out of the catechumens, and magnanimously offered themselves for the enterprise. This proposition was quite popular in many quarters; but some of the more respectable and influential people of the valley denounced it as outrageous and unreasonable, and hence the scheme was abandoned. As a dernier resort, it was now proposed to create a public sentiment against Christianity, and thus coerce the catechumens into submission. To accomplish this, every suitable occasion, public or private, was employed to extol the excellence and power of the idols they had so long worshiped. "Every good thing we possess," said these advocates of heathenism, "has been conferred on us by these idols, and we ought to worship them. Moreover," they continued, "the idols are highly incensed in consequence of the denunciations poured upon them by the Christians, and soon unheard-of calamities will come upon all the people of the valley." Our catechumens conducted themselves with much prudence during this time of excitement. Every failure of their enemies to harass them served only to establish them the more firmly in the principles of their new faith, and to all threats and maledictions they replied by blameless lives or by the "soft answer" which "turneth away wrath." Time passed on, and still, notwithstanding the declared anger of the idols, there was no deviation from the ordinary course of nature. The sun, moon, stars, and seasons passed through their courses as of yore; no floods or storms devastated their fields; no pestilence invaded their dwellings. In the Li family heathenism opened the struggle with considerable vigor but soon was compelled to change its tactics. The contest in this family was very interesting, and the following brief sketch of it will be gratifying, I think, to the reader. I give the incident just as it was narrated to me, without attempting to explain how the parties communicated with the spirits:

The heathen members of this family declared that when the foreign missionary entered their house the spirits of the idols all ran away; and hence on each occasion of our leaving the premises these members of the family would go up on the mountain just back of the house and beg the spirits to return, assuring them the missionary had gone from the place. The spirits at first, and for some time subsequently, responded to these calls, and resumed their respective positions on the altar. On the occasion of one of our visits to the place, however, we spoke with considerable liberty and power, the congregation was unusually solemn, and the exercises were continued to a late hour. Next morning I left for home, and after my departure the heathen members of the family went out as usual to call back the spirits. To their utter astonishment they found the spirits unwilling to return. A famous exorcist was then sent for, and he tried all his incantations upon the spirits; but, strange to say, they still remained incorrigible. To all interrogations and entreaties their uniform reply was, "Jesus is very powerful, and unless you keep him out of the house we dare not re-enter it." Surprised and confounded by this unexpected occurrence, the exorcist and two heathen members of the Li family began to attend our meetings, and attached themselves to our class of candidates for baptism.

After passing through a course of Christian instruction, and giving satisfactory evidence of their fitness for the ordinance, seven of our adult candidates were approved for baptism, and Sunday, March 13, 1859, was appointed as the day for administering the rite. At an early hour on that day our rude chapel was filled with attentive hearers, and after a discourse from: "Behold, we have left all and followed thee; what shall we have, therefore?" the approved candidates were admitted first to baptism and then to the Lord's Supper. Let us linger for a moment over the material aspects of the scene. Our so-called chapel is a small earth-floored room in a country farm-house, destitute alike of ceiling or windows. In one corner are piled plows, hoes, drags, and other agricultural implements; at my back stood the grim, smoked images, still worshiped by a few members of the family; while scattered round the room, on backless benches or on the threshold of the door, sat the rustic congregation. The occasion reminded me of the time when in my native land the Gospel was preached in log-cabins, country school-houses, and tented groves; and as I thought of the rapid process by which those log-cabins had become palatial residences, those school-houses beautiful church edifices, and those forests populous cities, my faith descried the day when the same transformations shall appear in China; and I felt that, despite the humble incidents of the present hour, it was a glorious privilege to aid in laying on Chinese soil the foundation of that kingdom which is to endure forever. August 21, 1859, five more candidates were approved for baptism, and admitted by that rite into the communion and fellowship of the Christian Church, thus increasing our class at the Peach Farm to twelve members.

The following incidents, growing out of our work at this appointment, will show that everywhere the labors and experiences of the minister of Christ preserve a wonderful identity. It matters little, indeed, where the faithful minister's field of labor may be; whether among the ice-glaciers of the North, or the sunny plains of the South, or the broad prairies of the West, or in the old storied lands of the East, his work in all its prominent outlines and characteristics is ever the same. The great wants of humanity are not essentially modified by degrees of latitude or longtitude; the text of the Gospel message has been authoritatively settled by infinite wisdom, and the leading appliances for its propagation are indicated by the same high authority.

One beautiful Sabbath, after concluding our public services at the Peach Farm, I went out with some of the native brethren to make some pastoral visits. Our first call was on an old man who had once expressed an interest in the Gospel, but who had grown indifferent on the subject, and was now confined to his bed by sickness. We found him very low, unable to converse or even to think consecutively on any subject. He seemed stupefied by the conviction that he could not get well. To all our questions and remarks his uniform reply was: "I am old; I am dying of old age. The fortune-teller says the turning of the spring will decide my fate." I tried in various ways to arrest his attention, but in vain. He turned his face to the wall and groaned out his melancholy refrain: "I am old; I am dying of old age." After lying in that position for a few minutes he turned himself on the couch, and, fixing on me his dull leaden eye, asked: "Who are you?"

"It is the foreign missionary," said the brethren. "He has come to see you and to tell you about the Saviour?"

"Yes," I added, "I have come to tell you of a wonderful Saviour and a glorious home in the skies."

He looked steadily into my face, as though he wished me to go on; but in a moment his mind again wandered, and, shaking his head, he sighed: "No, no, it is of no use; too late, too late!" and then continued muttering to himself in a low, indistinct tone of voice, "too late." O what saddening thoughts and reminiscences were called up by the sound of those ominous words! Finding it impossible to converse with him, we tried to commend him to God, and then with heavy hearts turned away to other duties.

A five minutes' walk brought us in sight of the house of a man notorious throughout the valley as the ringleader in everything reckless and wicked. The man had attended our services on the forenoon of that day, and though he listened respectfully to all that was said, yet the contemptuous sneer on his countenance, and the jeering remarks he uttered as he left the place, indicated the true character of his thoughts, and showed but too plainly that a deeply rooted hostility to the Gospel rankled in his heart. We approached his dwelling with some trepidation, and with many misgivings as to the result of our visit. The native brethren, indeed, had tried to dissuade me from calling; but I felt desirous of at least trying to lead him to the Saviour. Entering the yard in front of his house, we found him surrounded by his wild companions. Seeing us approach, he rose to receive us with an air of assumed indifference, for it was evident he felt embarrassed by our visit. After interchanging the customary salutations we proceeded at once to speak of the Gospel.

"I have heard my neighbors talk about these new doctrines," he replied, "but they don't suit me—they are too profound. I am a rough, ignorant man, and can never arrive at their meaning."

The brethren spoke of some important Christian doctrines, and sought to show their simplicity and adaptation to our wants; but he parried all their appeals by asserting his inability to comprehend them, though any one could see, in a moment, that this stupidity was all assumed.

"And what do you think of your idols?" I inquired, changing the subject.

"I don't care anything about them," he quickly replied. "They don't do any good. All they want is something to eat and something to wear. Give them a bowl of rice and a suit of paper clothes, and they are entirely satisfied." These remarks were delivered in a flippant, jocose manner, and called forth bursts of laughter from the company.

"And is it indeed true," I continued, "that your idols cannot help you?"

"Certainly it is true," he replied. "These idols are nothing but wood, or earth, or paper; how can they assist us?" Here he took hold of a small clay idol, and tossing it about he continued: "See! the thing cannot help itself, how can it help me?"

"And is there no power," I asked, "to protect and help us?"

"I don't know," he replied; "everything is determined by fate."

"What is this fate which determines everything?"

"I don't know," he replied; "all I know is, that there must be somewhere a power superior to man which controls all things."

It was now sufficiently apparent that the person before us was a man of no ordinary shrewdness and native ability. Pleased with the vigor of his thoughts, and wishing to hear him speak further on this topic, I asked:

"What evidence have you that there is such a power as that to which you have referred?"

"Plenty of evidence," he replied; "you can see it everywhere—in the motions of the heavenly bodies, in the changing seasons, in the phases of human life, and in the mysterious phenomena constantly puzzling and alarming us."

"And does this power concern itself about us and our affairs?"

"No," he replied. "We are too insignificant to attract its notice. Why should it, possessing all the sources of happiness, concern itself with us or our paltry affairs?"

At this point I interposed some remarks on the love of God, as exhibited in the gift of his Son to be the Saviour of the world.

"Yes," joined in one of the brethren, "and now Jesus receives sinners and pardons them."

"And who is this Jesus," he fiercely retorted, 'who goes about granting instant pardon to every rebel who asks him for it, thus thwarting the claims of justice, degrading the law of heaven, and throwing everything into confusion?"

He uttered these words with such vehemence and apparent sincerity that it was evident we had touched on one of his strong objections to the Gospel. I embraced the opportunity to dwell, at some length, on the character of Christ as mediator between God and man, and to state as clearly as I could the *conditions* on which he is willing to receive and pardon the guilty. Apparently satisfied, he then changed his ground, and asked, with an air of triumph: "But where is Jesus? I cannot *see* him; consequently I do not believe there is such a being."

"Did you ever *see* the Emperor of China?" I quietly inquired.

A general laugh from the company anticipated his reply, and showed him that even they could now detect the fallacy of his apparently irresistible argument. Availing myself of the advantage thus gained I turned to more practical subjects, and tried to give him some idea of his own sinfulness in the sight of God. To my great surprise he promptly responded: "What you say is true; I am a bad man; I know it, and am neither afraid nor ashamed to acknowledge it." He uttered these words with so much earnestness and apparent sincerity that for a moment it seemed as though the Holy Spirit were just about to lead him to the Saviour; but a change soon came over him, and, resuming his former reckless manner, he turned aside all my appeals by pleading old age, ignorance, and the power of habit.

"Will you allow me to pray with you?" I inquired as we rose to leave.

"Thank you," he replied, "I'd rather not."

Warmed by our previous conversation, and feeling a deep interest in his case, I ventured to urge the point; but he persistently refused, and finding that my importunity irritated him I desisted. He accompanied us to the gate, invited us to call again, and then bade us a pleasant good-by. "Blessed are they who sow beside all waters," I recited to myself as we walked slowly away from this den of wickedness.

After a brief interval of rest we started to make our third call. In a retired cove on the side of the mountain stands a solitary farm-house. One portion of it is occupied by a farmer with his family, while the other part is the home of a lone widow whom we had recently baptized and admitted into the Christian Church. A sacred atmosphere seemed to surround the place as we approached it, and the scenery was so quiet and homelike that it was difficult for me to believe myself in a heathen land. Entering the dwelling, our good sister received us with a cordial welcome. It was most interesting to listen to her simple experience.

"I am so glad you have come," she said as she took a seat beside me. "This is a lonely place, and I am sometimes tempted to fear that the idols which I have forsaken will in some way injure me. Here is where I pray," pointing to a corner of the room; "and at night, when disturbed by unpleasant dreams, I get up from my bed, kneel down there, and pray. And prayer to Jesus always makes me feel better," she added with great earnestness.

We talked to her for some time about the way of salvation through a crucified Redeemer, and then proposed prayer.

"O yes," she quickly replied, "I do want you to pray in my house. After you have prayed in it I shall feel that it is consecrated to the true God, and that henceforth the idols will not dare to enter it."

While engaged in these exercises the farmer came in from his work and sat down with us in the room. We conversed with him some time, urging him to abandon heathenism and embrace Christianity. He listened attentively to all we said on the subject, and expressed a desire to become a Christian. "But," said he, "I am a poor man, and have a large family to support; I fear I should come to want if I were to cease work every seventh day."

"As to that," I replied, "if you will be diligent in business during six days of the week, I believe God will not suffer you to starve on Sunday. Besides," I continued, "you have now been toiling for perhaps fifty years under the fancied protection of your idols, and I suspect you are more heavily in debt now than you were at the beginning."

"True," he responded; "every word you have said is true."

"Then," said I, "just give up this way of living and try Christianity."

"But," he replied, "my landlord says he will turn me off the farm if I become a Christian."

"He'll not do anything of the kind," I said with some earnestness, for I had some knowledge of the facts in the case; "and even if he should do so you can find as good situations elsewhere."

"Well, I'll think over the matter," he replied solemnly, "and you must pray for me."

We assured him we would do so; and after a few months it was our privilege to receive himself and wife into Church fellowship.

CHAPTER XVI.

INCIDENTS.

"Are the Chinese capable of appreciating the doctrines of the Bible?" "Can the Chinese be converted?"

The following incidents are given, partly as answers to these and similar questions which recently have been addressed to the writer, and partly as illustrations of our field and work in China:

In the autumn of 1859, a few weeks before leaving Fuhchau for the United States, I visited our two out-stations, Peach Farm and Ngu-kang. After the forenoon sermon at the Peach Farm we held the usual class-meeting. All the members spoke, giving a simple and, to me at least, most interesting account of their Christian experience. One brother said the *Bible*, to the Christian, was like the *compass* to the mariner; and another, carrying out the figure, spoke of *faith* in the Bible as our *rudder* in the voyage of life. Toward the close of the meeting old Father Li arose and said:

"Brethren, I am an old man, too old to think clearly and consecutively on any subject. I am not able to comprehend everything the Bible contains; it is not probable I shall understand all its doctrines in this life; *but, brethren, I just believe the whole of it.* Only assure me that what you say is contained in the Bible, and I'll believe every word of it."

Never shall I forget the simple earnestness with which these words were uttered; and never shall I forget the delightful emotions they excited in my heart. In what school had the old man learned this sublime lesson of faith? I was the more gratified with these remarks, because, so far as I could remember, I had never presented the subject to him in this light, and I could not but feel that this beautiful experience was due to the teachings of the Holy Spirit.

After dinner I walked two miles to the other appointment at Ngu-kang; and at the conclusion of the discourse the members, as usual, remained for class-meeting. When a goodly number had spoken old Father Ting arose, and with evident emotion said:

"What a wonderful mercy it is that I, so old a man, have heard and obeyed this glorious Gospel! Had I died a few years since, or had this Gospel been delayed a few years more in reaching this place, I should have been lost forever. Thank God, I am here to-day, permitted to hear the joyful sound and to believe on the Lord with all my heart! There are many things of which I am ignorant, brethren, but this one thing I know: *I do love the Saviour, and living or dying I'll never leave him!*"

Tears gushed from the old man's eyes as he uttered these words, his large frame quivered with emotion, and he sank into his seat sobbing like a child.

At a previous class-meeting held at Ngu-kang, a young brother rose to speak. He was a blacksmith, had lost his parents years ago, was now the eldest member of the family, and had recently embraced religion. He said:

"Some two or three months ago, when I became interested in these doctrines, my neighbors tried to frighten me. They said I would starve if I became a Christian, for I would not be allowed to do any work on Sundays; and that if I did really embrace Christianity they would never give me any more work. These statements," he continued, "startled me at first, and I scarcely knew what to do; but after thinking over the matter, I concluded that God would take care of me if I sincerely tried to obey his will; hence I embraced these doctrines, and became a Christian. And now what is the result? Why, with regard to keeping the Sabbath, I find that I now do more work in six days than formerly I did in seven; and with regard to losing my business, I never had as much work in my life as I have had since I became a Christian. My shop is frequently crowded with people who bring their farming tools to be repaired; and while I am doing their work, they keep me busy answering their questions about these new doctrines. I fancy, indeed, that some of them bring me their hoes and axes only as a pretext for getting into a conversation with me; for I occasionally notice that the tools they bring require scarcely any dressing at all."

The case of this young man is full of interest. Before hearing the Gospel he was not able to read a word; but after he commenced attending our meetings he addressed himself to the task of learning to read, and within two months from that time he was able to read the entire Gospel of Saint Matthew. He possesses a mind of more than ordinary clearness and vigor. Some of his prayers and addresses in our social meetings are remarkably pertinent and efficient. We have already, indeed, designated him the "learned blacksmith," and I most earnestly pray that he may consecrate all his gifts to the advancement of Christ's kingdom in China. I remember his rising on one occasion in class-meeting to narrate his experience. Referring to his faith in Christianity, he said:

"Brethren, a man must believe something. What a man believes should be good, for a man's practice will always approximate his theory. If what a man believes is good, he will become virtuous; but if what he believes is bad, he will become vicious. Now," said he, "just look for a moment at our systems of idolatry. Suppose we were to become like the idols we worshiped; why, we should be devils incarnate, and the world would be made a pandemonium! Hence I conclude that our heathenism is bad. But look at Christianity. If we become like Jesus we shall possess characters of the highest excellence and purity, and the world will be like heaven. Hence I conclude Christianity is good, and in believing it we are simply obeying the voice of reason."

During one of our examinations of candidates for baptism at Ngu-kang, I observed that one woman and some three or four young people had the same surname. This circumstance led to the following conversation between myself and one of the young men:

"I observe you all have the same surname. Are you members of the same family?" I inquired.

"Yes," one replied; "this is mother, and these are my brothers."

"Where is your father?" I continued.

"He is at home attending to business."

"Does he approve of your embracing Christianity?"

"Yes, he is entirely willing."

"Why does not your father himself become a Christian?"

"He says it would not answer for *all* the family to embrace Christianity."

"And why," I asked with some curiosity, "does he think so?"

"He says that if we all become Christians our heathen neighbors will take advantage of that circumstance to impose on us."

"How will they do that?" I inquired.

"Christians are not allowed to swear or fight; and father says that when our wicked neighbors ascertain we have embraced Christianity, they will proceed at once to curse and maltreat us. Hence father says to us: 'You may all become Christians, but I must remain a heathen so as to retaliate on our bad neighbors. You can go to meeting and worship, but I must stay at home to do the cursing and fighting for the family.'"

An incident occurred at Ngu-kang which will furnish some illustration of our work in China. One Sunday afternoon we commenced our usual service in the house of one of the brethren. The room was crowded, and many were standing about the door.

We had sung the opening hymn and kneeled for prayer, the entire congregation kneeling with us. I had uttered only a few sentences of the prayer when whir-*whiz*-WHACK came a blow so close to my face that for a moment I felt sure it had been aimed at me. Somewhat startled, I opened my eyes, and there, right before me, stood a strapping field-woman, armed with a stout bamboo cane. She seemed frantic with rage, and poured her blows with furious energy upon the shoulders and back of a young man kneeling at my side. Her voice, never musical I should suppose, was now gratingly harsh, and pitched on a particularly high key, so that the volleys of objurgations and curses with which she interlarded her blows fell on the ear like rapid discharges of fire-crackers. A moment's thought explained the character of this unexpected episode in our services, and, as all the congregation remained quietly kneeling, I determined to continue my prayer notwithstanding this unwelcome disturbance. The execution of this purpose was more difficult than I had anticipated. The woman was in a towering passion, her arms and tongue moving with astonishing velocity, and, in self-defense, I found myself compelled to lead the devotions of the sanctuary in an elevation of tone and a prolixity of address quite unusual with me. The storm, however, gradually subsided. Finding that the meeting was going forward in spite of her disorderly proceedings, the woman began to restrain herself, and the young man, acting on the advice of the brethren near him, arose from his knees and accompanied her from the place. After our exercises were over the brethren gave the following explanation of the disturbance: The woman was the mother of the young man she thus publicly chastised. The son had become interested in Christianity, and began to attend our meetings. His mother opposed him, and threatened to beat him if he did not change his course. On the Sunday preceding the above occurrence the mother had dragged him out of the prayer-meeting and gave public notice of her intention to beat him if he ever dared again to disobey her commands on this subject. Greatly to the surprise of the brethren the young man appeared in the congregation on the present occasion, and hence the scene that ensued. Shortly after this I left China, and have not yet learned the final issue in the case, but hope and pray that the young man may persevere in his desire to become a Christian.

I was much interested in some remarks made by one of our converts in class-meeting on one occasion. He was speaking of the blessings Christianity confers, and after enumerating a goodly number of its more prominent gifts, he proceeded: "And then, brethren, in addition to all these, Christianity institutes a new order of kindred. While a heathen I had parents, brothers, sisters, cousins, and so on, and I never thought of even caring for any one beyond these; but since becoming a Christian I really love every person in the world who believes on the Lord Jesus Christ. This is a new bond which attaches me to the entire Church of Christ, and I now love Christians of all countries more cordially and thoroughly than I ever did my kindred after the flesh. Indeed, while I was a heathen there was but little if any love between the members of our family; contentions and quarrels never ceased among us. But now all is changed; we live together in peace and harmony, and it is really delightful thus to dwell together in unity of faith and love."

The following conversation passed between a member of our Church in Fuhchau and one of his unconverted neighbors. It may be well for me to state here that in Fuhchau the Chinese are accustomed to assert, with great boldness and persistency, that foreign missionaries bribe the people to embrace Christianity, though they must very well know that the charge is utterly without foundation. Shortly after the conversion of the brother referred to one of his neighbors called to see him, and the following dialogue ensued:

"How much did you get for embracing Christianity?" inquired the neighbor.

"I do not wish to name the sum," replied the convert; "how much do you think it was?"

"I suppose you received at least ten dollars."

"More than that."

"Twenty?"

"More than that."

"Fifty?"

"More than that."

(With eager curiosity) "One hundred?"

"More than that."

(In utter amazement) "Why, how much did you get? pray do tell me!"

"Something more valuable than the bulk of

Kushan in solid gold," (pointing to a mountain of that name some six miles off, and measuring three thousand feet in height.)

"You confound me," exclaimed the excited neighbor; "pray explain your meaning."

"Why I have received this," (holding up a copy of the Bible.) "This is the word of God, and is worth more than all the combined treasures of earth."

Shortly after I entered upon my public labors as a missionary in Fuhchau the following incident occurred, and I give it here to show how the principles of Christianity, when embodied in individual life, may break down the prejudices and win the affections of the heathen. I was preaching in our street chapel from: "Blessed are ye when men shall revile you and and persecute you," etc., (Matt. v, 11;) and I was saying that Christians frequently endured persecution in consequence of their faith in Christ. The Chinese have beautiful theories in ethics and politics. They can depict in glowing colors the superior excellence of virtue; but from these intellectual exercitations they will pass without compunction to the grossest sensual indulgences. They conceive it to be impossible for a man's practice to approximate, in any good degree, his own ideal of excellence. I referred at some length to this discrepancy between theory and practice among the Chinese, and then spoke of Christians as approximating the Bible standard of excellence. As I was presenting this point a man seated near the door arose and, addressing me, said:

"May I interrupt you, sir, for a moment?"

"Certainly," I replied, and then waited to hear what he had to say. Turning to the congregation the man proceeded:

"What the teacher says is true. Christians will endure reproach and persecution. Why, from the first day this teacher came here to live I have taken every suitable occasion to revile and injure him. I have sought to thwart his plans in every possible way, and yet to this hour he has never answered me a harsh word. It seemed, indeed, as though he took pains to treat me kindly. His conduct in this respect has always puzzled me; but what he has just been saying seems to throw light on the subject." Then addressing me, he said: "Will you please tell me whether or not your conduct with reference to myself has been dictated and controlled by the doctrine you have just been explaining?"

"Your surmise is correct," I replied. "Your persistent abuse has often pained me; but for Christ's sake I have endured it, hoping you would see the wickedness of such conduct and abandon it."

"Well," said he, addressing the congregation, "this doctrine is good, and it has a power over the heart of which we are ignorant. There is not a man here who would have borne a tithe of what this teacher has endured from me; now, henceforth, I am this teacher's friend. He is a good man, and we ought to treat him kindly."

It affords me pleasure to state that the man has been true to his promise. Since that day I have never received from him the slightest disrespect. He has shown himself in many ways to be my friend, and on all suitable occasions he never fails to speak a good word for me. I believe he has not yet become a Christian; but it rises before me in the light of a blessed probability that I shall be permitted to lay my hand on his head, and, at a Christian altar, baptize him in the name of the Father, the Son, and the Holy Ghost.

On one occasion I preached a missionary discourse to our native Church in Fuhchau, and endeavored to impress on their minds the duty of contributing according to their ability for the support of the Gospel. When the congregation had been dismissed one of our aged members came forward and took a seat beside me near the pulpit. He was much agitated, and seemed anxious to speak to me. An opportunity was soon given him to do so, and he said:

"I was thinking, while listening to your discourse, of God's great goodness to me. I was advanced in years when the missionaries came to Fuhchau and I had been living in sin all my life. At first I was unwilling to believe the Gospel. I was ashamed to confess Christ before my neighbors; but the Lord graciously enlightened my mind, and through grace I was made willing to accept Jesus Christ as my Saviour. And then here is my wife, also a member of the Church, and there are my sons and their wives, all converted and united with me in Church-fellowship. Such mercies are truly wonderful; and then to think that I have never made any returns to God for his wondrous love!" Here the old man's emotions choked his utterance, and he sobbed aloud, while the tears streamed from his eyes. After gain-ing control over his feelings, he resumed: "I often feel like going out among my countrymen to preach the Gospel, and, indeed, I have started occasionally to visit certain places where I thought I could persuade the people to become Christians; but after walking a short distance my strength would fail, and I had to abandon the effort. I am old and feeble. O if I were only a young man how I should love to go everywhere proclaiming the glorious Gospel! But, alas! this can never be my privilege. I can only stay at home, talk a little to my neighbors, and, by my prayers and contributions, try to aid in advancing this holy cause."

I was much gratified by this incident at the time of its occurrence; and I now remember it with the greater interest, because since I left China (1859) the old gentleman has died in the faith. The following account of his death, from the pen of the Rev. Otis Gibson, a member of our mission in China, will doubtless be acceptable to the reader:

"FUHCHAU, 1860.

"DEAR BROTHER MACLAY: About one o'clock A. M., on Saturday, the 11th of February, 1860, Father Hu Ngieng Seu died in piece. During the last few years of his life, while prostrated by sickness, he seemed much more humble, patient, and submissive than before. You remember that he has always been a source of some anxiety for fear he had not met with a radical change of heart. I am sure you will rejoice to learn that his last days, and especially his death, have left strong grounds for believing that

Father Hu.

he was truly a child of God. He regretted very much that he was not able to come and bid you good-by before you left for America. The first time I saw him after your departure, with a sad countenance, he said: "What are we to do now? We native Christians are too young and too weak to walk alone. Teacher Maclay has left us; you and Teacher Wentworth cannot hold us all up; some of us will fall." I tried to impress upon his mind that Jesus is able and willing to support, to strengthen, and to bless; that it is much better for us to trust in Christ than in man. He seemed thoughtful a moment and then said: 'We must now put our trust all in Christ.'

"I was soon away on a long trip up the river visiting Minchang, Chuikau, Yenping, and Kienning. On my return no one manifested more joy to see me than Father Hu. He said that I was more precious than ever, now that I had been away, and that I must not go away so far for fear bad men might lay violent hands upon me. I often talked with him on the subject of saving faith in Christ. Sometimes with tears he would confess himself so great a sinner that he feared he could never reach heaven. I made it a point to call and see him once a week, and pray for and with him during his confinement to his room. He always seemed very glad to see me, and joined earnestly in prayer. The second day after I was so violently mobbed in the streets I visited Father Hu, and I shall perhaps never forget the reception he gave me. As I was going up stairs the old man got up from his bed, and came with feeble steps (his wife assisting him) to meet me. They both shed tears. Father Hu cried like a child, took hold of me with both hands, and with affecting earnestness thanked the heavenly Father for saving me from the violence of those who had laid snares for my life. Said he: 'It is well that I am sick. Had I not been sick when I heard how the mob abused you I could not have endured it, but would have taken an ax and cut the wicked fellows to pieces.' It was at this time that I asked him if he thought he was ready to die, and he answered: 'My *body* is a miserable wicked thing, and God will not suffer it much longer. My *soul* trusts in Christ, and in him alone, for salvation, and I hope soon I shall be in the heavenly country.'

"The watch-night this year was held at Tienang Tong. Nearly all the Church members were present, and Father Hu was left entirely alone nearly all night. He passed the hours in a rigid self-examination, and the next day, in attendance at a 'Union Prayer-meeting' (Chinese) held in the Ching Sing Tong, he received such a blessing that from that day he seemed a different man. He took less interest in worldly matters, and seemed only interested in the things of God. Brother Iong Mi's letter, I think, alludes to this. On the night of his death Iong Mi and his wife, Sing Mi, Seng Mi, and Kiu Taih were with him. About midnight he asked to be raised up on the bed, and then he called on them to pray, saying that his time had come, that the Saviour was calling him, and that he must go. After prayer they asked him if he had peace of soul. He placed his hand on his breast, and pointing to heaven, said:

'The Saviour does not leave me; the Saviour is with me.' He was laid down on the bed at his own request, and without a struggle or a groan his spirit passed away. His remains were interred in the family vault some four or five miles out from the east gate of the city. Brother Baldwin and myself attended the funeral, and buried the remains of Father Hu in 'sure and certain hope of the resurrection unto eternal life.'

"Father Hu was born and brought up in this city, (Fuhchau.) He had reached the fifty-ninth year of his age. He was the father of eleven children, eight of whom, six sons and two daughters, are now living. The oldest four sons are acceptable members of the Church, and two of them are licensed exhorters. The youngest two boys and the youngest daughter are in the mission schools. It was through Father Hu, then an idolater, that we purchased the lot for building the Ching Sing Tong, (Church of the True God,) and you will remember with some interest that Father Hu dissuaded his neighbors from building a temple which they had commenced next to our church. He told them that the one we had erected was large enough for all purposes, and proposed that they inquire into the doctrines there preached.

"He became interested in the Gospel about 1855, and was baptized in May, 1858. During the most of his life he was connected with the military service of his country, and in 1858 he received from Hienfung, the present emperor of China, an honorary title for services rendered in the imperial cause.

"Yours truly, OTIS GIBSON."

CHAPTER XVII.

INCIDENTS.

In the spring of 1859 we were holding a quarterly meeting in Fuhchau, and on Sunday morning had the usual "love-feast." There was a full attendance of the members at this meeting, and the exercises were interesting and edifying. Toward the close of the services a boy, whose head alone was visible over the top of the pew, arose near the center of the church, and in a clear though tremulous voice said:

"Friends, I am a little boy, and am very ignorant; but I wish to become a Christian, and I desire you all to teach me and pray for me."

The evident sincerity of the little fellow greatly interested me in his case, and at the close of the love-feast I made some inquiries concerning him. Our brethren from the country knew him very well. They said he was about sixteen years of age, that he lived about twelve miles from Fuhchau, and that he had walked all the distance that morning to be present at the love-feast. The brethren then gave the following history of the case, and I place it on record for the edification and encouragement of the Church:

"About four weeks since," said they, "we noticed this boy in our Sunday prayer-meeting at Koi-hung, but we paid no attention to him, supposing he had come merely through idle curiosity. The following Sunday he was again at meeting, and we thought it somewhat strange he should remember both the day and hour of our meeting; still we did not say anything to him. On the third Sunday, to our surprise, he was again at the meeting, and manifested such a hearty interest in the exercises that we entered into conversation with him.

"'Do your parents know you are attending this meeting?' we inquired.

"'I have no parents,' replied the boy.

"'Where then do you live?'

"'O with Mr. ——; he is my guardian.'

"'Well, does Mr. —— know you attend this meeting?'

"'Yes, he knows it.'

"'Is he willing you should attend?'

"'At first he was not, but afterward he changed his mind, and said I might come.'

"'What induced him to change his mind?'

"'I'll tell you how it happened. About a month ago I heard of this meeting, and was very anxious to attend. So one day I said to my guardian: "The people at Koi-hung are learning the new doctrines, and I would like to attend their meetings." He became very angry, and said: "Who has been telling you about these doctrines? Go to your work, and never mention the subject to me again." I went to work feeling very badly, for I thought it would be impossible for me ever to get to your meetings. One day, however, Mr. —— was in a very pleasant humor, and I ventured to approach him again on the subject, assuring him that if he would release me from work on Sundays, I would make up the lost time by working harder all the rest of the week. He scolded me sharply for daring to speak to him again on the subject, and I began to give up all hope of succeeding. But after a while he changed his manner, and spoke to me more kindly. I then repeated to him my proposition about making up the lost time; and after thinking over the matter for a few minutes, he said: "Well, if you are so anxious to hear these new doctrines, you may go on the condition you name; but remember, *you shall have nothing to eat on Sundays!*"'

"'And have you been going without food every Sunday since that time?' we asked with eagerness.

"'Yes,' said the little fellow; 'but I do not regard that as any great hardship.'"

I may add that the boy continued to grow in Christian knowledge and grace, and before I left China he was admitted by baptism to membership in our native Church at Ngu-kang.

Mr. Wong, a young landscape painter in Fuhchau, was an intimate friend of one of our Church members. Both being painters, their business often threw them into each other's society, and a strong attachment sprung up between them. After the conversion of Brother Hu Iong Mi, he felt a great desire for the salvation of Mr. Wong, his cherished friend. He prayed fervently for him, and never failed, when opportunity offered, to urge upon him the claims of

Christianity. It soon became apparent that these pious efforts were producing a salutary impression on Mr. Wong's mind. He began to read the Scripture, and was present frequently at our meetings. Gradually he acquired confidence, and began to speak and pray in our class-meetings. We all felt a lively interest in his case, for he was a young man of excellent character, possessed more than ordinary mental ability, and always evinced a humble, docile spirit. That he could embrace Christianity without encountering opposition, was more than could be expected; and yet no one had formed an adequate conception of the trying ordeal that awaited him.

While he was embracing every opportunity to attend our meetings, and was giving us every evidence of his sincere desire to become a Christian, some persons called to see his mother, and said:

"You must look after that son of yours; he is running into danger."

The old lady was a widow, tenderly attached to this son, and the information communicated by the persons just referred to startled her. "What is wrong!" she exclaimed; "my son has always been industrious and dutiful; what has occurred?"

"He attends the foreign church," they replied, "and it is said he has determined to become a Christian."

"Impossible!" cried the old lady; "it cannot be that my son is about to do such a thing."

When the young man came home his mother thus interrogated him: "Son, it is said you go to hear these foreign doctrines; is the report true?"

"Why, mother," replied the young man, "everybody goes to hear them. The church is on the main street, and when the church door is thrown open and the bell rung all the people go in for a few minutes to see and hear. I too have gone in to listen."

"Is it possible you can listen to the abominable lies uttered by those foreigners?" continued the mother.

"I am quite young yet and cannot understand all that is said; but, mother, what they say seems to be reasonable."

"Don't talk in that way to me," retorted the old lady; "you must cease to hear those foreigners; they are crafty, unprincipled fellows, and you are not able to resist their blandishments. I dare not trust you out of my sight; henceforth you must not cross the threshold of my door to go abroad. Stay here and work, and when you have prepared the pictures I will attend to selling them."

"I shall do as you direct, mother," quietly replied the son.

The old lady kept her son in close confinement, narrowly watching him to see that he did not leave the house. She tried in every way to shake his determination to become a Christian, weeping, scolding, and threatening by turns. It was a terrible trial to the young man; he sought help in prayer; morning, noon, and night he would kneel in his chamber to pray, and at times, in the earnestness of his feelings, the petitions would find expression in audible words. The old lady soon heard sounds proceeding from her son's chamber, and occasionally, as she drew near to listen, the name "Jesus," or the petition, "Lord bless my mother," would fall on her ear. These words troubled her; it made her uneasy to hear in her own house the name Jesus; it filled her with strange fears to have that name ringing in her ears. And then that oft-repeated prayer, "Lord, bless my mother!" it was too much. After enduring it as long as she possibly could, she determined to change her tactics. Calling her son into her presence, she said:

"Son, you must stop this praying."

The young man replied: "Mother, hitherto I have obeyed all your commands, but now, when you tell me to cease praying to God, I dare not obey you."

"But the noise disturbs me," continued the old lady; "I cannot stay in the house with you."

"Mother," replied the young man, "I did not know I prayed so loudly. Hereafter I will pray in a whisper, so that you need not be disturbed."

"You shall never pray in my house again," sternly responded the old lady. "If you continue to pray you must leave the house."

"Mother," said the young man, "I cannot cease to pray."

"Leave my house then this moment," exclaimed the mother. "I disown you forever as my child. Never again enter this house; and when I die dare not to join with the family in celebrating my funeral obsequies."

A mother's malediction is one of the direst calamities that can befall a Chinese; but in the present instance the terrible anathema failed to move this humble, patient young man. Driven from his own home he came directly to his friend, Brother Iong Mi, and asked permission to live and labor with him in his shop. The request was at once granted; and now, in the congenial society of his friend, within reach of sanctuary privileges, and surrounded by our Church members, he seemed to be perfectly happy. The Bible was his constant companion, and his Christian experience developed rapidly.

After spending some time in this manner, he came to me one day in great perplexity, saying:

"My mother sends for me, and I understand they have determined to get me into their power and then beat or kill me; what shall I do?"

It was a solemn moment. O how profoundly I felt the need of heavenly wisdom to direct us in that trying emergency. "Follow the teachings of the Bible," I replied. "The fifth commandment says: 'Honor thy father and thy mother;' and then the Lord Jesus has said: 'He that loveth father or mother more than me is not worthy of me.' Were I in your place I would go, but maintain my integrity at all hazards."

It was a trying moment for the young man. A fierce struggle was going on within his bosom, and for a time it seemed as though he could not decide the question. The decision, however, was made; and never shall I forget the solemnity of his manner as he deliberately uttered the words, "I'll go; pray for me!" He went, and with many prayers for his deliverance we awaited the result.

The next day he returned with a joyful countenance, saying:

"It is all right; there was no trouble at all. When I reached home mother was sitting in her chair waiting for me. She said: 'I have sent for you to ask you for the last time whether or not you will abandon your purpose to become a Christian.' I replied: 'Mother, I have forsaken the evil and am following the good; how can I now abandon the good and turn again to the evil?' 'You are fully determined then,' said mother, 'to become a Christian?' I felt that my answer to this question would decide my fate, and raising my heart in prayer to God for grace to meet even death itself, I ventured to reply: 'Mother, I have so determined.' She looked at me steadily for a minute, and then said: 'If I cannot change your determination I shall change mine. I shall not oppose you any further. You are at liberty to become a Christian, and I wish you to live with me as formerly.' These remarks were so utterly unexpected that my emotions completely overpowered me, and falling on my knees I poured out my grateful acknowledgements to God for this wonderful deliverance. And now I wish to be baptized and received into the Church, and I wish you all to pray for my mother's conversion."

On the following communion Sabbath he was admitted to baptism, and now he is a licensed exhorter in our Church at Fuhchau. Since my return to the United States I have received a letter from him, of which the following translation is here presented to the reader:

"To Rev. R. S. Maclay:

"My Dear Sir,—I desire that you will be pleased to give thanks for me to our heavenly Father for all his goodness to me, as I am sure my one mouth cannot sufficiently praise him for his mercies. I know, indeed, that you do most certainly offer thanksgiving on my behalf, and that you do pray for all the members of our Church in China. I am assured also that it was God who guided you to China and enabled you to endure so much persecution and reproach without ever once leaving China or ceasing to compassionate the Chinese, during a period of nearly thirteen years. It was not by your own strength that you accomplished all this; surely it was in the strength of God you did it. Before there were any Christian converts in Fuhchau, with whom did you associate? Truly it must have been with the Saviour, Jesus Christ; otherwise you could not have passed the time. When I think of these things I give thanks to God for his great grace toward you. I pray you constantly to cherish the recollection of these mercies, and never suffer Satan to lead you astray. In former years also our heavenly Father has crowned your life with many blessings; but you can yourself readily understand these matters. Our heavenly Father regards you as gold, which, after a refining process of thirteen years, now exhibits the unclouded luster; and most assuredly he will use you as a righteous instrument for the accomplishment of his purposes. Remember, I beseech you, how the Lord has purified and honored you, and do not fail to come back to China. All the brethren desire this;

we long for you as the parched mouth longs for the grateful tea. In all our thoughts we desire this one thing, that the Holy Spirit may quickly lead you back to China.

"We pray God to preserve you and your family while on the ocean, and to grant that both your body and soul may have health. I believe God will give you great joy on your voyage to America; and the Saviour says: 'Your joy no man taketh from you.' This joy, granted you by the Lord, you will communicate to all the brethren and sisters of the Church in America; and then I am sure your hearts will overflow with joy, and God will be glorified.

"During the past nine weeks Satan has tried to take away my charity, my faith, and my love for God. He has sought to carry on his devices in my heart; but, thank God! the Saviour has cast him out and driven him from me. I praise the Lord because he answers my prayers. For some time past I have desired to preach the Gospel, but supposed I should not be able to do it, as my mother was unwilling. When thinking over the matter a great mountain seemed to rise before me, and I was able to enjoy peace of mind only because I supposed it was not the will of God that I should preach. About a month since, however, my mind became greatly troubled, and I was unable to decide upon the matter. At one time I felt the greatest compassion for men, and then I would feel that if I refused to go and preach the Gospel I never could see the Saviour in heaven. But still I asked myself, 'How can I climb this great mountain?' and Satan suggested that it was far better for me to travel on a level road. Thank God, the Holy Spirit enlightened my mind by suggesting: 'Do you not believe that with God all things are possible? Doth not the Scripture say, "He that loveth father or mother more than me is not worthy of me;" also, "Strait is the gate and narrow is the way?" Where then is the level and easy road for you to walk on?' At that moment, through the mercy of God, I remembered that formerly, when I thought of becoming a Christian, then also there seemed to be a high mountain in my way, but the Saviour mercifully aided me in climbing it. These thoughts induced me to cry to the Saviour for assistance in my present distress, and, blessed be his name! he heard and delivered me. I was a condemned criminal, exposed to the punishment of hell, and had I been sent to that place of torment the sentence would have been just. But the Saviour did not seal my guilt; he gave me grace to repent, granted me, through faith, a confident hope of eternal life, changed all my purposes, and opened the eyes of my understanding, so that I could dig for the hidden pearls and search in the Scriptures for the words of life. Truly the Saviour has loved me with an unspeakable love in enabling me to become a disciple; and how can we express that love wherewith he hath loved the world! Please pray for me that I may not be an unprofitable servant. And may I trouble you to present my Christian salutations to the bishops, pastors, members, and friends of the Church in America? May the peace of the triune God, Father, Son, and Holy Ghost, be with your body and spirit!

"As I close this letter I ask myself, When shall I see you? Will it be on earth or in heaven? Will you first enter the heavenly country, or shall I first touch its shore? The Lord knoweth. While yet in the flesh, let me urge you to return soon to China. I am very thankful for this privilege of writing to you, and beg you will send me a letter as soon as possible. From your unworthy pupil,

"WONG KIU TAIH."

My latest advices from the Fuhchau mission represent Brother Wong Kiu Taih as a most devoted and exemplary Christian; and in a letter I recently received from the Rev. Otis Gibson of that mission, he says: "We have just granted exhorter's license to Brother Wong Kiu Taih. When he received the license he went directly home, disposed of his business, supplied himself with Christian books and tracts, and at once commenced itinerating through the country, preaching the Gospel and distributing the books." Will not all who read these pages unite in fervent prayer to God in behalf of this most interesting and promising Chinese Christian?

After the conversion of Brother Hu Po Mi, one of our early converts, he was very diligent in talking to his neighbors about the Gospel. One of the persons whom he most frequently visited was a basket-maker, and Brother Hu cherished the hope that he would become a disciple. In this hope, however, he was disappointed; the man could not think of meeting the opposition which a profession of Christianity would inevitably excite against him. But there was a young apprentice in the shop, who had quietly listened to all that had been said, and upon whose mind Brother Hu's exhortations had produced a profound impression. This young man, under the gracious influences of the Holy Spirit, determined to become a Christian. When Brother Hu next visited the shop, there was only the young apprentice present, and he embraced the opportunity to make known his determination to Brother Hu. It was a most grateful surprise to Brother Hu to hear the young man speak in this way, and after conversing on the subject of Christianity for some time they engaged in prayer. When they rose from their knees the young man said: "I feel very happy; my heart is as light as a feather; I never before felt as I do now. May I not at once be baptized and become a Christian?" Brother Hu was puzzled by the sudden change that had come over the young man, and not wishing to assume any further responsibility as his spiritual instructor, advised him to wait till some of the missionaries could converse with him. Next morning Brother Hu was awaked by a loud rap at his door, and on opening it there stood the young apprentice. "I have come to see you," he said, "about my becoming a Christian. Here is my ancestral tablet; I went home for it last night, and now I wish you to take charge of it." They then conversed and prayed together, and Brother Hu was astonished at the fluency and intelligence of the young man's prayer. After breakfast Brother Hu came to see me on the subject, and after giving me a history of the case, we at once went to see the young man. He gave us a full account of his experience, and I examined him closely, thinking it possible there might be some mistake either in his language or in my interpretation of it. The result of the examination was entirely satisfactory, and I felt assured that the young man had really experienced a change of heart. We then engaged in prayer, each one leading in turn, and it was delightful to notice the pertinency and fervor of our young brother's petitions when he led in prayer. He was entirely illiterate, being unable to read even his own name, and it was surprising now to notice the vigor of his thoughts and the appropriateness of his language. We all felt a deep interest in the young man, and assisted him in making arrangements with his employer by which he was able to attend public worship and rest on the Sabbath. After passing through a course of Christian instruction, he was admitted to baptism and membership in our Mission Church in Fuhchau. When his friends learned that he had become a Christian they made a violent assault upon him, charging him with multifarious crimes and misdemeanors, demanding from him a recantation of his Christian vows, or large subsidies of money in the way of bribes, and proceeding even to blows in their efforts to coerce him. The young disciple bore himself with meekness and dignity through the storm, and steadily refused in any way to compromise his Christian character. His employer, apprehensive of trouble, dismissed him from his service, and thus our young brother, without home or employment, was thrown out upon the world. Hearing of his trouble, the Rev. Mr. Gibson called to see him, and offered him a place in our mission boarding-school; and he remained there, learning to read, until he succeeded in making satisfactory arrangements for going into business on his own account.

CHAPTER XVIII.

CHINA AS A MISSION FIELD.

We now notice the opening up of China to Christianity and Western commerce by the provisions of the treaties recently formed at Tientsin. Before proceeding to state the provisions of the new treaties with reference to Christianity and foreign intercourse, let us glance at the previous attitude of the Chinese government on these points.

Among the "fundamental laws" of China there is one section (162d) headed, "Wizards, Witches, and all Superstitions, prohibited." Under the Emperor Kiaking, A. D. 1814, a sixth clause was prepared under this section with reference to Christianity. The clause was modified in 1821, and printed in 1826, by the late emperor, Taukwang. We quote part of this clause. It reads: "People of the Western Ocean, [Europeans or Portuguese,] should they propagate in the country the religion of heaven's Lord, [name given to Christianity by the Romanists,] or clandestinely print books, or collect congregations to be preached to, and thereby deceive many people, or should any Tartars or Chinese, in their turn, propagate the doctrines and clandestinely give names, (as in baptism,) inflaming and misleading many, if proved by authentic testimony, the head or leader shall be sentenced to immediate death by strangulation; he who propagates the religion, inflaming and deceiving the people, if the number be not large, and no names be given, shall be sentenced to strangulation after a period of imprisonment. Those who are merely hearers or followers of the doctrine, if they will not repent and recant, shall be transported to the Mohammedan cities (in Turkistan) and given to be slaves to the beys and other powerful Mohammedans who are able to coerce them. . . . All civil and military officers who may fail to detect Europeans clandestinely residing in the country within their jurisdiction, and propagating their religion, thereby deceiving the multitude, shall be delivered over to the Supreme Board and be subjected to a court of inquiry." This stringent prohibition was evidently directed against Romanism. It was hoped that the Chinese government would discriminate between Protestantism and Romanism; and in A. D. 1835–6 several voyages were made along the coast of China by Protestant missionaries, and Christian books were given to the Chinese, who were eager to receive them. These voyages aroused the attention of the local authorities, and representations on the subject were sent to Pekin from Canton. The emperor (Taukwang) immediately sent down an edict, commanding the governor of Canton to examine into the matter secretly and rigorously; and also to ascertain who were the intruders on the coast, and who were the "traitorous natives in Canton who had supplied them with books." The high authorities at Canton at once issued a proclamation on the subject. They first referred to the existing laws against Christianity, and to certain foreigners who in time past had clandestinely entered the country, and who, having been apprehended, were tried and either strangled or expelled; then they referred to the ships which, a few months before, had suddenly appeared in the waters of those provinces bordering on the coast distributing books, "to persuade men to believe in the Lord Jesus;" and after stating that half a year would be allowed any booksellers or others, who had received such publications, to deliver them up to the magistrates, thereby saving themselves from punishment for past crimes, they concluded their edict by warning the people to reject "corrupt doctrines," and to follow the ways of the ancient kings. These edicts sufficiently indicated the animus of the Chinese government with regard to all forms of Christianity.

The treaties formed with China in 1843–4 by England, France, and the United States, made no allusion to Christianity or Christian missions. In 1844 the French embassador, M. Lagrene, brought to the notice of Keying, Chinese Imperial Commissioner at Canton, the persecutions to which Chinese converts to Romanism were subjected in consequence of their faith. Keying memorialized the emperor on the subject, praying that "henceforth all natives and foreigners without distinction who learn and practice the religion of the Lord of heaven, and do not excite trouble by improper conduct, to be exempted from criminality;" adding, however, "as to those of the French, and other foreign nations who practice this religion, let them only be permitted to build churches at the five ports opened to commercial intercourse. They must not presume to enter the country to propogate their religion. Should any act in opposition, turn their backs upon the treaties, and rashly overstep the boundaries, the local officers will at once seize and deliver them to their respective consuls for restraint and correction. Capital punishment is not to be rashly inflicted, in order that the exercise of gentleness may be displayed." This memorial was approved by the emperor, and its publication was hailed with great satisfaction by the friends of Christian missions. A more careful examination of the memorial, however, dampened this joy, and the course of subsequent events showed but too plainly that the antichristian policy of the Chinese government was not abandoned. The influence of this so-called "Toleration Edict" was scarcely perceptible, and all the previous prohibitory laws on the subject remained, apparently, in full force.

We now introduce a translation, by a competent hand, of the articles referring to Christianity in the treaties recently formed at Tientsin. It may be well at this point to state that each of the four treaties contains an article or clause stipulating that the subjects or citizens of its government shall receive all the privileges granted by China to any other nation; thus any advantages granted to England or France accrue equally to Russia and the United States, and *vice versa*. The twenty-ninth article of the American treaty reads: "The principles of the Christian religion, as professed by the Protestant and Roman Catholic Churches, are recognized as teaching men to do good, and to do to others as they would have others do to them. Hereafter those who quietly profess and teach these doctrines shall not be molested or persecuted on account of their faith. Any person, whether citizen of the United States, or Chinese convert, who, according to these tenets, peaceably teaches and practices the principles of Christianity, shall in no case be interfered with or molested." Article eighth of the English treaty reads: "The Christian religion, as professed by Protestants and Roman Catholics, teaches the practice of virtue, and the treatment of others as ourselves. Henceforth all teachers and professors of it shall, one and all, be protected. No one of them peaceably following his calling, and not offending against the laws, shall in the least be oppressed or hindered by the Chinese authorities." Article thirteenth of the French treaty reads: "The Christian religion, having for its essential object to lead men to virtue, the members of all Christian bodies [communions] shall enjoy full security for their persons, their property, and the free exercise of their religious worship; and entire protection shall be given to missionaries who peacefully enter the country, furnished with passports such as are described in article eight. No obstacles shall be interposed by the Chinese authorities to the recognized right of any person in China to embrace Christianity if he pleases, and to obey its requirements without being subject on that account to any penalty. Whatever has been heretofore written, proclaimed, or published in China, by order of government, against the Christian faith, is wholly abrogated and nullified in all the provinces of the empire." Article eighth of the Russian treaty says: "The Chinese government, recognizing the truth that the doctrines of Christianity promote the establishment of good order and peace among mankind, promises not to persecute its subjects who may wish to follow the requirements of this faith: they shall enjoy the same protection granted to those who profess other forms of religion tolerated in the empire. The Chinese government, believing that Christian missionaries are good men, who seek no material advantages for themselves, hereby permits them to propagate the doctrines of Christianity among its subjects, and allows them to pass everywhere in the country. A fixed number of missionaries passing through the cities or open ports shall be furnished with passports signed by the Russian authorities."

Reference has been made to the passport system under which foreigners are now permitted to travel or reside in the interior of the country: I now present a translation of the ninth article of the English treaty on this subject, merely reminding the reader that its provisions apply equally to the other treaty powers. The article reads:

"British subjects are allowed to proceed to every place in the interior with passports, either for amusement or to trade. The passports will be issued by their consuls and stamped by the local authorities. When passing through any locality, if they are desired to produce it they must hand it up for inspection. If it is correct they will be allowed to go on.

There must be no obstruction to their hiring vessels or people to carry their merchandise or baggage. If they have no passport, or if that they have is irregular, or if they commit any offense against the law, they are to be sent to the consul nearest at hand for punishment. On their way to him they may be kept in custody, but must not be ill treated. Persons going out on excursions from the ports open to trade, so long as they are within one hundred *le* for a period of not more than five days, need not apply for a passport. Seamen and persons belonging to ships do not come under this rule. The local mandarins and the consuls will together draw up regulations for the purpose of keeping them in proper order. As to Nankin and other places which are rebel positions, on the recapture of these passports shall be given to them."

The preceding extracts indicate clearly and definitely the present attitude of the Chinese government with reference to Christianity and foreign intercourse. Let us refer to a few points:

1. There stands the imperial declaration that Christianity is good, that it inculcates the principles of virtue, that it promotes good order and peace among men, teaching them to do to others as they would have others do to them.

2. There is the imperial authorization to every Chinese in the empire to follow the dictates of his own judgment with regard to embracing Christianity.

3. There stands recorded the imperial pledge that no Chinese convert to Christianity shall be subjected to any persecution for his faith.

4. There is the imperial authorization to every

discreet foreigner, whether missionary or merchant, under the passport system, to enter the interior of the country either for trade or the preaching of the Gospel.

5. And there stands the solemn revocation, by imperial authority, of all those persecuting edicts which in the past have been fulminated against Christianity, native Christians, and foreign missionaries.

Such, we believe, is the present auspicious attitude of the Chinese government with regard to the important questions before us, and our view is supported by the highest authorities both native and foreign. The change is truly wonderful, and we incline to believe it will be permanent. However tardy the Chinese government may have been in recognizing the grave crisis that had arisen in its affairs, and however reluctant it may have been to accede to the reasonable demands of the allies, it now evidently begins to appreciate its true position, and is disposed to execute in good faith the provisions of the recent treaties. It is highly probable, indeed, that the Chinese government may hereafter seek to evade or misconstrue the clear purport of some provisions contained in the treaties, and possibly western nations may be compelled to support their rights by force; but we conceive it impossible for it now to retrace its steps or annul its recent action. Progress is inevitable; and we believe that China is now thrown open fairly, fully, and, we hope, finally, to Christianity and foreign intercourse.

We here present some of the aspects of China as a

mission field. The discussion of this topic brings us upon ground that cannot fail to interest all classes of readers.

The first point we notice is the entire absence, at the present day, of all healthy progress in the religious systems, literature, and civilization of the Chinese. Religious faith can scarcely be predicated of the Chinese in our day. Their present position on this subject differs widely and sadly from what we have supposed it was in the period of their early history. We have witnessed the utter materialization of their ancient religious faith; and the vagaries of Tauism and Budhism have so stultified and bewildered their moral sense, that now the Chinese apparently refuse to think at all upon the subject. A stoical indifference with regard to this vital question pervades all classes of society; indeed, the man who manifests any serious concern about it is regarded by his neighbors as a knave or a fool. Their religious practices are multifarious, and though frequently discordant and contradictory, they still exert great influence over nearly all classes of society. And yet the religious systems of China seem to be utterly incapable of inspiring the national mind with any definite aim, any concentration of energy or enthusiasm of faith. They contain no great idea, the development of which must stir the heart and mould the character of the nation; no popular divinity, whose fancied utterances sway the masses and control the public sentiment; no symbol of faith, deviation from which is at once sacrilege and treason. Their priests are fired by no missionary zeal; no new phases of idolatry are presented; no aggressive measures are devised for the propagation of their tenets; and all sects seem the victims of a deep and fatal atrophy, which already foreshadows their utter abnegation. It is possible, we think, to assign the causes that have produced this fearful apathy and infidelity with regard to religious subjects. The materializing philosophy, to which we have already referred, has fossilized the ancient Chinese faith. Tauism has forfeited all claims to public respect by its low jugglery and buffoonery; while the tenets of Budhism, by clashing with some of the noblest hereditary instincts of the Chinese character, have ever failed in China to receive hearty approval or belief.

Chinese literature exhibits similar symptoms of exhaustion. Centuries ago it reached the zenith of its excellence. Confucius, Mencius, Ma Twan Sin, Chu Hi, and others have successively impressed and enriched it by their powerful genius; but within the last six hundred years we search in vain for the names of profound scholars or original thinkers. The perfection of education now consists in a passionless imitation of the ancient masters; to-day every student in China is conning not merely the same ideas, but the very words that were written some two thousand years ago. The national mind is ever looking backward for its maxims, principles, and models. Its millennium is in the past, and each successive year is but drifting it farther away from those pure intellections and rapt harmonies. Occasionally, indeed, we meet with a Chinese scholar who seems desirous of increasing his stock of ideas, or find a modern work which gives evidence of an inquiring mind; but these instances are very rare, and serve only to indicate and intensify our conception of the utter stagnation of independent, joyous thought in Chinese literature. This comparative barrenness of the national intellect cannot be attributed to any fancied opposition of the present (Tartar) dynasty to the development of native genius. It is true, indeed, that some of the earlier Tartar emperors were inclined to undervalue, and even sought to destroy the admirable system of popular education that prevails in China, but under Kienlung this opposition was abandoned. Besides, it will appear on examination that during the period of this dynasty the native mind has been more active than it was during the Ming dynasty, which immediately preceded it. The causes of this intellectual sterility are radical and permanent. The Chinese mind has exhausted itself on the narrow range of subjects to which it has been confined. Deprived of the inspiration which springs from communion with the truths of revelation, and shut off from the stimulating influences of Western literature, the intellect of China has depleted itself by a blind, servile imitativeness, and by finical dissertations on topics destitute alike of any broad, genial basis of truth, and of any well-defined relations to any of the great practical questions of the day.

The civilization of China, under existing influences, is hopelessly effete. It has exhausted its inherent powers of progress. From the earliest period of authentic Chinese history it has possessed all the essential features of its present state; scarcely any change even has passed upon it for centuries. At this day the soil is plowed, the seed sown, the harvest gathered, the mulberry and silk-worm cultivated, the cloth woven, the China-ware prepared, the tea cured, society controlled, the state governed, the arts of handicraft practiced, and all the sources of wealth husbanded as they were two thousand years ago. It seems incredible that the civilization of any people should remain stationary at such an advanced state through so many centuries, but the fact is substantiated by the clearest historic evidence. One remembers how the civilization of all other ancient nations has culminated, and sunk into luxury, licentiousness, and barbarism. What are those conservative elements which have kept Chinese civilization steadily up to its present standard? The Christian need not pause for a reply. He finds such elements in the influences of those divine truths underlying the ancient faith of China, which in all ages have produced a powerful and highly conservative effect in the formation of the national mind. The thorough education of the Chinese, in the very reasonable teachings of their ancient classics, has done much to save them from utter demoralization under the vitiating influences of Tauism and Budhism. Even their respect for parents, heathenish as it has become, may have contributed toward securing to them "the length of days" in "the land given them by the Almighty," which is promised to those who obey the fifth commandment of our decalogue.

The second point we notice is that China now

gives the most convincing evidence of being on the eve of great changes. What will be the nature of these changes we do not now stop to inquire; it is sufficient for our present purpose to indicate and illustrate the fact to which we have referred. We confess to a hearty interest in this subject, though we fancy ourselves free from any untoward bias, or the swaying influence of any preconceived theory on the subject. No intelligent observer can look on the present aspect of affairs in China without noticing her unprecedented and critical position. It requires no magician to cast her horoscope, and detect in its struggling and conflicting elements the inception and proximate development of strange events. Let us notice some of these indications.

First, we refer to the fact that among all intelligent and thoughtful Chinese with whom we come in contact, there exists an almost unanimous conviction or presentiment that a great crisis in their national affairs is at hand. They state that every great change in their past history has been heralded by certain signs or omens, and that in the times through which we are now passing, both the heavens and the earth are giving out unequivocal indications of approaching great events. It is true, doubtless, that most if not all of these supposed omens are imaginary or fictitious, and it would be impossible to discover any legitimate connection between them and the results anticipated by the Chinese; still the fact of such a widely spread presentiment on the subject carries with it considerable force, even though we may explain away much of the evidence adduced in its support. History furnishes many instances of similar presentiments that have been fulfilled, and the circumstances of the present case forcibly remind us of that expectation which prevailed throughout the world when, "in the fullness of time," the Saviour was born.

Secondly, we may refer to the palpable weakness of the present government of China. We hope not to be misunderstood in introducing this topic. It is not our design to decry the present government of that great country; its abrogation is not at all essential to our line of argument. Its form is probably better suited to the character of the Chinese than any other that could be devised, and it is altogether unlikely that any succeeding dynasty would essentially modify it. The reigning dynasty is, perhaps, as liberal and enlightened as we could rationally expect. We believe foreign diplomatists find, on personal acquaintance, that the Tartar portion of the officers of China are less bigoted and arbitrary than those who are of Chinese origin. After all, however, the fact remains that hitherto the policy of the present dynasty has been antiforeign and antichristian; and it is entirely probable that the present emperor, if he had the power, would gladly carry out this exclusive policy to the furthest limit. Traditionally identified with such a policy, and persistently refusing to receive truthful information concerning other parts of the world, it is matter for gratulation that his power is unequal to his will, and that a consciousness of weakness constrains him now to adopt a line of policy for which, hitherto, justice and humanity have pleaded in vain. Poverty and official corruption are the powerful agencies operating to exhaust the resources of the present dynasty. It is saddening to observe the shifts to which the government is now driven to replenish its exchequer. Official rank and titles which, according to every high national instinct of the Chinese, had previously been conferred only on the successful candidates at the literary examinations, are now publicly sold to the highest bidder; and by all parties among the people gold is now considered more potent than brains in procuring these coveted honors. The national currency has been tampered with and depreciated until it would seem that political quackery had exhausted itself on the subject. Opium, which was long on the list of contraband articles, and against the use of which by its subjects all the power and influence of the government were ostensibly directed, is now placed on the list of imports, and from it the government expects to derive a large revenue. Official corruption prevails to a frightful extent. We are in possessiou of undoubted facts on this point, which, to those unacquainted with Chinese politics, would appear utterly incredible. Office is now sought as the only avenue to certain wealth. All departments of business are so oppressed by the extortions of government officials that it is almost useless for any private person to lay up money. His property is not safe for an hour; it is only the man of official rank who can revel in indolence and luxury, undisturbed by any fears of criminal charges and interminable processes of litigation.

Thirdly, we adduce the influence of the celebrated Tai Ping rebellion. Our train of thought in this paragraph is not predicated on the supposed triumph of this rebellion; so far, indeed, as our present purpose is concerned, it is about the same to us whether the movement succeeds or fails. Nor is it predicated on the supposed genuine conversion of the insurgents to Christianity. Even yielding this point, we still have sufficient for our present design. Among other prominent facts relating to this movement, we hold the following to be indisputable: About ten years ago a party of Chinese reformers in the Kwangsi province came into violent collision with the government authorities. Within a year from their first battle the forces of these reformers or insurgents had overrun most of the southern provinces of China, and in 1853 they made their triumphant entry into Nankin, where they established the capital of their *soi-disant* empire. During the past ten years they have waged an incessant though desultory warfare against the reigning dynasty of China, and in their fortifications at Nankin have, to the present hour, effectually held at bay the entire power of the government. They profess to believe the cardinal doctrines of the Bible, and to regulate their lives according to its precepts; have printed and circulated those portions of the sacred Scriptures in their possession, proclaim the existence of the triune God, denounce all forms of idolatry, demolish heathen temples, destroy idols, and, according to their imperfect notions on the subject, seek to establish the worship of the one living and true God. These are some of the great and significant facts presented by this most remarkable movement, and their influence among the

Chinese can never be fully counteracted by the hypocrisy, fanaticism, rapine, and bloodshed which, in too many instances, have attended and disgraced its career.

What will be the ultimate issue of this great struggle it is impossible now to foretell; we may, however, conceive somewhat adequately of the influence it must exert on the Chinese. The astonishing success of the insurgents has filled the nation with surprise, and compels the reigning dynasty to a restatement of its assumed divine right to govern the eighteen provinces of China. The respective claims of the reigning dynasty and of the insurgent chief to such high authority, are now freely discussed in the forum of public opinion; it is considered, indeed, a drawn game, which only the success of one of the parties can decide. In a religious aspect the influence of this movement must be profound and far-reaching. Such an authoritative assertion of their ancient, monotheistic faith, such an overwhelming judgment against idolatry, the Chinese never before witnessed.

The history of the world scarcely furnishes a parallel to the iconoclastic enthusiasm of the insurgents. The knowledge of their principles circulates everywhere, and the empire resounds with the reports of their prowess. China never before looked on such a Cromwellian chief, never listened to the heavy tread of such "ironsides." In no other land has Christianity ever had such a precursor, in no age has the Saviour ever had such a "John the Baptist."

Lastly, in this connection, we notice the influence of western diplomacy in the affairs of China. The days of China's fancied omnipotence are numbered. No dash of the vermilion pencil can now confine "outside barbarians" to their frozen latitudes in the "Northwestern ocean," and withhold from them the luxuries and "civilizing influences" of the "middle kingdom." No more flaming dispatches shall be forwarded to Pekin by bombastic governors or vaporing generals, delighting the imperial heart with poetical descriptions of "the blowing up of foreign ships," "the annihilation of foreign armies," "driving foreigners into the sea," "foreigners humbly supplicating the imperial clemency," and similar forms of speech. China is no longer isolated; no longer the *Ultima Thule* of nations. The religion, civilization, and commerce of modern times have all passed "the pillars of Hercules;" and henceforth, in the broad East also, are to develop their vast resources. It matters little who may now, or hereafter, fill the throne of China; the programme of his foreign policy is marked out for him by a power whose influence he cannot eliminate, whose utterances he may not disregard. During the past twenty years the influence of western governments has steadily and rapidly advanced in China. It requires no prophetic vision to foresee the changes which the introduction of this element will soon produce in the affairs of this vast empire.

We now briefly refer to the present appreciable results of Protestant missionary efforts for the evangelization of the Chinese. Preliminary thereto we present a brief historic *résumé* of the prominent facts bearing on the subject.

The Rev. Robert Morrison, D. D., the first Protestant missionary to the Chinese, arrived at Canton in 1807, but so bitter was the hostility of the Chinese government to Christianity that it was impossible for him to prosecute his labors as a missionary. To maintain any footing at all in China he was compelled to accept the office of translator to the East India Company in China, and to his great grief and disappointment he was never permitted to engage publicly in the work of preaching the Gospel to the Chinese. The utmost he was able to accomplish in this direction was a regular private service, in his own apartments, with his servants and a few others. Thus providentially shut up to the retirement of his study, he devoted his time and energies to the preparation of his celebrated dictionary of the Chinese language, to the translation of the Bible into Chinese, and to the prosecution of such other labors as might aid in forwarding the great cause so dear to his heart.

During the interim between Dr. Morrison's arrival in China and 1830, all Protestant efforts for the conversion of the Chinese were carried on at stations among the islands of the Malayan Archipelago, whither the Chinese had emigrated. The most important of these stations were at Malacca, Batavia, Penang, Rhio, Borneo, and Singapore, where the Chinese had colonized in large numbers. These missions were initiated in 1815 by the Rev. William Milne, D. D., who, under the auspices of the London Missionary Society, established a mission to the Chinese at Malacca. Considered in itself, the field thus entered was most difficult and unpromising, but at the time it was the best position the Protestant Churches could obtain; and in the hope that it would finally become a point of entrance to China, they entered on the work with a courage and perseverance rarely if ever surpassed in the history of missions. Honor to the heroic spirits who, under such disadvantages and against such fearful odds, commenced the glorious struggle with the heathenism of China!

Dr. Medhurst, in 1837, gives the following summary of their labors: "Since the commencement of their missions they have translated the Holy Scriptures, and printed 2,000 complete Bibles in two sizes, 10,000 Testaments, and 30,000 separate books, and upward of half a million of tracts, in Chinese; besides 4,000 Testaments and 150,000 tracts, in the languages of of the Malayan Archipelago, making about twenty millions of printed pages. About 10,000 scholars have passed through the mission schools; nearly one hundred persons have been baptized, and several native preachers have been raised up, one of whom has proclaimed the Gospel to his countrymen and endured persecution for Jesus's sake."

Dr. Williams, in 1848, says: "Since this [the foregoing extract] was written, the number of pages printed and circulated has been more than doubled; the number of scholars taught has increased to 12,000, and preaching has been proportionably attended to, while a few more have been baptized." Shortly after the close of the war between China and England (1843) these missions were transferred to China.

The first Protestant mission to the Chinese, on the territory of China, was commenced at Canton in 1830 by the Rev. E. C. Bridgman, D.D., under the auspices of the American Board of Commissioners for Foreign Missions. The government of China, however, continued its hostility to the Christian religion, and so persistently did it trammel and thwart the mission, in all its plans for aggressive action, that it was not till 1844 the mission was fairly established. During the period from 1844 to the present time (1859) Protestant missions have been established, and carried forward at Hong Kong and the five open ports of China. The entire number of Protestant missionaries to the Chinese is 213, of whom 69 retired from the work, 32 labored only in the archipelago; 21 labored partly in the archipelago, partly in China, and the others entered directly on the work in China. At present there are 110 Protestant missionaries to the Chinese, either in China or absent expecting soon to return to their field of labor. Thirty nine have died in connection with the work.

The foregoing statement, meager as it is, may perhaps indicate the embarrassments and difficulties against which Protestant missionaries to the Chinese have contended from the commencement of their operations to the present time. And when we bear in mind the vastness of the field, both in geographical area and amount of population, the labor necessary to acquire the general language and local dialects of the empire, and the deeply rooted superstitions of the Chinese, we shall be ready to accept anything short of utter discomfiture and defeat as a positive success in the prosecution of this work. We hope, however, to show that the results, already apparent, are of the most substantial and cheering character; that they amply compensate the Church for all her past efforts, and furnish sure promise of a glorious consummation in the future.

First, we notice that, with regard to the ultimate evangelization of China, a great work of preparation has already been accomplished. This has been effected both among the home Churches and in China. At home we observe a rapidly increasing interest on the part of Christians in the spiritual welfare of the Chinese. We have convincing proof of this in the advancing contributions of the churches for the cause of God in China, and in the growing desire on the part of young men to devote themselves to this work. This result is to be attributed mainly, we think, to the published narratives of missionary operations in China, to the correspondence of missionaries with the home societies and Churches, to the books they have published on the subject, to their translations from the original Chinese, and to their public addresses and appeals during occasional visits to their native lands. In China a great work has been done in the preparation of dictionaries, vocabularies, grammars, and other books designed to facilitate the acquisition of the general language and local dialects of the empire. A vast fund of practical wisdom has been accumulated from experience in the field with reference to the conservation of health, the best methods of labor, the regions of country most accessible to missionary labor, the classes of people most likely to listen to the Gospel message, and the best appliances for the promotion of the general cause. Four complete translations of the Old and New Testaments have been made into the general language of China; and many other translations of the New Testament, either in whole or in part, have been made both into the general language and local dialects.

It is impossible to estimate with accuracy the number of Christian books that have been published and distributed in China since 1843. Taking, however, as the basis of our calculation the operations of one society in this department, whose report is now before us, we estimate that during the past seventeen years there have been published annually in China, about twenty millions of pages of Christian books. These books have been sent throughout the empire. Carried by the native merchant and student, they have gone where the foot of the missionary has never trod, and have silently and surely sown the good seed of the kingdom. Schools for the Chinese have been connected with nearly all the Protestant missions at the open ports, and thousands of the youth of China have received in them the rudiments of a Christian education. We do not suppose that all thus educated have or will become Christians, but we must believe the amount of Christian knowledge thus imparted is doing something to prepare the way of the Lord in China. At the open ports, and at Hong Kong, the different missions have erected suitable edifices for churches, chapels, school-houses, and private residences; and when we bear in mind the exigencies of a strange climate, and the fact that for many years to come these open ports will continue to be great centers of missionary operations and interest, we can estimate the value of these appliances in connection with the prosecution of the work.

Secondly, we notice some of the results already obtained. There are now about twenty Chinese Churches, comprising nearly two thousand members, connected with the Protestant missions in China. Of these perhaps one hundred are trained evangelists, engaged in preaching the Gospel to their countrymen. The work has spread beyond the limits of the open ports. In spite of government opposition and the restrictions of the former treaties, the Gospel has sounded out into the regions beyond, and some of our most flourishing Churches are in the country towns and villages.

We notice also the growth and recent triumph, in the imperial cabinet of China, of a policy favorable to Christianity and foreign intercourse. It is not our wish to magnify our office as missionaries, but we think it only fair that the Church should know the truth on this important and interesting subject. The thoughtful observer of Chinese politics, during the past seventeen years, could scarcely fail to notice that in the imperial cabinet at Pekin a fierce controversy was going on between the respective advocates of what might be designated the foreign and the anti-foreign policy. The complete history of this interesting and momentous struggle is for the present concealed from our view; but the vicissitudes of its progress were indicated, with tolerable distinctness, by frequent and significant movements in the outer field of Chinese politics; and from the character of those sent to fill the posts of high authority throughout the empire, it was always possible to ascertain whether the foreign or antiforeign policy was in the ascendant at Pekin. We do not mean to say that the operations of Protestant missions in China forced this question upon the imperial cabinet, and necessitated the controversy referred to; but we do mean to declare our earnest conviction and belief, that in the discussion and final adjustment of this question by the statesmen of China, the influence of Protestant missions was powerfully and favorably felt; and that for the future maintenance of her integrity and sovereign independence, under the action of her recent treaties with England, France, Russia, and the United States, China regards the influence of Christian principles over these nations as the sheet-anchor of her safety and hope. We have not space at command for all the evidence that might be adduced in support of this statement. It will be sufficient perhaps for us to state that until quite recently nearly all the diplomatic intercourse of both England and the United States with China has passed through the hands of Prostestant missionaries; that by means of the press the Bible has been scattered throughout the empire, entering alike the cottage of the peasant and the palace of the mandarin; that the lives and teachings of Protestant missionaries have furnished to the Chinese convincing proof of the superior excellence of Christian doctrines; that Chinese officers, in their interviews with foreign diplomatists, have sometimes shown a surprising familiarity with these doctrines;

and that in some of their official communications the Chinese authorities have assumed it as a primary truth, that the motives and principles which control the conduct of western nations are drawn from the Bible. We therefore feel authorized to assign to Protestant missions in China a prominent place among the influences which have contributed to open up the Chinese empire to Christianity and foreign intercourse.

The last result to which we shall refer is the great Tai Ping insurrection, which during the past seven years has marched its victorious legions through most of the southern provinces of China, and on more than one occasion has sent trembling even within the walls of Pekin. We are not yet in possession of sufficient data for a thorough analysis of this wonderful movement. Enough is known, however, to show that it is a direct result of Protestant missionary operations, and that as a religious system, notwithstanding its great and lamentable defects, it is far in advance of the hoary heathenism of China.

These results, we conceive, challenge the confidence and gratitude of the Church, and furnish the most convincing evidence that even in our day, and operating through the appliances of modern missions, the Gospel comes, "not in word only, but also in power, and in the Holy Ghost, and in much assurance."

With regard to the future progress of the Gospel in China the following encouraging facts should be considered:

1. The Chinese are a gregarious or clannish people. They move in masses, the crowd always following in the wake of a few courageous leaders.

2. The missionary work in China is simple evangelism. In most mission fields the missionary must combine in his own person the farmer, the tradesman, the schoolmaster, etc.; but in China his one great work is to "preach the word."

3. The Chinese have been trained to support their systems of religion, and it is altogether probable they contribute more money in proportion to their pecuniary ability for the maintenance of their idolatrous worship than it will cost them to support the institutions of Christianity.

4. China will supply Christian pastors just as fast as they are required in the progress of the work. The following remarks on this topic, by the Rev. J. Doolittle, of the American Board mission at Fuhchau, are here introduced, and commended to the serious attention of all interested in this important subject:

"Last Sabbath evening I attended the usual Chinese service held in the church belonging to the mission of the American Board at this place. Three young men, members of the native Church under care of that mission, two of whom are employed as native helpers, addressed the congregation, followed by closing remarks by the missionary in charge of the meeting.

"The first speaker, aged twenty, had a very bashful appearance. His delivery was rather monotonous. His remarks, however, indicated him to be a sober and earnest thinker. He took as his subject the closing part of the fifth chapter of Matthew, and explained at considerable length the manner in which Jesus taught his disciples to treat their slanderers and enemies. The way in which he handled this subject, as well as the subject itself, conciliated and interested the audience. He alluded to several customs of the Chinese, and quoted some of their maxims, relating to their treatment of enemies, and exhibited in marked and impressive contrast the principles which the Saviour laid down as rules for the guidance of his followers, in regard to those who 'cursed,' who 'hated,' and who 'despitefully used and persecuted them.' I could not but be grateful for such plain and earnest remarks on this subject, so different from anything which exists either in theory or practice among the Chinese.

"The second speaker, aged twenty-five, so far as concerned his manner of delivery, was much more pleasing and oratorical than the first. He announced as his theme John xv, 25, 'They hated me without a cause,' and proceeded to show the unreasonableness of the common objections made by the Chinese against Jesus. He declared that his text was fulfilled in Fuhchau, in that Jesus was hated without a cause. While he exposed, in a masterly manner, the sophistry of the popular excuses and objections against the Christian religion, he did not fail to notice the real reasons why the Chinese do not believe in the Saviour. His words were simple, yet pointed, and his meaning unmistakable. His appeals were bold and searching. I felt grateful when he closed that the truth had been spoken so earnestly, and at the same time so kindly.

"The third speaker, aged twenty, discoursed from Matt. x, 28. His voice was sharp and quick, yet quite distinct. He explained and enforced, in a pleasing and direct manner, the duty of every one to fear God more than man. He spoke of the nature, the value, and the immortality of the soul in a way which rivetted the attention of the congregation.

"He denied the sentiment which seems to be entertained, in theory at least, by not a few learned Chinese, that the soul perishes when the body dies. The audience listened with a kind of wondering interest, while he urged them in a bold and spirited manner to fear and obey that Being 'who is able to destroy both soul and body in hell;' and not to fear man, who can only kill the body, but cannot kill the soul.

"What has been said, as well as what has been left unsaid about the exercises of that evening, illustrates two interesting facts, which I believe to be eminently true of the native helpers at this port. I have had ample opportunities of judging in this matter ever since any converts were employed as helpers in the missionary work at Fuhchau.

"1. The native helpers select very practical and important subjects when addressing their countrymen. They do not love to dwell on abstruse, metaphysical, or far-fetched themes, nor are they fond of presenting exclusively doctrinal points. There is not much science or philosophy or history embodied in their public addresses, but there is a great deal of most important truth relating to the most practical subjects, prescribed by them in an earnest and kind manner.

"2. They are not ashamed to speak out boldly for Jesus. They literally and emphatically 'stand up for Jesus' in all their discourses. Indeed, their preaching and their addresses are so full of Jesus, and contain so many allusions to the life and the doctrines of the Saviour as the only proper example and standard for men of all ages and all nations, as frequently to irritate many of their hearers. It is a very common occurrence to hear some of those who have been listening to their addresses say in substance, on leaving, that of every ten sentences three or four have Jesus in them, or are about Jesus. Another form of expressing the same idea is that 'one word out of every three is Jesus.' Not a few leave the chapel or the church in anger, uttering the above sentiment with loud and bitter curses on the native helpers.

"Prayer in behalf of foreign missionaries, of native converts to Christianity in foreign lands, of Christian schools among the heathen, and of the heathen generally, is very common among Christians in Western countries. But I fear that especial prayer for *the native helpers as a class*, laboring for the conversion of their heathen countrymen, is rarely offered. So far as my experience and my recollection serve, such prayer was never or very seldom presented before the mercy-seat in family worship, in church or neighborhood prayer-meetings, or even in the monthly concert in America previous to my sailing for China. Has there been a great change for the better as regards this subject? Would that I knew such a change had already been extensively made!

"The subject of prayer for native helpers is one of great and general importance, considered with reference to the progress of the work in every missionary field. But I shall briefly present the subject viewed from China as my standpoint, for I feel that there are some grave considerations, some special reasons, why frequent and fervent prayer in behalf of the native helpers in China should be offered by the Church.

"1. China is so immense and so populous, its distance so great from America and England, (the present centers of interest in the missionary cause,) and the necessary expense connected with the foreign missionaries so large and constant, that it is idle to expect the evangelization of this empire mainly by the labor of foreigners. And besides, the number of missionaries and of candidates for the missionary work is immensely inadequate. The Church, at least in the present state of her zeal in the cause of missions, has neither the money nor the men to spare for the work in China. Can she send and support annually several scores or hundreds, not to say thousands, of her sons and daughters in this empire to labor for Jesus? No; China must be saved by the divine blessing resting principally on the labors of her own converted sons and daughters. *Native preachers, under God, are her main hope.* How important, then, that suitable persons should be raised up at the right time and place, and in sufficient numbers to meet the growing demands of the work—to respond to the loud call of Providence for more laborers in this empire! Is it reasonable and consistent to believe that the evangelization of China will be achieved without the importunate and effectual prayers of the Church in behalf of the native agents or instruments in the work? Are the present or the future missionaries in this land, on whom will devolve the responsibility of selecting, training, and superintending the native helpers, sufficient for such a responsibility, unaided by the sympathies and the prayers of western Christians, poured out before God in behalf of these helpers?

"2. 'As the twig is bent the tree is inclined,' is an old adage, which has a moral application of peculiar significancy and force in such an empire as China, where *custom and precedent* are generally more powerful than law or than right. The foundations should be properly laid if the superstructure is to be firm and durable. A low standard of piety and devotion to the work in those who are first or among the first to be employed as native helpers or native preachers would be a calamity to be peculiarly dreaded and deprecated in this empire. Now may not, should not a deep and powerful interest be taken in this matter by those at the West who are coworkers in the promotion of the cause of missions in this land?

"Ought they not, and will they not offer up special and frequent prayer in behalf of native helpers or native preachers in China, in view of the transcendent importance of rightly *beginning* as well as of rightly prosecuting the work by the instrumentality of converted Chinese?"

CHAPTER XIX.

APPEAL TO THE CHURCHES.

We pass to notice the claims of this new era in Chinese history upon the Churches of Christendom. We feel authorized to use this expression to designate the present aspect of affairs in China. The former things have evidently passed away, and this nation now stands on the threshold of a new era in her history. The abrogation of her exclusive policy, the rescinding of her persecuting edicts against Christianity, the permission to her subjects to embrace the Christian faith, and the authorization of missionaries to travel and preach the doctrines of this faith throughout the empire, are all significant indications of the great change that has passed over the government of China. Observe also the spread of liberal ideas in China, the steady growth of foreign influence in its councils, and the rapid extension of foreign trade and intercourse, with capacities for future unlimited expansion. While I am penning these lines an English expedition is steaming some eight hundred miles up the broad bosom of the Yang-tsze-kiang, through waters never before cut by foreign keels, right into the heart of China. The expedition is expected to reach Hankow, the great inland commercial mart of China, situated in the province of Hupeh, to examine this celebrated city, and at the same time to test in this practical manner the value of the recent treaty provisions, and the sincerity of the Chinese with regard to their execution. What, then, are some of the most urgent claims of China in this new phase of her history in the Churches of Christ? She demands,

1. A CORDIAL APPRECIATION OF HER CHARACTER AND WANTS. The discovery of a new planet in the solar system at once changes the previously supposed relations between its bodies, and necessitates a reconstruction of theories and a readjustment of the recognized celestial influences. The discovery by Columbus of the Western continent gave a new phase and direction to history, and initiated a series of political evolutions which has culminated in the ascendancy of Protestantism, and the enthronement of Protestant governments as the ruling powers of the world. The advent of China into the great family of nations introduces a new and potent element into the world's politics, disturbs the previously existing relations and affinities, and necessitates a stern conflict of principles and interests, the development of which is yet future, and the history of which is yet to be written. The time has gone by when ignorance of China characterized alike all classes of society, and when Christians might innocently shut out from their sympathies and evangelism its myriads of people. By her own recent and authoritative acts China has placed herself as it were within the pale of Christendom, and has precipitated the inevitable conflict

between truth and error. The grand tournament has already opened; Christianity and heathenism, in utter antagonism, have entered the lists, and further evasion or procrastination is impossible. For weal or woe, the question of supremacy must now be decided; and when heathenism shall quail and expire in the presence of a purer faith, then will commence the final struggle between Protestantism and Romanism for supremacy in this the grandest empire of the world.

It would be impossible, within the limits of this chapter, even to name all the wants of China; we can now refer only to those of a moral or religious character, and of these we can present only the more prominent. First, then, we conceive *a pure and saving religious faith* to be one of the great and imperative wants of China at the present day. The present position of China, with reference to this vital subject, is most lamentable. She has, indeed, no clearly defined principles of religious belief; the subject is practically ignored by nine tenths of the Chinese. They have banished the Almighty from their thoughts, and by a daring apotheosis have enthroned man as the object of their faith and trust. The few rays of divine truth that may have illumined the minds of their ancient sages have been lost long since in the thick darkness of heathenism; the light that once shone feebly on their altars has been extinguished by a cold and sensuous atheism. The entire range of Chinese literature furnishes no possible basis for a rational religious faith, touching those subjects that most nearly and powerfully affect man's destiny.

We search it in vain for those principles and influences which purify and exalt humanity. As a nation, the Chinese are utterly "without God and without hope in the world." This we consider the radical and fatal defect in their social and political compact. If proof or illustration of this remark is needed, we refer to the patent facts of their past history and present condition. For centuries the Chinese have possessed, in different degrees of excellence and efficiency, civilization, literature, social order, and political government; and yet they have failed to obtain the grand results contemplated. Their civilization, literature, and political economy have become *effete*, while their ancient religious faith has degenerated into bald atheism. Never was there a more promising field for the trial of those godless humanitarian theories of social organization so fulsomely lauded by some modern writers in Christendom, and yet the experiment has resulted in utter failure. All healthy progress ceased centuries ago; conservatism even has exhausted its resources, and henceforth there remains for China no alternative but the introduction of a new element into its political system, or utter deterioration and ruin. This new element is to be found only in the pure and simple faith of the Gospel. Christianity is China's last and only hope.

Another want of China, pertinent to her present position, is *the exemplification of this pure and saving faith in the lives of holy men and women.* It is probably true of men, in all countries and in every stage of intellectual culture, that their conceptions of the good and the true are always in advance of their actual performances. It certainly is most strikingly characteristic of the Chinese in our day. They are prone to revel in dreams or fancies of ideal probity and virtue; they seem to possess a delicate appreciation of those higher and mental traits which result from superior education and refinement; and yet no other people in the world furnish such an utter contrast between their conceptions and practice. The Christian missionary descants on the pure morality of the Gospel, and the educated Chinese will express their enthusiastic indorsement of every sentiment uttered; and yet at the close of the discussion which they appeared so highly to appreciate as a mental exercitation, they pass, without the slightest compunction, to lying, cheating, idolatry, and licentiousness, from the debasing influences of which you would suppose they were invincibly shielded by their refined mental tastes. They, in fact, conceive it to be impossible for one's practice even to approximate his own ideal of moral excellence, and fortify their position by the corroborating experience of their entire nation.

The last want of China to which we shall refer in this connection, is the *Christian preacher to expound and enforce the principles of this faith.* "How shall they hear without a preacher?" It has pleased God, by "the foolishness of preaching," to carry forward his kingdom in the world. This agency is admirably suited to the character and wants of the Chinese. Their written language is so concise and arbitrary that more than one half of the Chinese can scarcely use it at all. Throughout perhaps three fourths of the empire, colloquial dialects have grown up alongside this written language; and it is in these dialects the mass of the Chinese think, and feel, and speak. Most of these dialects are readily and accurately acquired by a foreigner, while to master the most difficult of them requires only a moderate amount of industry and perseverance. Under present circumstances, the first supplies of Christian preachers for China must come from abroad. She can furnish the congregations, but the men of God, the "embassadors for Christ," must come from other lands.

We proceed to state,

2. THAT, IN VIEW OF HER GREAT AND URGENT WANTS, CHINA NOW DEMANDS FERVENT, PREVAILING PRAYER IN HER BEHALF FROM THE CHURCHES OF CHRIST. In introducing this topic we are not careful to guard ourselves against the charge of enthusiasm, or to conciliate any of our readers who may be disposed to turn away from the discussion of this topic. We are too thoroughly in earnest to be greatly affected by such considerations. The interests involved in this discussion are so stupendous, the events transpiring around us are so startling, and the issues before us are so momentous and far-reaching, that we are willing to sink ourselves in the grand results contemplated. Our concern is for the ark of God, the cause of Christ; and we shall be only too happy if what we now write on the subject shall contribute to the consummation of its glorious designs in that vast empire. We believe in the pertinency and efficacy of faithful prayer in this connection, and

we rest our belief on the sure foundation of God's written word. It is unnecessary, we conceive, to quote those passages of Holy Writ which support this view; their general purport has been well expressed by Charles Wesley in his hymn:

> "O wondrous power of faithful prayer!
> What tongue can tell the Almighty grace?
> God's hands or bound or open are,
> As Moses or Elijah prays."

We love to dwell upon this theme. Its important bearings on the present subject can scarcely be exaggerated. As a power for good, too, it possesses the singular excellence that every Christian may wield it. Whether rich or poor, learned or illiterate; called by the Spirit to go forth preaching the word, or directed by the same Spirit to the soil, the anvil, the loom, the study, or the forum, all can pray for China. Apart from the word of God, and the power of his Spirit to make that word effectual in the heart of the believer, nothing in all our experience as a foreign missionary has so cheered and supported us as the thought that the holy cause in which we are engaged is remembered in the prayers of God's people. And we have asked, What if all the Christian hearts throughout the world were to unite in earnest persevering prayer to God for the conversion of the Chinese? What if for a year, for a month, for a week, for a day, or even for an hour, the entire body of Christian believers were to unite in prayer for the immediate conversion of the population of this mighty empire! It is not our prerogative to indicate or estimate the direct results of such an act of intercessory faith. What riches of grace, what treasures of mercy, what streams of instant salvation it would open for China, is known only to Him from whom nothing is hidden, and who has declared his willingness to be inquired of by the house of Israel concerning such things.

Passing, however, from those "secret things" which "belong unto the Lord our God," we may conceive somewhat of the influence this grand act of faith would exert upon the Church. How it would rouse the sympathies, stir the energies, and fire the zeal of every Christian! What searchings of heart it would produce; what willing offerings of means and men for the evangelization of China would at once be laid on the altar of consecration! We see no good reason why the Church should not now come up to the exercise of this high, commanding faith. No Christian doubts its possibility, and no one acquainted with the subject can suppose it would be unacceptable to the Lord of the harvest. The times in which we live, and the present aspects of China, seem to demand just such faith. The world is manifestly approximating that grand epoch concerning which "glorious things are spoken;" in the foreground of which stand the promises of the Gospel's marvelous spread and unprecedented triumphs in the world. We proceed to remark,

3. THAT IN VIEW OF HER PRESENT WANTS, CHINA DEMANDS FROM THE CHURCHES OF CHRIST A THOROUGH AND COMPREHENSIVE SYSTEM OF IMMEDIATE EVANGELISM. We do not stop now to argue the

question of the Church's duty with regard to the proclamation of the Gospel throughout the world; the great body of Christians in our day recognize and accept their high commission on this subject, with all its vast and solemn responsibilities. We proceed at once to state the grounds on which China bases her demand upon the Christian Church for such a system of evangelism.

First, we notice the cheering fact that China is now fairly and fully opened to receive the Gospel. We have already presented the evidence on which this statement rests. The Chinese government, in the recent treaty compacts, has publicly and solemnly pledged her faith and honor on this subject to the four leading nations of the world. It does not invalidate our position to assert that the government of China entered into this compact reluctantly, and only in consequence of an external pressure which she could no longer withstand, and that she will gladly avail herself of the first favorable opportunity to annul her action on this question. Without entering into a full discussion of the subject, it is sufficient for our present purpose to state that the previous exclusive policy of the Chinese government was opposed alike to the word of God and the highest instincts of humanity; that it was unjust to the people of China, and at variance with their views and wishes; that its abrogation, without derogating from the sovereignty of the government, has conferred a priceless boon on the Chinese; that, according to all recognized principles of analogy and evidence, the forces which have accomplished the overthrow of this exclusive policy must inevitably and rapidly increase, and that, meanwhile, the progress of Christianity among the people will prepare them so fully to appreciate the propriety and necessity of intercourse with Christian nations, that any return of their government to its former barbarous policy will be utterly impossible. It is a fact, substantiated by the clearest historic evidence, that the Chinese have always been a commercial people, and that, in former periods of their history, they solicited intercourse with foreign nations; it is a fact that the exclusive policy of their government originated with the present dynasty; it is a fact that, in spite of the restrictions of their government, the Chinese have always carried on a foreign commerce; it is a fact that foreign influence is now sufficiently powerful in China to control the general policy of the government; and it is now, we believe, universally conceded that foreign influence in China must steadily increase for many years to come. In view of these facts, therefore, we feel entirely authorized to announce, distinctly and emphatically, that China is now fully open to the Gospel; and that, in view of this fact, she is entitled to the best efforts of the Church for her evangelization.

Secondly, we observe that, by her recent acts, China has placed herself within the power of influences that must effect her utter demoralization, unless counteracted by the principles of Christianity. The nation is breaking away from its ancient moorings; the conservative influences that hitherto have controlled the national mind are fast losing their potency; and if not succeeded by those ennobling influences which spring only from the principles of the Gospel, we can forecast nothing but disaster and ruin for China. The lucrative trade carried on with China by Western nations has already attracted to her shores merchants and traders of all countries, religious creeds, and social habits, and under the new treaty provisions their numbers will indefinitely increase. The commercial world now turns to China with the most absorbing interest. Western capital is moving eastward for investment; business men look to China for the rapid accumulation of wealth; young men press to it as the most quick and certain road to opulence; and the flags of all nations float in its capacious harbors. Within a few years that empire will be overspread by a vast net-work of commercial agencies and enterprises, the influence of which on the future character of the Chinese who can estimate? A bald atheism, correlated by a stolid fatalism, has long been a prominent trait of the Chinese mind; and when to this are superadded the jealous competitions of extending commerce, and the maddening thirst for gold, we can, in some degree, appreciate the dangers to which China is exposed. It is vain to talk of the civilizing influences of commerce. Alas! the history of the world shows only too plainly that commerce is a dangerous civilizer; the wake of its progress is ever the engulfing maelstrom of licentiousness and barbarism. Apart from the influences of Christianity, there is no hope for China in foreign intercourse, western commerce, or western civilization and literature. Evangelization or demoralization is China's only alternative.

Thirdly, we notice that the forces of Romanism are already in the field, and are pushing forward their operations with resources and zeal worthy of a better cause. We are not in possession of very recent statistics with regard to the operations of Roman Catholic missionaries in China. According to the "Annales de la Propagation de la Foi" for June, 1839, there were then in China eight bishops, fifty-seven foreign priests, one hundred and fourteen native priests, and three hundred and three thousand converts, connected with the Romish Church. It is difficult to know just what amount of credence to assign to these statistics. Our impression is, however, that they do not overstate the case. Indeed, we think the number of foreign priests in China has considerably increased since the foregoing statistics were published. The provisions of the recent treaties with China are exciting the liveliest interest throughout the ranks of Romanism. In the thirteenth article of the French treaty there is a clause declaring that "whatever has been heretofore written, proclaimed, or published in China, by order of government, against the Christian faith, is wholly abrogated and nullified in all the provinces of the empire." Under cover of this clause, the Romish missionaries in China declare their purpose to institute claims against the Chinese government for the recovery of all their ancient Church property at Pekin and elsewhere throughout the empire, which was confiscated during former persecutions. If successful in this measure, as seems entirely probable, they at once will be in possession of wealth, prestige, and Church appliances which will be of immense advantage to them in the propagation of their faith among the Chinese.

The preceding remarks indicate, with perhaps sufficient clearness, what we conceive to be the grounds of China's claim upon the Christian Church for a thorough and comprehensive system of evangelism. There is, however, one point more to which we wish briefly to refer. No thoughtful observer, we think, can fail to perceive that China has now reached a great and eventful crisis in her history; that she is now in a transition state, passing through a formative process, during which she receives for weal or woe the impression of those influences which at the time are brought to bear upon her. If then it is desirable that China should ever be brought under the influence of Christianity; if it is, indeed, the duty of Christians to proclaim to her people the words of life and salvation, now is the time to engage in this work with resources and energy commensurate with the imperative demands of the enterprise. Christians must at once gird themselves for this conquest, or the present golden opportunity may pass away forever. Again, it is well understood in political and commercial circles, that though China is theoretically and legally open to foreign intercourse, yet practically it will remain closed until foreign enterprise shall push its way and proclaim its immunities throughout the empire, and that, in order to give efficiency to the recent treaty provisions, and make them the recognized laws of the land, foreigners must at once and in earnest avail themselves of all the privileges to which they are now entitled. These remarks apply with equal pertinency and force to the Christian Church in her great work of evangelizing China. Civil authority has now done its work in opening the way; it remains to be seen whether the Church possesses sufficient faith and zeal to go up and claim this land in the name of her Lord and Master.

We proceed now to notice briefly the character and proportions of that system of evangelism which China now demands from the Christian Church. What we have already written must convince every candid mind that the field now opening in China before the Christian Church is of an extraordinary character; that the demands now made on the aggressive energies of the Church are unparallelled in her history, and that to meet these demands her preparations and plans must be on a scale of unprecedented magnitude and efficiency. It is the loudest and most urgent call ever made on the Church of Christ. What shall be her response? We confess to an unutterable solicitude on this subject; it presses upon us at times with a power and solemnity absolutely overwhelming. Let us, however, try to look at the subject calmly and faithfully. And, first, what is the character of that evangelism which China now demands from the Church? Does she demand regular and stated pastors for native churches which may be gathered, or does she demand missionaries in their extraordinary character of apostle or evangelist? The latter view seems to us the more reasonable and pertinent to the present aspects of the subject. We conceive the present need of China to be an adequate supply of holy, zealous missionaries, who, through the pulpit, the press, and the school, shall proclaim the glad tidings of salvation to all classes of Chinese throughout the empire. It is not, indeed, our idea that each missionary shall take the empire for his parish; this is rendered impracticable by the vast extent of the field and by the conflicting dialects of the people; but that the aggregate body of missionaries shall suffice to bring the Gospel message clearly and forcibly to every soul in China. A bold, triumphant evangelism, such as was instituted by the Saviour, is now the urgent want of China. Pastors for the Churches which may be gathered will be readily supplied, partly from the ranks of the missionaries, but mainly, in the progress and development of the work, from the class of native helpers whom God shall call and qualify for that purpose.

What then must be the proportions of that system of evangelism which shall meet the present demands of China? We present a few facts and suggestions to aid the Church in answering this question. Within the eighteen provinces of China are fourteen hundred and seventy-three districts, each containing, on an average, eight hundred and eighty-one square miles, and a population of two hundred and fifty thousand. What number of missionaries shall we assign to each of these districts? Suppose, at our lowest estimate, we say two; we shall then have one missionary to an area of four hundred and forty-one square miles, and to a populution of one hundred and twenty-five thousand, and the required number of missionaries will be two thousand nine hundred and forty-six. If we divide this number equally between the Churches of

Europe and the United States, we shall have fourteen hundred and seventy-three as the number of missionaries China now demands from the Churches of Christ in America. What will it cost to send out and support such a force of missionaries? If two thirds go out married, at a cost, in each case, for outfit and passage, of $1,000; and one third go out unmarried, at a cost, in each case, for outfit and passage, of $600, the entire expense of sending out the proposed re-enforçement is $1,276,600. For their annual expenses in the field, including personal support, house-rent, chapel and school purposes, etc., suppose we allow $1,200 for each married, and $800 for each unmarried missionary, and we have as the entire cost of supporting such a body of missionaries $1,571,200. Are the Churches of the United States able to meet this expense? According to the estimate of a recent writer on the subject, ("Gift of Power," p. 91,) the amount of taxable real and personal estate of evangelical Christians, and those identified with them as members of their respective Church congregations in the United States, in 1854, was $6,332,542,679; "one tenth of the simple interest of which, at six per cent. per annum, makes $37,995,256 as, at the lowest computation, the annual available means of the Church of God in our land." Deduct now from this sum the annual cost of supporting the proposed number of missionaries in China, and there remains as the annual income of the Church in the United States, for the support of its home work, and its operations in other foreign mission fields, the immense sum of $36,424,056.

If the statistics on which this calculation is based are reliable, (and we see no good reason to doubt their accuracy,) is it not evident that the Christian Churches of the United States are abundantly able, at this moment, to send out and support their one thousand four hundred and seventy-three missionaries for China? and that, too, without the slightest detriment to any of their home or other foreign interests. Distribute the evangelical Christians of the United States into eight great missionary organizations, represented respectively by the American Board of Commissioners for Foreign Missions, the Presbyterian Board, the Protestant Episcopal Board, the Dutch Reformed Board, Baptist Board, North, Baptist Board, South, Methodist Episcopal Board, and Methodist Episcopal Board, South, and to each assign an equal portion of the aggregate annual resources of the Church, and also of the expenses of the proposed missionary re-enforcement. We shall then have $4,749,407 as the annual available income of each society, while the annual demand on its funds for China is only $196,400; thus leaving in its treasury for other claims the enormous sum of $4,628,017. But why multiply proof or illustration of the point under discussion? No one, we think, can doubt the ability of the Church in the United States to send out and support the proposed re-enforcement of missionaries; and no one acquainted with the wants of China can believe that the number proposed is at all in excess of the demand.

What response shall we make to this call? No one acquainted with the subject can suppose we have made an exorbitant demand in behalf of China; and no Methodist can doubt the ability of our Church to meet, at once and fully, her portion of the claim. The heart of Christendom now turns toward China with unprecedented solicitude and conviction of duty. Many Churches are already discussing and arranging their plans for aggressive operations in this great field on a scale of surpassing magnitude and thoroughness. Shall the Methodist Episcopal Church in the United States have a worthy part in this great aggressive movement of modern Christendom for the evangelization of China? Shall we march our column to the front? Shall our banner float above the smoke of battle in this glorious war, or shall we abide in our cities, and jeeringly ask the gathering tribes of our Israel, "Are the hands of Zebah and Zalmunnah now in thine hands?" Shall we be those who willingly offered themselves? or those of Meroz, against whom the angel of the Lord hurled his bitter, scathing curse? As Methodists, we conceive ourselves bound, by all our historic precedents and denominational instincts, to give an affirmative response to this call. Such a response, in part at least, we have already given. In 1847, when only the five consular ports were open to foreign intercourse, and while Christianity was still under the ban of the Chinese government, we established our China Mission; and to the present hour, in the face of no ordinary difficulties and discouragements, the Church has never failed to give it cordial and generous support. It is evident, however, that to meet the present demands of China, missionary zeal and contributions must increase beyond all modern precedent. Are we ready for this advance?

We have endeavored to present a clear and truthful picture of the character and demands of the field before us in China. We have shown that its immense population are living "without God and without hope in the world;" that by the recent treaties the entire empire is now thrown open to Christianity; that, to give effect to these treaties, Christians must, at once and in earnest, avail themselves of all the privileges to which they are now entitled; that the antagonistic forces of mammon, atheism, and Romanism are already in the field; that the heart of Christendom is now turned toward China with intense interest, and that other Churches are already preparing for the great struggle. We have shown also, by reliable statistics, that our Church possesses at this moment a superabundance of means to meet the demands of China without the slightest detriment to any of her home or other foreign interests. What now is your response? We beg to urge this subject upon your attention. Its importance and urgency justify our boldness and importunity. We entreat you, by your regard for the name and honor of God; by your sympathy with Christ, in his great work of saving a lost world; by your compassion for one third of the human race, destitute of the blessed Gospel; by your oft-repeated vows of consecration to the service of God; by your love for the Church of your choice; by your desire for an approving conscience in the last mortal agony, and by your hopes of heaven; by all these motives and considerations we entreat you, members of the Methodist Episcopal Church, turn not away from the supplicating wail of the perishing 400,000,000 of China; turn not away from the voice of God, now solemnly calling you to this field; falter not in this hour of crying need to the cause of Christ in the world! Shall it be told in Gath, shall it be published in the streets of Askelon, that the Methodist Episcopal Church, with a membership of nearly a million, and an estimated annual income for purposes of evangelism of more than three millions of dollars, refuses to furnish annually the sum of, say $250,000 for the evangelization of China?

But the Church must go as well as give. The spirit of consecration to this work must come upon the ministry of our Church with unprecedented definiteness and force. And yet, after all, what a mere fraction of our ministry is demanded for China! Over six thousand traveling and over seven thousand local preachers in the Methodist Episcopal Church minister to a membership of about a million; while, for our entire work in China, we have estimated only one hundred and eighty-four missionaries. We appeal to the thirteen thousand preachers of the Methodist Episcopal Church, and to the hundreds of young men in our communion whose minds are turned toward the Christian ministry, and we ask, How long shall the perishing millions of China plead in vain for one hundred and eighty-four Methodist missionaries to break unto them the bread of life? Are there not in the ranks of the Methodist ministry, or among the candidates for that ministry, one hundred and eighty-four capable and willing men to give themselves to the cause of God in China? We beg respectfully and earnestly to put this question to all the students in Methodist seminaries, colleges, and universities; to all our theological students at Concord, Evanston, or elsewhere; to all our traveling and local preachers; to all our presiding elders; to all our Church editors; to all our ministerial professors and presidents in institutions of learning; and finally to our bench of bishops. We should like to propound it in our preachers' meetings, in all our annual conferences, and in the General Conference of our Church. When God, by a series of wonderful providences, has opened up the Chinese empire to Christianity, and when, in one year, he has added hundreds of thousands of converts to the Churches in the United States, is it true that out of the thirteen thousand preachers of the Methodist Episcopal Church it is impossible to obtain one hundred and eighty-four missionaries for China? Shall we throw open the doors of our churches and proclaim this fact in the ears of the mocking infidel and scoffing libertine? or in the presence of the Jesuitical emissaries of that Church whose boast is that her temples and missions girdle the globe? Shall we pass beyond the limits of Christendom and proclaim it to the millions of heathen perishing for lack of knowledge? Suffer, brethren, the word of exhortation. We must, we must awake to the subject! we must listen to the call China now sends to us across the waters! we must consecrate ourselves to the work of the Christian ministry among the people of China!

What shall be done? We invoke the aid of the

pulpit. Man of God! we charge you to sound the alarm on this great subject. Bring it before every congregation you address, and see to it that your trumpet gives no uncertain sound. We invoke the aid of the forty-six thousand class-leaders of our Church! Take the subject with you to the class-room; speak of it, pray over it. Come up yourself to the proposed standard of systematic giving, and then urge, persistently urge every member of your class to do the same. We invoke the aid of the press! We appeal to every Methodist editor, and to that large and influential class of writers who quarterly, monthly, and weekly discourse, through the press, to the thousands of our Zion, and we say, Plead for China! Circulate information on the subject! arouse the conscience of the Church! and, if circumstances favor, add example to precept and offer yourselves for the work of God in China. Finally, we appeal to the nine hundred thousand members of our Church. Hear the Saviour's command to you: "Go ye into all the world, and preach the Gospel to every creature!" What says it? Go! What say the signs of the times? Go! What say the wants of China? Go! Go, then, either in your own person, or in the persons of those whom your missionary contributions aid to send and support as foreign missionaries!

We now present some of the considerations which we think should induce the Church to give China the system of immediate evangelism to which we have referred. We cannot expect, within the small space remaining to us, to present all the important aspects of this subject; our remarks must necessarily be of an eclectic character.

First, we notice obedience to Christ's command, "Go ye into all the world and preach the Gospel to every creature," as a consideration that should have great weight with the Church in deciding this question. We have no time now to argue the question of the Church's duty with regard to this high commission. Alas for her and for the world if she has yet to learn its grand scope and meaning! We have supposed that the great body of Christians in our day accept the literal import of the Saviour's command, with all its vast responsibilities, and are honestly seeking to know their present duty with reference to its execution. We have shown that China is now fairly and completely open to the Gospel; that the present time is apparently her day of grace; that the tendencies of the age corroborate the teachings of Scripture on this subject, and that auspicious omens cheer the Church in girding herself for the battle. In view, then, of these recognized facts and claims, we put to every Christian the solemn question: Will you obey our Saviour's last command? will you now, according to your ability, aid in the evangelization of China? will you? We protest against indifference on this subject. It is no time for evasion or procrastination. The inevitable conflict is at hand; momentous issues are just before us, and the hour has come for action, instant, bold, decisive action. Dare not to dismiss this subject from your thoughts. We appeal from the caviling of the advocate to the calmness of the judge, from the subterfuges of the carnal mind to the dictates of an enlightened Christian conscience, and we ask, Will you at once come up to the measure of your duty with reference to this important subject?

Secondly, a regard for the name and honor of God should now impel the Church to engage in this work. No Christian can be insensible to the force of this consideration. To him the name and honor of God are infinitely precious. He prefers them to all the treasures of earth, and guards them with a ceaseless vigilance. Is it nothing, then, to him to know that in China this holy name is openly and maliciously given to reproach? that among the myriads of that land the names designating the triune God are contemned, and his honor trampled in the dust? We appeal to you, O Christian, on this subject, with an intensity of feeling that finds but feeble expression in these words. You can no longer plead ignorance in extenuation of indifference. Christendom is now ringing with indignant protests against this defiant sacrilege. The pens and tongues of scores of devoted missionaries are electrifying all hearts with disclosures on this subject, more painful and startling than any with which "Peter the Hermit" ever thrilled the hearts of the faithful.

Thirdly, sympathy for the perishing millions of China should rouse the Church to instant action in their behalf. China's claim to this sympathy, we conceive, is predicated of her spiritual or moral rather than of her physical destitution. Bad as her social condition confessedly is, fearful as are her physical wants, they are as nothing when compared with her moral destitution. It is utterly impossible to form an adequate conception of this subject; the mind is alternately bewildered and sickened in the effort to grasp it. No one can think of China's immense population, the depths of guilt and pollution into which they have sunk, and the awful doom awaiting them in eternity, without a painful consciousness of the utter impotence of human language to convey a complete description of her true condition. Such an appeal was never before made to the heart of the Church. She cannot, we think, hear this appeal with indifference; she dare not drive from her altars the supplicating millions of China.

Fourthly, the essentially aggressive character of Christianity should constrain the Church to meet, at once and fully, the present demands of China. It is unnecessary, we conceive, in this connection, to furnish proof of the statement that Christianity is essentially aggressive, that progress is the inherent law of its existence. No truth is traced more legibly than this in the original charter of its being, or can be more thoroughly substantiated by the great facts of its history, or more certainly deduced from the predicted glories of its future triumphs. The Church, as the representative of Christianity, is impelled by her organic elements to action, instant, ceaseless action. With her mere conservatism is deterioration, inaction is defeat, and passivity is atrophy. By every consideration and aspect of duty she is bound to a spirit of indomitable enterprise and sleepless vigilance in the discharge of her high commission. She must stand ready, with all her resources of energy, faith, and means, to enter every open door for the propagation of the Gospel. Woe to her if she prove recreant to her sacred trust! woe to her if she turn away from the cries of those ready to perish! woe to her if, like the great Carthagenian, she find her Capua this side the Tiber and the seven hills! The present crisis calls for that spirit of immediate, triumphant evangelism which thrilled the heart of the primitive Church. Alas for the world if this call is unheeded by the Church in our day! The scoffing infidel could ask no more convincing proof that she has passed into a fearful decadence of faith and energy, that she has lost her ancient spirit of battle and conquest, and is utterly unworthy both of the high character she claims, and of the glorious destiny to which she aspires.

Lastly, a regard for her own safety should induce the Church to supply this evangelism. The present times are fraught with danger to the Church of Christ. Omitting from our view those perils which are patent and appreciable to home observers, we wish now to notice a source of danger which has not as yet attracted the attention of the Church. We have already referred to the frightful social demoralization of the Chinese, and to the immense and growing commerce which they carry on with foreign countries. This trade is conducted chiefly by England and the United States. It would startle Christians of the United States to learn the amount of American capital and the vast network of American mercantile interests identified with this trade. It would startle them to be told how much of the wealth that glitters in New York, Boston, Philadelphia, Baltimore, and Charleston, or finds its way into the interior of the country, has been drawn from China. It would startle them to know the extent to which, even now, American sentiments, tastes, and habits are influenced by this Oriental heathenism, and it would astound them to discover at how many points the civilization of China and the United States are approximating each other. It is not our design or wish to denounce our trade with China; but we do wish to send out this distinct voice of warning to ring through the Churches of our land. We mean to call the attention of the Church to the subject, and we are bold to declare our solemn conviction that, unless Christians bestir themselves, the commerce of the United States with the far East will prove to her a sink of unutterable infamy; its atmosphere will be more deadly than the simoon of the desert; and at this moment we are prepared, in the presence of Christendom, to inscribe over its portal, "This way ruin lies!" The Church must give her earnest attention to this subject; it is at her peril she hesitates or delays. A conflict, more fierce and protracted than any through which the Church has ever yet borne her triumphant banner, is approaching. The enemy, victorious on his own soil, now boldly and defiantly scales the bulwarks of Christendom, and plants his standard within the shadow of the cross. Is it not time for the Church to marshal her forces and gird herself for the war? Rise, then, ye men of God! Go forth to this great battle, and plant your standards on the ramparts of heathenism.

ADDENDUM.

CHRISTIAN CHINESE WEDDING.

THE following account of a Christian Chinese wedding near Fuhchau, China, will doubtless interest the reader. It is from the pen of an American missionary at Fuhchau, and was originally published in the "American Presbyterian."

"My invitation to the wedding, given in the name of the eldest living paternal uncle of the bridegroom, was received on New Year's day. It consists of a red piece of paper, nine and a half by four and a half inches. On one side was written, in Chinese, of course, the name of said uncle, the nephew to be married, the time selected, and a few other items, all in Chinese style, inviting me to 'enlighten' the occasion by my presence. This card was inclosed in an unsealed envelop of red paper, ten inches by five and a half. My Chinese name was written on a narrow slip of red paper, extending the whole length of the envelop and attached to it at the top and bottom. All those who receive such a formal invitation to a wedding, whether they attend or not, are expected to make a present of money to the bridegroom, which goes toward defraying expenses.

"Among the foreigners who accepted their invitations were two missionary ladies and the Rev. Otis Gibson, a member of the American Methodist mission, located at this city, who had been invited to perform the marriage ceremony in accordance with the principles of the Christian religion. We went on board the Chinese boat furnished to take us a part of the way, about half past four o'clock in the morning. We had provided ourselves with provisions for a cold breakfast to be eaten on the boat, to which we did ample justice. The boat was propelled by Chinamen, who rowed standing, as Chinese usually do. The tide was favorable, and we made good progress. We reached the landing-place about day-break, distant from Fuhchau some eight or nine miles. But here we were disappointed in ascertaining that the coolies who were to be in readiness to carry the sedan chair, brought thus far in the boat for the accommodation of the ladies, were nowhere to be found. The original plan was for the ladies to walk and ride alternately from the landing place to the scene of the wedding. It was too late to send to the neighboring villages to endeavor to hire other bearers unless we were willing to make a considerable delay, so the ladies undertook to walk the distance yet to be passed over, some four or five miles. Our way lay for a mile or more across a large paddy or rice field. The autumnal crop of rice had been harvested, and some of the ground was covered with winter wheat, sown in beds, in drills, or in rows of hills about seven or eight inches apart. The wheat was already some eight or ten inches high, and presented a very fine appearance. After we had walked nearly three miles we succeeded in finding men who could carry the sedan chair when holding a living person, it having been brought on from the boat by one of the hands and another Chinaman. Those who carry the sedan well must have considerable practice and be trained to the work. The ladies now rode in turn for a short distance. Our path soon leaving the paddy fields led us along the side of a valley, and gradually became more and more inclined. We soon found ourselves in very romantic if not grand scenery; we were in the midst of lofty hills, covered principally with a kind of stinted pine, wild fern, and a singular species of very tall grass. On our left, a hundred or more feet below us, a small rivulet wound its way down toward the Min. In due time, about half past eight o'clock, we arrived at the residence of the bridegroom, all delighted with the sublime beauty of the scenery around us.

"We found a large company already assembled at the residence of the bridegroom. He and several of his family relatives were converts to Christianity, and were members of one of the native Churches connected with the Methodist mission. His intended bride was not a Church member. On inquiry we found she had been bought when a child, and had been brought up in the family as his betrothed wife. The custom of buying female children, or of receiving them as gifts from their parents when quite young, and of bringing them up as the future wives of some of the boys in one's family is very common among the poorer classes in Fuhchau and vicinity. It implies no particular disgrace, but is an index of the low pecuniary circumstances of the family which buys or receives the girl thus to be brought up.

"The ceremony was performed in a covered court, the reception room of the house. A plain table was placed in the front part of it, and on it were set two old-looking goblets, tied together by a common red cotton string, about three or four feet long. The arrangements having been completed the bridegroom took his position, and the bride was led along by her bridesmaid, a married woman some forty years old. The parties stood facing the missionary clergyman. The foreign guests stood along the two sides of the court and in front on the outside.

"The bridegroom was about twenty-six years old, of pleasant manners, dignified, and composed. He wore a pair of Chinese boots, the uppers of which were made of satin, and the Chinese cap of ceremony, which had a brass button and red silk tassels on its top. His outer garment was made of fine blue black silk and extended nearly to his feet. The bride was about nineteen, and seemed much discomposed during part of the ceremony. She belonged to the large-footed class of Chinese women, and of course her dress was made according to the fashion which prevails among such women at Fuhchau. Her shoes, worn on feet which were stockingless, were of black cotton cloth, embroidered with red silk, having thick white soles and red silk tassels on the top. Her outside dress was made of black cotton cloth, and extended only a little below her hips. Beneath were pantaloons of the same color and same kind of material. Her costume resembled, in general, the Bloomer costume, more nearly than the popular style of ladies' dress in America. She wore no vail or bonnet, but had ear-rings about three inches in diameter. From the top of the hair on her head projected a metallic ornament, washed with gold, some six or eight inches long, resembling, as much as anything I can think of, the crooked end of some plow handles, or, as others say, a cow's horn turned backward. Some ten or twelve artificial flowers, of several different kinds, were so arranged in a sort of wreath around her head as to stick out three or four inches from her hair.

"The minister commenced the services by giving out an accommodated translation of the hymn familiarly called, in English, 'The Happy Land,' and the Christian part of the congregation united in singing it as follows:

'Tieng tong tu mo ku nang, muang hok hu tie,
Ho neng chieng chieng uang uang, ing iew la kie,' etc.

"He then proceeded to read the marriage ceremony of the Methodist Church, which had been translated, with some modifications, to meet some peculiarities in Chinese customs. The portion which challenges the audience to object now or never, if there were good grounds of objection, to the marriage of the parties, was wisely omitted, in view of the fact that they had been engaged for quite a number of years, as all their acquaintances knew. In the estimation of the Chinese friends such a challenge would be eminently ridiculous and unnecessary. When that portion was reached which, in the original form, requires the parties to join their hands in token of their willingness to take and acknowledge each other as husband and wife, the reading was suspended for a moment. A person stepped forward with some hot Chinese wine in a small stone pitcher, and poured a portion of its steaming contents into the two goblets standing on the table by them, and tied together by the red string. These goblets were then taken by the bridesmaid, one in each hand, who first presented one to the mouth of the bridegroom, who sipped a little of the wine, but without touching the goblet with his hands, and then held the other to the lips of the bride, who sipped some in a similar manner. This drinking of wine from these goblets, which is a Chinese custom, invariably practiced at marriages among themselves, was substituted in place of the parties taking each other by the hand.

"All the parties (bridegroom, bride, and clergyman) knelt down in their places, while the reading of the ceremony was continued to the end. A long meter doxology was sung in conclusion. The husband made, slowly and respectfully, a low bow toward his wife, which compliment she returned, by the assistance of the bridesmaid, by bowing thrice toward him. They then retired to the bride's room, accompanied by some of their relatives and friends, and the company broke up.

"As soon as convenient several tables were arranged in the court where the ceremony had been performed, for breakfast for the male portion of the guests. I noticed five square tables, which seated forty persons, each table accommodating eight guests. In a room in another part of the house two or three similar tables were spread for the entertainment of the female guests. The sexes never eat together on public festive occasions. It is said that about one hundred guests were expected to breakfast. Some might have been entertained in another place, not observed by us.

"We foreigners were provided with an entertainment of the foreign fashion. It seems that one or two young men, who had lived in missionary families, and who knew how to provide food for foreigners, had been engaged to prepare breakfast for us. We had sausages, roast chicken, pork chops, boiled pork, ham and eggs, rice and potatoes, wheat bread, with fruit, figs, dates, two kinds of oranges, etc. The bridegroom, with his cap of ceremony still on his head, did us the honor to sit down with us, and testified to the quality of the provisions and the keenness of his appetite by eating very heartily. He managed foreign knives and forks much more dexterously than we should have managed chopsticks under similar circumstances. The bride during part of the meal sat down at our table, but remained in perfect silence, and could not be prevailed upon to eat a morsel, which taciturnity and fasting were in complete accordance with the rules of Chinese etiquette on such occasions. To attribute her conduct to moroseness or displeasure would be doing her manifest injustice, for she evidently enjoyed the dinner. Several times she came very near laughing outright on catching a glimpse of some of her female friends in an adjoining room, who were looking at our company. But she strove to maintain her gravity, for to laugh would have been as much out of the way as to eat heartily, according to Chinese notions of propriety.

"We were cheered by what we saw and what we heard at the marriage yesterday, in the country, in proof of the Christian character of the household. They greeted us as Christians on our arrival. We heard no improper language, nor did we see any traces of heathenism remaining about the premises. We observed, with great satisfaction, that around three sides of the reception room, or the court where the ceremony was performed, there were suspended from the walls seven large paper hangings, on which were written, in large characters, quotations from the Old and New Testaments. One of these, some four or five feet wide by seven or eight feet long, contained a translation of the Ten Commandments, the characters for which were written in a bold and beautiful style. On most of the posts of the house, and on the doorposts, we noticed also that a large number of pieces of red paper had been pasted up, containing sentiments, prepared in Chinese style and according to Chinese taste, alluding to the Bible or to the truths of the Bible. They reminded us of the command recorded in Deuteronomy vi, 9. They consisted of couplets of five or seven characters in each line, written on slips of paper several feet long and a few inches wide, and were substituted for the heathen sentiments or quotations from the Chinese classics which formerly occupied their place. For example, on the posts of the doors of the bride's room was posted up a couplet, which taught that 'males and females ought to learn the true doctrine,' and that 'children and grandchildren should listen to the Gospel.'

"There being no necessity for a longer visit, we started on our way back to the river about eleven o'clock, the ladies walking the whole distance. We stopped for a short time about half of the way, at a place where the Methodist mission have an out-station. A young native exhorter is living there with his family. That mission are building there a small substantial chapel, assisted by a voluntary contribution of some available material and two hundred and seventy days' work from the native converts living in that vicinity—a large amount, considering their great poverty. Just before we left we had a season of prayer, suggested by one of the native brethren."

THE END.

www.ingramcontent.com/pod-product-compliance
Lightning Source LLC
LaVergne TN
LVHW020113110826
845151LV00001B/141

* 9 7 8 1 4 2 5 5 4 3 1 1 2 *